Treasures of the World's Religions
Series

World Wisdom
The Library of Perennial Philosophy

The Library of Perennial Philosophy is dedicated to the exposition of the timeless Truth underlying the diverse religions. This Truth, often referred to as the *Sophia Perennis*—or Perennial Wisdom—finds its expression in the revealed Scriptures as well as the writings of the great sages and the artistic creations of the traditional worlds.

For God's Greater Glory: Gems of Jesuit Spirituality from Louis Lallemant, Jean-Pierre de Caussade, and Claude de la Colombière appears as one of our selections in the Treasures of the World's Religions series.

Treasures of the World's Religions
Series

This series of anthologies presents scriptures and the writings of the great spiritual authorities of the past on fundamental themes. Some titles are devoted to a single spiritual tradition, while others have a unifying topic that touches upon traditions from both the East and West, such as prayer and virtue. Some titles have a companion volume within the Perennial Philosophy series.

Cover: St Ignatius of Loyola

For God's Greater Glory
Gems of Jesuit Spirituality

From Louis Lallemant,
Jean-Pierre de Caussade, and
Claude de la Colombière

Edited by
Jean-Pierre Lafouge

Foreword by
Fr Raymond Gawronski, S.J.

World Wisdom

For God's Greater Glory: Gems of Jesuit Spirituality from Louis Lallemant,
Jean-Pierre de Caussade, and Claude de la Colombière
© 2006 World Wisdom, Inc.

Library of Congress Cataloging-in-Publication Data

Lallemant, Louis, 1588-1635.
  For God's greater glory : gems of Jesuit spirituality / from Louis Lallemant,
Jean-Pierre de Caussade, and Claude de la Colombière ; edited by Jean-Pierre
Lafouge ; foreword by Raymond Gawronski.
     p. cm. – (The library of perennial philosophy)
  Includes bibliographical references and index.
  ISBN-13: 978-1-933316-11-6 (alk. paper)
  ISBN-10: 1-933316-11-X (alk. paper)
  1. Spiritual life–Catholic Church. 2. Jesuits–Spiritual life. I. Caussade, Jean
Pierre de, d. 1751. II. La Colombière, Claude de, Saint, 1641-1682. III. Lafouge,
Jean-Pierre, 1944- IV. Title. V. Series.
  BX2350.65.L34 2006
  248.4'82–dc22

                                                                    2006014763

Printed on acid-free paper in Canada.

For information address World Wisdom, Inc.
P.O. Box 2682, Bloomington, Indiana 47402-2682

www.worldwisdom.com

Table of Contents

PART III—CLAUDE DE LA COLOMBIÈRE

FOREWORD

A Jesuit Appreciation

According to its founder, one enters the Society of Jesus to save one's own soul and to help in the salvation of others. The marvelous anthology that Professor Lafouge here presents sinks deep shafts into the treasure trove of the wisdom of the sons of St Ignatius, from one of its most glorious expressions, a period and religious culture that produced the classical spiritual masters of France. The three Jesuit writers here presented all explore the depths and heights of the spiritual path, and all do so in profound resonance with the spiritual illumination with which St Ignatius was blessed.

Long overlaid by various other concerns, more recent reflection has been uncovering an earlier image of St Ignatius as a man of profound contemplation and of the highest mystical gifts. And these graces, given to the Church through him, are clearly present in the work of these spiritual sons. His "Spiritual Exercises" are a profound expression of the Catholic spiritual tradition, in which grace is seen as wedded to nature, faith with reason. In them, all human powers are marshaled to the service of Jesus Christ as portrayed in the Gospels. Most notably, the imagination—the heart—is engaged and given the lead in contemplating the form of Christ that the Holy Spirit is eliciting from the heart of the believing soul, and which, ultimately, the Trinity is drawing from the created universe.

This spiritual project is vast and all-comprehensive. It is willing to develop all the tools of mind and heart, all the asceticism known to human wisdom, and placing them at the service of the God who addresses man and comes to Him in Christ. The response to this is, as our Jesuit authors remind us constantly, a simple and humble faith.

Each of the authors presented tends to emphasize a different moment in the spiritual vision of the "Exercises." In Fr Lallemant, it is the central "Meditation on the Two Standards." In the spiritual battlefield of the created universe, everyone must choose between serving either under the standard of Christ or under the standard of Satan. Fr Lallemant is clear that in discerning the standard of Christ, the humility and meekness of Jesus, which evoke the same spiritual condition in His disciples, is essential. This means a willingness to endure contempt and humiliations. As he writes: "Humility and patience are, so to say, the shoulders of charity..." (p. 61). The inner despoliation is so great that "even prayer and converse with God" must be abandoned to draw near to God (p. 63), but this in union with Christ who Himself experienced the deepest abandonment.

This draws us to the language of the darkness of faith, naturally reminiscent of St John of the Cross who surveys the same landscape, and is characteristic of the higher ascent in the thought of Jean-Pierre de Caussade. For him, "After a soul has climbed the first rungs of the ladder of perfection it can make little progress except by ways of despoliation and spiritual darkness, and the way of self-obliteration and death to all created things including the spiritual" (p. 111). Characteristic of the Jesuit vision, the only sure guide through the dark night, in which one must abandon one's ego—one's own judgment—is blind obedience.

De Caussade especially celebrates the culminating vision of the "Spiritual Exercises," the *Contemplatio ad Amorem*, where a most intimate embrace of, and participation in, God's work in all of creation is the heart of the contemplation. In everything, in every moment, God can be found by surrendering ourselves to Him entirely, for His will is at work in everything that happens, and everything that happens is for God's greater glory. "The will of God is the presence, the reality, and the virtue in all things, adjusting them to souls" (p. 78). For the Society of Jesus, of course, the humanity of Christ is at the center of the vision, calling forth the fullness of humanity in those who contemplate Him: "It is the will of God that gives everything, whatever it may be, the power to form Jesus Christ in the center of our being" (p. 78). Beautifully celebrating this *Contemplatio*, he writes: "Jesus lives and works among us, throughout our lives, from the beginning of time to the end, which is but one day. He has lived and lives still. The life he began continues in his saints for ever..." (p. 86).

The way to discover this will is to "Listen to the heart: it interprets His will in everything that happens" (pp. 76-77). The heart must be the master: the mind is a "dangerous slave" which if rightly ordered can yet serve "to great advantage" (pp. 83-84). And for there to be true peace of heart, the heart must rely entirely on grace.

The spiritual progeny of St Ignatius are to be "contemplatives in action": and our Jesuit authors remind us of the indispensable primacy of contemplation. Anticipating temptations to activism, de

Caussade writes: "Human activity, being substitute for fulfillment, leaves no room for the true fulfillment of divine purpose" (p. 84). Instead, with "total mistrust in ourselves and perfect confidence in God, which are like the two poles of the spiritual life, humility forms the foundation and guardian of all the virtues" (p. 138). And this humility—and its resultant virtues—can never be found where the heart does not lead, and herself receive all from God. The mind must know emptiness: a total emptiness "of every thought of either God or of the world" (p. 149). In the phrase Fr de Caussade made famous, one can only fully "abandon oneself to God's Providence."

In recent years, the Catholic Church has recognized the spiritual greatness and authenticity of Fr Claude de la Colombière by placing his name in the canon of saints. St Claude, sharing this complete abandonment to God's Providence, dwells on what is called the "First Principle and Foundation" and its consequences. That is, as man is created to praise, reverence, and serve God and by this means save his soul, everything else on earth—and everything else in man's life—is to serve this goal. In ordering his life this way, he finds perfect freedom, and that means perfect indifference to what humans consider earthly goods. So, health or sickness, a long or short life, riches or poverty, success or failure, all become matters of perfect indifference, that is, perfect freedom and availability to God's directing will. More: in line with the "Meditation on the Two Standards," St Claude goes on to celebrate those who, imitating Christ, actually prefer illness or poverty to health and riches (p. 164). The only alternative to the peace of abandonment to God's will is the instability and eventual shipwreck of those who try to guide themselves (p. 177).

The "Spiritual Exercises" offer a school in the discernment of spirits, and our writers are agreed that spiritual consolation with its sweetness—welcome as it is—all too easily offers the soul a "tender trap" while times of desolation and dryness are the best for drawing close to God. "There is nothing so dangerous and so much to be suspected as sweetness" (p. 187). Abandonment of inner states is part of this radical ascent, which is all based in the darkness of faith.

Finally, the Jesuit spiritual tradition is radically incarnational and thus sacramental and ecclesial. One lives a life of faith in communion with "so many saints and doctors of the Church" (p. 185). If we are to distrust inner states in a dark faith, we yet have the consolation that "Jesus is in the midst of us in the Blessed Sacrament" (p.

198). And if we surrender all creatures, and all inner states, we do so in the confidence and love of Jesus: "Jesus, be my friend, since thou commandest me to be thine" (p. 199). The prayer of the *Suscipe*,[1] in which one surrenders all to God and trusts God to return all in His own way and time, is at the heart of this spirituality, summarized in St Claude's words: "Provided that I am with thee, and thou with me, I am content" (p. 200).

The world is always prone to forget the primacy of the spiritual. People of seemingly good intentions in our times are perhaps especially tempted to an idolatry of human means in creating an earthly utopia cut off from spiritual wisdom, indeed, cut off from God Himself. In *For God's Greater Glory*, Professor Lafouge splendidly presents spiritual treasures that richly reveal the depth and breadth and the very core of the Jesuit spiritual tradition, a way of contemplative action in the world. It is a way that shares with the best of humanity's traditions an asceticism of the heart that purifies and leads to God, and which gently guides the longings of the human heart and mind to answer the "upward call of God in Christ."

—Fr Raymond Gawronski, S.J.

---

[1] Perhaps the most beloved prayer of the Society of Jesus is the prayer called the *Suscipe*: "Take, Lord, receive, all my liberty, my memory, understanding, my entire will, all I have and possess. You have given all to me, and I return it. In return, give me only Your love and Your grace, and these are enough for me."

INTRODUCTION

This anthology is not intended to be a comprehensive presentation of Jesuit spirituality. This form of spirituality is so rich that it could fill volumes of detailed analyses. Three authors were selected: Louis Lallemant, Jean-Pierre de Caussade, and Claude de la Colombière. But if they do not comprehensively represent Jesuit spirituality, they are are among what we would call its "gems" because of their deep contemplative orientation.

Before reviewing why these three authors were chosen, it is important to define first what is understood by the word "spirituality," and what is the origin and general history of Jesuit spirituality.

When deciding upon a choice among Jesuit writings, my first principle was to avoid repeating what is commonly known about the Jesuits: it has become fashionable to deal with this religious society by referring to the most spectacular or sensationalist activities of the Jesuits in the Catholic Church. This very outward aspect of things, often controversial and not always accurately reported, is not part of what we here consider as "spirituality." Much has been written to reconstruct, deform, and even defame the reputation of this order, and it is certainly not the goal of this book to enter again into this useless debate.

On the contrary, our goal is to present to the public something less known, more profound, and more contemplative, thereby providing a more objective insight into an extraordinary world of sanctity, wisdom, and spiritual knowledge. Indeed, "spirituality" is nothing else if not sanctity and wisdom and a method with which to realize them. It does not consist of "building a better world" (such a goal could in any case only result from universal sanctity), but of "saving souls" at whatever level—from avoidance of sin to the purest form of love and knowledge of God. It is true that many people nowadays find it difficult to accept such words as salvation and sin. Perhaps the reading of the following texts, although written around three centuries ago, will help them realize that "spirituality" differs from ordinary "psychology" (in the modern sense of the word) and from "morality"—although it is obvious that fundamental virtues are the necessary basis of any spiritual path.

As to the meaning of the word "spirituality," George E. Ganss, S.J. writes:

> For a century or more the English word *spirituality* has been used
> to designate a person's interior life, manner of praying, and other
> such practices. It also designates the spiritual doctrine and prac-
> tices characteristically formulated in the writings of some person
> or group.... In this light, Christian spirituality is a lived experience,
> the effort to apply relevant elements in the deposit of Christian
> faith to the guidance of men and women toward their spiritual
> growth.[1]

It is true that Jesuits are mainly known for their activity in the
world: their vocation is not one of cloistered monasticism but of
"contemplation in action." It is also well known that a number of
them were, and still are, eminent in various intellectual pursuits.
But the goal of this anthology is to present the other side of their
lives: the spiritual method—beyond the famous "Exercises"—in
which they are rooted. Much of Jesuit life is learned and practiced in
novitiates where Jesuits undergo an intense spiritual training based
on Ignatius of Loyola's "Spiritual Exercises". This anthology will
not enter into the details of these "Exercises," this having already
been done quite extensively in other works. In fact, the only way to
really understand what they are all about is to spend a month, or at
least a few days, practicing these "Exercises" with a knowledgeable
director.

However, we can briefly summarize their use. Since the vocation
of man is to conform himself to God's will as perfectly as possible,
the very general goal of the "Exercises" will be to place his soul in a
disposition that allows him to discern this will without interference
from the ego, and then build—or rebuild—his life accordingly. Of
course, there are many degrees to this discernment, from knowing
what God asks us to do in our life in the world (profession, vocation,
family, etc.), to how to respond to more contemplative calls. Every
individual case differs from others, and that is why it is not possible
to enter into the details of the "Exercises."

It should be emphasized that the spirit of these "Exercises"
resulted from an extraordinary spiritual illumination (we could
also say enlightenment) on the part of St Ignatius: he saw and
understood in a lightning fashion many spiritual insights which
determined the rest of his life. We are referring here to the grace

---

[1] *Ignatius of Loyola: The Spiritual Exercises and Selected Works,*, edited by George E.
Ganss, S.J., Paulist Press, Mahwah, NJ, 2002, p. 62.

that Ignatius received in Manresa, a grace which was, according to the best spiritual Jesuit commentators of the time, a real "descent" of the Holy Ghost. The supernatural nature of this inspiration is *a posteriori* confirmed by its "fruits" in Ignatius and in his successors. As Ganss writes: "St Ignatius of Loyola ... had a dynamic spirituality which was ordered toward both personal spiritual growth and energetic apostolic endeavor."[2]

And also:

> One prominent characteristic of his spirituality, especially important for understanding his *Spiritual Exercises* and his *Constitutions*, is his sharp focus on ends with accompanying means. His ends were clear in his mind and arranged in a series leading up to God. The one supreme and inspiring end, the keystone to which all the other elements in the arch of his thought were supports, was "the greater glory of God," with "glory" meaning praise and implying service. To pursue this single aim was his own constant endeavor.... God should be found in all one's actions, and one should order them all to his glory.[3]

What is specifically Jesuit in this spirituality comes therefore from the "Exercises" and from Ignatius himself. But on the other hand, as Ganss indicates, Ignatius was deeply inspired by the religious orders of the Middle Ages and by the Fathers of the Church, even though he lived mostly in the sixteenth century. No Jesuit spirituality could be radically different from the spirituality of St Bernard, St Benedict, or St Francis of Assisi. The appearance of a fundamentally different spirituality would have amounted practically to the advent of a new Christianity, *quod absit.*

> Ignatius was the founder of ... a school of spirituality, one with an emphasis directed especially toward personal spiritual growth and that of others. Emphasizing a desire to bring greater glory to God, here and hereafter, it has propagated a message of service through love and discernment. His spirituality—like that of others—is simply Christian spirituality with emphasis on those elements in the deposit of faith which he stressed.[4]

[2] Ibid., p. 9.
[3] Ibid., p. 12.
[4] Ibid., p. 62.

And again:

> The beginnings of Ignatius' spirituality must be sought in the Catholic faith, which he inherited with its sixteenth-century trappings amid the cultural environment of his youth. When he turned to serious spiritual living at the age of thirty, he began the lengthy formation of his personalized concept of God's redemptive plan by drawing particularly from writings of the Dominican, Carthusian, Cistercian, and Franciscan schools.[5]

What this anthology would like to point out, however, is that the Jesuit movement arose during a time in need of synthesis and adaptation. The Society appeared at the end of the Renaissance, when people, especially in Europe, were becoming more individualistic, more characterized by psychological and reflexive tendencies, as Maritain noticed. In such a context, it became more and more necessary to discern between true spirituality and egoic concerns. Consciousness became more "subjective," more complex, and the task of spiritual masters became more difficult because of the imbroglio raised by sentiments, emotions, and passionate reasoning—to such an extent that it became difficult to realize the meaning of the love of God and the salvation of the soul. Since we have inherited this complexity, it seems quite appropriate to include authors who were best at discerning these intricacies thanks to their experience with aspirants in novitiates, and because of their own sanctity of soul.

The texts of Louis Lallemant serve as an excellent introduction to the anthology because they have the merit of presenting in a comprehensive and very organized fashion the diverse aspects of spirituality in its most general compass. Jean-Pierre de Caussade's texts direct the reader more towards the everyday life of a spiritual path, with concrete examples of the numerous problems the soul encounters when it tries not only to master itself, but to transcend itself, which is precisely what the ego is very reluctant to allow because it corresponds to a kind of death. Caussade's writings on the prayer of the heart emphasize in a systematic way his spiritual method. Lastly, Claude de la Colombière's writings enter even more deeply into the psychological analysis of the soul; and they do so with such clarity that he proves—if proof be required—that spiritu-

[5] Ibid., p. 13.

al masters and saints knew—well before the advent of psychoanalysis—the complex functionings of the human soul and, above all, how to help it escape from its self-inflicted suffering without it thereby losing the *raison d'être* of human existence.

Louis Lallemant (1587-1635)

Louis Lallemant was born at Châlons-sur-Marne and died at Bourges. After completing his studies under the Fathers of the Society of Jesus, he entered that order in 1605 and followed the usual course of study and teaching. He then taught philosophy and theology for some time until he was made master of novices, an office he filled for four years. He was then appointed director of the fathers in third probation;[6] but after three years in this difficult post he broke down in health and was sent to the college of Bourget, in the hope that change of occupation would restore him. This hope was not to be fulfilled, and he died a few months later. He is known today mainly for his *Doctrine Spirituelle*, a collection of maxims and instructions gathered together by Fr Jean Rigoleuc, one of his disciples, which details very thoroughly his spiritual method.[7]

The Spiritual Teaching of Father Louis Lallemant, from which we have excerpted the texts that follow, "was compiled by Father Champion, S.J., from manuscript notes made by Fathers Rigoleuc and Surin, the two chief disciples of Father Lallemant, and was first issued in 1694."[8] The structure of this book is still under discussion by specialists in the field, but it does not prevent it being considered as "one of the most important monuments of French [and Jesuit, we would add] spirituality."[9] Since the book is 300 pages long, we have made a selection of those passages of more "universal scope," spiritually speaking, while excluding those *pro domo* texts specifically addressed to future Jesuits and to their religious communities, as also those which deal with the more specific points of Catholic theology. Such passages would have required extensive contextualized explanations, at the expense of the spiritual focus of our anthology.

---

[6] Tertianship represents the final phase of training for a Jesuit.

[7] After a text at http://www.newadvent.org/cathen/08752e.htm.

[8] *The Spiritual Teaching of Father Louis Lallemant of the Society of Jesus, Preceded by an Account of His Life by Father Champion, S.J.,* edited by Alan G. McDougall, Benziger Brothers, New York, Cincinatti, Chicago, 1928, p. v.

[9] Ibid., p. v.

Since the goal of this anthology is to reach as wide an audience as possible, we thought it necessary to exclude these more circumstantial and specific passages. But since the value of these passages cannot be denied, whoever wishes to enter into these theological aspects can refer to the original texts.

The extracts of Fr Louis Lallemant's *Spiritual Teaching* come first both for chronological reasons, and also because they inspired generations of readers. They provide an excellent "theoretical" and "practical" overview of spiritual life with such clarity, precision, and order that they constitute, as we mentioned earlier, an excellent introduction to the rest of this book. As Robert M. McKeon writes:

> This school promoted contemplation as the way to stand humbly before the Holy Spirit, who resides at the center of the human soul. The aim of prayer was to withdraw into one's center to rest in God's presence, to discern his will, and to carry it out. The life of prayer required discipline and mortification, for devotees have to die to themselves if they want to make a place for God. For instance, Lallemant outlined seven principles of the spiritual life:
>
> 1. to know our goal: only God can make us truly happy;
> 2. to pursue the ideal of perfection: specifically as outlined by the rules and procedures of the Jesuit order;
> 3. to purify the heart: what we should purify ourselves of; purity of action and purity of mind;
> 4. to be docile to the promptings of the Holy Spirit: working with the gifts and fruits of the Holy Spirit;
> 5. to lead an interior life of inner quiet: the only true source of peace;
> 6. to be united with our Lord by knowledge of his life and teachings, by love, and by imitation of his virtues;
> 7. to follow the three steps of the spiritual life: Ignatian meditation, affective prayer, and contemplation.[10]

Jean-Pierre de Caussade (1675-1751)

Little is known about the life of this Jesuit priest beyond the bare facts of his career. He was born in 1675 and entered the Jesuit novitiate in Toulouse at the age of eighteen. Later, he taught classics in

---

[10] Cited from his introduction to Jean-Pierre de Caussade's *A Treatise on Prayer from the Heart: A Christian Mystical Tradition Recovered for All*, translated, edited, and introduced by Robert M. McKeon, The Institute of Jesuit Sources, St Louis, 1998, p. 13.

the Jesuit college in Aurillac. He was ordained a priest in 1705 and took his final vows in 1708. From 1708 to 1714, he taught in the Jesuit college in Toulouse, and then devoted himself to the itinerant career of a missionary and preacher.

Between the years 1730 and 1732 he was in Lorraine, and, as John Joyce, S.J., mentions,

> it was during this period that he made his first contact with the nuns of the Order of the Visitation in Nancy, to whom we are indebted for having preserved his letters and the notes of his conferences. In 1731 he was sent as spiritual director to the seminary in Albi, but two years later was back in Nancy in charge of the Jesuit Retreat house there. During his seven years in this office he gave frequent conferences to the Visitation nuns and undertook the personal direction of several of them.[11]

After some administrative responsibilities in various institutions in the south of France, he had more and more difficulty with his eyes but "he bore [this blindness] with courageous fortitude and in the spirit of his own great principle of self-abandonment to the will of God."[12] He died in 1751 at the age of seventy-six.

The choice of Jean-Pierre de Caussade for this anthology could appear inappropriate *at first view* considering the controversy over his method. But, as Robert M. McKeon has indicated, this very contemplative approach to Christian spirituality is one of the best answers, in the Western tradition, to the needs of those Christian laymen and laywomen who are drawn to interior silence and contemplative prayer rather than to ordinary piety and outward activity. For hundreds of years Christianity promoted contemplativity and inwardness as the first characteristic of its method and Caussade is consequently very *à propos* in this respect. As Robert M. McKeon remarks:

> We are all called to contemplation and mystical union with God. But how do we proceed, especially those laypeople among us who lead full, active lives? Has anyone written an accessible guide book

---

[11] In Jean-Pierre de Caussade, S.J., *Abandonment to Divine Providence*, translated from the standard French edition by Algar Thorold, newly edited by Fr John Joyce, S.J., Burns and Oates, London, 1959, p. xix.

[12] Ibid., pp. xix-xx.

on prayer like Francis de Sales's *Introduction to the Devout Life?* The answer is a resounding yes! Jean-Pierre de Caussade's *Treatise on Prayer from the Heart*, written around 1735, leads the reader step by step into deep mystical prayer. He answers our thirst for prayer by showing a simple and direct path to prayer.[13]

"Without me, you can do nothing" said Christ.[14] In keeping with Christ's recommendations, and the graces of the apostolic tradition, it should be strongly emphasized here that Caussade's method should not be practiced outside an authentic and orthodox religious framework.

Caussade's writings occupy the largest part of this anthology given the relevance of his method in the modern world. Three sets of texts were chosen: the first one is *The Sacrament of the Present Moment*; the second is *The Fire of Divine Love: Readings from Jean-Pierre de Caussade*; and the third *A Treatise on Prayer from the Heart: A Christian Mystical Tradition Recovered for All*, which is given here almost in its entirety.

Claude de la Colombière (1641-1682)

Claude de la Colombière was born of noble parentage in France in 1641 and died at Paray-le-Monial, in 1682. He entered the Society of Jesus in 1659. In 1674 he was made superior at the Jesuit house at Paray-le-Monial, where he became the spiritual director of Saint Margaret Mary and was thereafter a zealous apostle of the devotion to the Sacred Heart of Jesus. In 1676 he was sent to England as preacher to the Duchess of York, afterwards Queen of Great Britain. Although encountering many difficulties, he was able to guide Blessed Margaret Mary by letter. His zeal soon weakened his vitality and throat and lung trouble seemed to threaten his work as a preacher. While awaiting his recall to France he was suddenly arrested and thrown into prison, denounced as a conspirator. Thanks to his title of preacher to the Duchess of York and to the

---

[13] Cited from his introduction to *A Treatise on Prayer from the Heart*, p. 4.

[14] John 15:4-6: "Abide in Me, and I in you. As the branch cannot bear fruit of itself, unless it abides in the vine, neither can you, unless you abide in Me. I am the vine, you are the branches. He who abides in Me, and I in him, bears much fruit; for without Me you can do nothing. If anyone does not abide in Me, he is cast out as a branch and is withered; and they gather them and throw them into the fire, and they are burned."

protection of Louis XIV, whose subject he was, he escaped death but was condemned to exile in 1679. The last two years of his life were spent at Lyon where he was spiritual director to the young Jesuits there, and at Paray-le-Monial. His principal works, including *Pious Reflections, Meditations on the Passion,* and *Retreat and Spiritual Letters,* were published under the title, *Oeuvres du R. P. Claude de la Colombière* (Avignon, 1832; Paris, 1864). His relics are preserved in the monastery of the Visitation nuns at Paray-le-Monial. Claude de la Colombière was beatified on 16 June 1929 by Pope Pius XI and canonized on 31 May 1992 by Pope John Paul II in Rome.[15]

Although St Claude de la Colombière lived before Jean-Pierre de Caussade, we have placed his writings at the end of the anthology because he represents a culmination: his psychological and spiritual knowledge of the human soul is of the greatest interest. As Mother M. Philip, I.B.V.M., puts it:

> St Claude ... was also a clever psychologist who easily read the hearts of others. His sure judgment, aided by grace, enabled him to understand the difficulties of each soul and give the advice most needed for each person.[16]

Two texts are presented here: the first one is Parts IV and V of *The Secret of Peace and Happiness,* by Fr Jean Baptiste Saint-Juré and Fr St Claude Colombière, S.J., while the second is a selection of themes taken from *The Spiritual Direction of Saint Claude de la Colombière.*

How to use this anthology?
This book is not structured to be read from beginning to end, except perhaps for Caussade's *Treatise on Prayer from the Heart.* Readers can locate an entry in the Table of Contents or in the Index according to their present spiritual need. It will be noticed, however, that there are unavoidable "repetitions," but each paragraph contains nuances of approach and expression which may be helpful to different readers, each having their own spiritual needs and experience.

---

[15] Summarized from *The Catholic Encyclopedia,* http://www.newadvent.org/cathen/16026b.htm.

[16] Back cover of *The Spiritual Direction of Saint Claude de la Colombière,* translated and arranged by Mother M. Philip, I.B.V.M., Ignatius Press, San Francisco, 1998.

Finally, while reading these texts, one can see that Catholic spirituality does not differ fundamentally from the spirituality of other great religions, at least as to its goal, which is to live according to the truth and to master the ego. For no spirituality can be successful, as Frithjof Schuon reminds us, without (1) detachment from the world, hence purity of soul; (2) struggle against our passions and individualistic tendencies; (3) contentment with the will of God, hence peacefulness; (4) fervor and confidence in God, hence generosity towards our neighbor; (5) discernment between the Real and the unreal; and (6) union with the Real.[17] These three Jesuit authors, while putting the accent on the love of God, which is the main characteristic of Christianity in general, are indeed of great help for those seeking to practice these fundamental virtues.[18]

—Jean-Pierre Lafouge

---

[17] See Frithjof Schuon, *Stations of Wisdom*, World Wisdom Books, Bloomington, IN, 1995, pp. 147-157.

[18] To obtain a comprehensive view of Jesuit spirituality see *The Jesuits: Their Spiritual Doctrine and Practice, A Historical Study, A Posthumous Work*, by Joseph de Guilbert, S.J., translated by William J. Young, S.J., edited by George E. Ganss, S.J., The Institute of Jesuit Sources in cooperation with Loyola University Press, Chicago, 1964.

St Ignatius (1491-1556)

PART I

LOUIS LALLEMANT

1587-1635

THE SPIRITUAL TEACHING OF FATHER LOUIS LALLEMANT[1]

GOD ALONE CAN MAKE US HAPPY

There is a void in our heart which all creatures united would be unable to fill. God alone can fill it; for he is our beginning and our end. The possession of God fills up this void, and makes us happy. The privation of God leaves in us this void, and is the cause of our wretchedness.

Before God fills up this void, he puts us in the way of faith; with this condition, that if we never cease to regard him as our last end, if we use creatures with moderation, and refer to his service the use we make of them, at the same time contributing faithfully to the glory which it is his will to draw from all created beings, he will give himself to us to fill up the void within us, and make us happy. But if we are wanting in fidelity, he will leave in us that void which, left unfilled, will cause our supreme misery.

Creatures desire to take the place of our last end, and more than all, we desire to be our own last end. A creature says to us, "Come to me; I will satisfy thee." We believe it, and it deceives us. Then another and another holds the same language to us, deceives us in like manner, and will go on deceiving us all our life long. Creatures call to us on all sides, and promise to satisfy us. All their promises, however, are but lies; and yet we are ever ready to let ourselves be cheated. It is as if the bed of the sea were empty, and one were to take a handful of water to refill it. Thus we are never satisfied; for when we attach ourselves to creatures, they estrange us from God, and cast us into an ocean of pain, trouble, and misery—elements as inseparable from the creature, as joy, peace, and happiness are inseparable from God.

---

[1] Selections from *The Spiritual Teaching of Father Louis Lallemant of the Society of Jesus, Preceded by an Account of His Life by Father Champion, S. J.*, edited by Alan G. McDougall, Benziger Brothers, New York, Cincinatti, Chicago, 1928.

We are like jaded epicures, who taste a dish, then leave it, and immediately stretch out their hand to another, to leave it also in its turn, finding nothing to their liking. We seize upon every manner of thing, without being able to satisfy ourselves with any. God alone is the sovereign good who can make us happy; and we deceive ourselves when we say, "Were I in such a place, had I such a situation, I should be satisfied. Such a one is happy; he has what he desires." Vanity! Were you Pope, you would not be content. Let us seek God; let us seek God only. He only can satisfy all our desires.

Of old the devil disguised himself as God, presenting himself to the heathen in idols as the author and the end of everything in the world. Creatures do much the same thing. They disguise themselves as God, cheating us into the belief that they will satisfy us by giving us wherewithal to fill our souls. But everything they give us serves only to increase our emptiness. Now we do not feel it; it is only truly realized in the next life, where the soul, separated from its body, has an almost infinite desire to see itself filled with God, and disappointment in this causes it to suffer a pain in a manner infinite.

At the hour of death we shall know how miserably we have let ourselves be deceived and deluded by creatures. We shall be astounded that for things so low and vile we should have been willing to lose that which is so great and precious; and our punishment for this foolish conduct will be, to be deprived for a time of the sight of God, without which nothing can satisfy the soul. The desire it has to see him and possess him is as much beyond conception as the pain caused by such desire when it is unsatisfied.

This is why we must resolve generously to renounce all designs of our own devising, all human views, all desires and hopes of things that might gratify self-love; and, in short, everything that might hinder us in promoting the glory of God. This it is which, in the words of Scripture, is called "walking before the Lord," "having an upright soul," "walking in truth," "seeking God with all our heart." Without this we shall never be happy.

Why do we cling to creatures as we do? They are so limited and so void of any solid good, that all the pleasure and satisfaction we may promise ourselves from them is but a vain imaginary happiness, which only famishes instead of filling us, because, our appetite being infinite, it can be satisfied only by the possession of the sovereign good. Add to which that creatures endure but for a while and soon leave us, or we are ourselves compelled to leave them.

And as for men in particular, we do not know that they love only themselves, and in all things seek but their own interest? The little property, credit, authority which they possess, they economize for themselves; and if they had all manner of goods in abundance, they would not act otherwise. Everything which they do not do purely for God, they do from self-love; and in anything which they do for others, they never lose sight of themselves. They are our benefactors and our faithful friends only so far as they find their own advantage in it. What reliance, then, can we place on the favor and the friendship of men?

OUR HAPPINESS DEPENDS ON OUR PERFECT SUBMISSION TO GOD, WHO OUGHT TO REIGN ALONE IN OUR HEARTS

Our true greatness consists in our submission to God. We depend upon God in three ways. First, we cannot so much as exist but by him. Secondly, we cannot have the means of arriving at him, but from him. Thirdly, we cannot take possession of our end and sovereign good but by him. Herein the ancient philosophers deceived themselves, seeking their happiness in themselves and in human things.

God alone has right of sovereignty over our hearts. Neither secular powers, nor the Church herself, extend their dominion thus far. What passes there depends not on them. There God alone is King. It is his own proper realm. There he establishes his throne of grace. This interior kingdom is what constitutes his glory. Our perfection and our happiness consists in the subjection of our heart to this empire of God. The more our heart submits to him, the more perfect and happy shall we be.

The supernatural government of one heart in which he reigns, is the object of more special care to God than is the natural government of the whole universe, and the civil government of all empires. God sets value on the heart alone; if only he see that subjected to his power—if only he possess that, he is content. So, again, it is God alone that can satisfy our heart. The heart is a void, which can be filled only by God.

The delight of God is to converse with hearts; there is the place of his rest; and so likewise God alone is the center of hearts, and they ought to find their rest only in God, and to have no movement but for God.

O blessed interior life, which causes God alone to live in hearts, and hearts to live but for God alone, and to take no pleasure save in him! Blessed the life of that heart wherein God reigns, and which he possesses fully! A life separated from the world, and hidden in God; a life of love and holy liberty; a life which causes the heart to find in the kingdom of God its joy, its peace, trite pleasures, glory, solid greatness, goods and riches, which the world can neither give nor take away.

We imagine that a man must pass a sad and melancholy existence when he gives himself to recollection and the interior life. The very reverse is the case. Happiness even on this earth consists in possessing God; and the more we renounce ourselves to unite ourselves to God, the more we cease to be miserable, and the more happy we become. But the devil takes advantage of our ignorance and our weakness, to plunge us into constant errors and infirmities, whence we must needs extricate ourselves, if we would be capable of the sovereign happiness of this life, which consists in seeing God, and in enjoying the gift of his holy Presence, without which the highest seraphim would be wretched. A soul which, contemplating God incessantly, should hold itself ever ready to execute his will, would be blessed.

THE FIRST ACT OF A SOUL SEEKING PERFECTION

How we ought to seek God in all things, and to seek but him alone
To seek God truly, we must represent him to ourselves, 1, as the first Principle of nature and of grace; 2, the Preserver of all creatures; 3, as the sovereign Lord who governs everything and disposes everything by his providence. Thus we ought to regard all events, even the smallest, as flowing from the will of God and his good pleasure.

To seek God is to wish for nothing and to desire nothing but that which he wills, and which he ordains by his providence. We ought to consider how in God there are, as it were, two acts with reference to us.

One by which he wills to bestow upon us such and such graces to conduct us to such a degree of glory, if we are faithful to him. The other, by which he wills not to bestow upon us further graces, nor to raise us to a higher degree of glory. Few have sufficient courage and fidelity to accomplish the designs of God, and by their cooperation to reach the point of grace and of glory which God desires for them. We ought to regard the will of God, his judgments, and the decrees of his providence, with so much esteem, love, and submission, as to desire neither more grace nor glory than that which he is pleased to give us, even were it in our power to have as much as we would. We must confine ourselves to these limits, out of the unbounded respect which we ought to have for the dispositions of divine providence.

Another excellent way of seeking God is to have no other object in all things but the glory of God.

This maxim, applied to literary studies, teaches us to seek to know only that which tends to the greater service of God. The devil has beyond comparison more knowledge than we have, but we surpass him in this, that we can refer our knowledge to the greater glory of God, which the devil cannot do.

The same maxim may be applied to all our employments and to all things generally. We ought to be so detached from ourselves, our own interests, our own tastes, our own individual inclinations and designs, as to be in a disposition to renounce everything for the sake of the service of God, and of that which may help us to seek and find God; for nothing is desirable in itself but God, and all else is desirable only with reference to God. So that to seek that which does not lead us to God, to bestow care upon it, or to take a pleasure in it, is an error and delusion.

When we desert this rule, and prefer that which is most agreeable to ourselves to that which most conduces to the glory of God, it is as if a king were to sell his kingdom for a glass of water; the greatest folly in the world, seeing that everything is but vanity, everything is but a lie, which has not God for its object. And hence it follows, that every day we suffer immense losses; for we lose as much glory for ourselves as we ought to have procured for God when we had the power of doing so.

To act in all things for the greater glory of God, this is the noblest end imaginable. All that God himself can give to the highest seraph without this is less than this; neither is it possible for God to raise a creature to a sublimer end than this; even were that creature a thousand times more perfect than the highest seraph.

Let us, then, seek God in all things, and make everything serve as an instrument of his greater glory; prosperity and adversity, consolations and dryness of spirit, our very sins and imperfections. Everything is of use to those who know how to seek God, and to find God in everything that happens to them.

There is still another way of seeking God, which it is difficult to understand unless it be put in practice. It is not only to seek his will and his glory, not only to seek his gifts and his graces, his consolations and sweetness of devotion but to seek himself, to repose in him alone, and to find no sweetness save in him.

Otherwise, if we make his favors and sensible sweetnesses our object, we expose ourselves to great dangers, and shall never reach the end at which we aim. Whereas, when it is God himself and him only that we seek, we rise above all created things, and esteem the crowns and glories of the whole universe—nay, a thousand worlds and everything that is not God—even as nothing.

Our greatest care and our constant study ought to be to seek God in this way; and until we have found him, we must not so much as stir abroad to seek to serve our neighbor, except in the way of experimental essays. We must be like hounds held at half leash. When we have arrived at the possession of God, we shall be able to give our zeal a greater freedom, and then we shall do more in one day than we have hitherto done in ten years.

When a soul has no longer any affection but for God, when it seeks but God, and is united to God, and feels no pleasure but in him, when it finds no rest save in him alone, nothing can cause it any pain. Thus the saints, though persecuted by men, and assaulted by devils, laughed it all to scorn. It was but the outside that felt the blows, the interior was in peace.

Until we attain to this state, we shall always be miserable. Let the body be decked out with a thousand jewels, if the soul have departed, it turns to corruption, and is but a corpse loaded with infection. In like manner, let the soul possess all the advantages that can be desired, if it has not God, everything else it has cannot prevent it being wretched.

When creatures display their attractions in order to tempt us, the best way to secure ourselves from being surprised is to retire at once into God, to sigh after God, to gain a sweet savor of God by some devout and holy thought, instead of stopping to contend and dispute against the allurements of the temptation, which has more in it of perplexity and danger. We ought to pursue the same course at the first pressure of sufferings, crosses, and adversities.

Our study must be to seek God, and our end to fill ourselves with God. We shall only perfectly attain to this after we have thoroughly purged ourselves from our sins. However, we must be always tending to it, and for this end we must avail ourselves of all creatures as means, without yielding our heart to them.

THE EXERCISE OF THE VIRTUES THAT ARE MOST NECESSARY TO PERFECTION

Of faith

Faith being, next to the clear vision of God, the most excellent participation of the uncreated wisdom, it must not be based upon natural reasons nor our own human inventions. Nevertheless such reasons may serve to subdue the repugnance and opposition of our mind, to rid us of our dullness, and to dispose us to believe, though they cannot be employed as a support to that which we believe by faith; for faith implies the whole authority of God, and is founded on his sovereign and infinite wisdom, which makes it impossible for him to be deceived, and on his infinite fidelity, which makes it impossible for him to deceive us.

Some tremble at the sight of the truths of faith, and are unwilling to reflect upon them; not that they doubt them, but they avoid the thought of them, because they have not used themselves to it. This is a great error, and at death the devil will be able to assault them on their weak side.

As it is faith which makes perfect that knowledge which prompts the will to act, and as, according to St Thomas, it resides partly in the will, it facilitates the exercise of all virtues. For a knowledge of the faith touching temperance, for example, will make me perform an act of temperance more easily than the simple propriety of this virtue, and at the same time it will render my act supernatural.

We must endeavor, therefore, to ground ourselves more and more firmly in faith, walking always in its light, putting it in the place of those reasonings in which the human mind is always prone to indulge upon all kinds of subjects, and making it serve as the guiding torch and principle of all our actions. An act of the will grounded on faith is worth more than ten sentiments that have their source in spiritual taste.

When God desires to make himself perfectly master of a soul, he begins by gaining the understanding, communicating to it a high degree of faith. Thence he descends into the will, then into the memory, the imagination, and the concupiscible and irascible appetites, possessing himself little by little of all these faculties. Next he passes to the senses, and the bodily movements, and in this manner he succeeds in completely occupying the interior and the exterior; and all this by means of faith, which comprises in an eminent degree all virtues, as theologians say, and is the first spring of their action. This is why we must render the exercise of faith familiar to us, and guide ourselves by it in all our actions.

It is truly sad to see how, in religion, some, and often even the majority, guide themselves only by human reason and natural prudence, scarcely using faith, except so far as not to go against it. They apply themselves to the perfecting of reason and good sense, without taking the trouble to increase in faith. It is exactly as if a man were to take great pains with the education of his servant, and neglect that of his son.

How much our want of confidence displeases God and injures ourselves
One of the things in which we most dishonor God is our want of confidence in him; and this fault arises from our not sufficiently considering what has been bestowed upon us in the Incarnation, and what God made man has done for men. For God so loved the world as to give his only-begotten Son, and seeing that he spared not even his own Son, but delivered him up to death for us all, how hath he not also, with him, given us all things?

That the son of a king should be willing to die to expiate the crime of a subject whom he loved, or that a king should be willing to give up the life of his son for a favorite—this would be an instance of admirable mercy and goodness. But that this son should be willing to die, and this father be willing to give the life of his son for their special mortal enemy, is an excess of mercy and goodness inconceivable. Yet this it is that God has done, giving his Son to human nature, his enemy, not only to save it, but also to raise it to the throne of the Divinity. This it is that the Son of God has done, who, when he might have saved men by a word, by a single tear or a single sigh, willed to merit for them the grace of salvation by a life of so much labor and poverty, and by a death of so much agony and shame.

And after this shall we have no confidence in so much mercy? Shall we refuse to hope that a Redeemer so full of goodness, who has ransomed us at the price of his own Blood, will deliver us from our sins and imperfections?

Distrust is extremely displeasing to God, above all in souls which he has endowed with extraordinary graces. It was in punishment for a slight distrust that Moses entered not the land of promise. He died in sight of that land so often promised, and so ardently desired; but he entered not, and God would not let himself be turned by any prayers.

We wrong God when we say, "When shall I attain to indifference? when shall I gain the gift of prayer?" As if God were needy or grudging of his gifts, as if he had not himself undertaken the work of our perfection. Let us only follow his will, let us cooperate with his graces, let us study purity of heart, and rest assured that he will not be wanting to us.

Many will never arrive at a high perfection, because they do not hope sufficiently. We must have a strong and solid hope, grounded on the mercy and infinite goodness of God, and on the infinite merits of Jesus Christ. Thou, O Lord, singularly hast settled me in hope.

We must hope and expect great things from God, because the merits of our Lord belong to us; and to hope much in God is to honor him much. The more we hope, the more we honor him.

Of humility

St Lawrence Justinian says that we do not know what humility is, unless we have it in our heart. It is only those who are humble in heart that are capable of understanding it. Therefore our Lord said, "Learn of me, because I am meek and humble of heart." To acquire humility, we must, in the first place, never omit any outward actions in which we may be able to practice it according to our condition, and on such occasions as present themselves; and we must ask of God true feelings of humility, that we may perform well those exterior acts of this virtue which sometimes are done in a spirit of vanity. In the second place, we must make frequent interior acts of humility, acknowledge our own nothingness and wretchedness, love our own abasement, exercise continually a rigorous judgment, and inwardly pass sentence upon ourselves and upon everything we do.

We must never reprove anyone without being previously convinced, and acknowledging before God, that we do far worse ourselves, and are more guilty than he whom we are about to reprove. Offices of humility and charity are the best, because humility preserves within us the peace and the gifts of God, and charity keeps us occupied about our neighbor.

Let us be humble, patient, mortified, united to God, and he will bless our labors; their success depends absolutely on the blessing of God; for without it all our talents and all our exertions are nothing.

God ever reserves to himself dominion over the gifts with which he favors us. He desires to have the sole glory of them. It is not for the display of our excellence that he confers them upon us; it is to manifest his own. We have not, neither ought we to have, more than the simple use of them solely for the glory of God, and not for our own interest. And this must be understood of all kinds of graces, gifts, and privileges, and even of natural talents and endowments.

In the good we do, and in the good we possess, God leaves to us the profit and advantage, reserving to himself the glory; he will not have us attribute that to ourselves.

We are not content with this allotment; we take God's share to ourselves; we desire to have the glory as well as the profit of our possessions. This injustice is a kind of blasphemy; for nothing is due to nature, considered in itself—and thus we ought to consider it—but vileness and abasement. It is to that we ought incessantly to tend and aspire with a desire and a thirst insatiable, since therein consists our true greatness; all else is but presumption, vanity, illusion, and sin. So much so, that they in whom this desire of abjection is most ardent are the greatest in the sight of God. It is they who, above all others, walk in the truth, and they are so much the more like unto God, as with him they seek only his glory. This is his own property; glory belongs to him alone. As for us, all our estate is nothingness; and if we attribute anything to ourselves, we are robbers. If we love the esteem and applause of the world, we are fools; we feed ourselves with wind.

We commonly form to ourselves a false idea of humility, imagining it to be something degrading to us. It has quite the contrary effect; for as it gives us a true knowledge of ourselves, and is itself unmixed truth, it brings us near to God, and consequently it confers true greatness upon us, which we seek in vain out of God.

Humiliation degrades us only in the estimation of men, which is nothing; it raises us in the estimation of God, in which true glory consists.

Upon such occasions, so trying to nature, we must reflect, that if men behold us despised, defamed, and made a mock of, God looks upon us as exceedingly exalted; in the very things which lower us in the eyes of men, Jesus Christ rejoices to see us wearing his livery, and the angels envy us the honor.

Someone will say, "I cannot persuade myself that I am a greater sinner than others. If I break one rule, I see others who break many; if I am guilty of certain faults, I see others who are guilty of greater."

The difficulty we feel in conceiving this humble opinion of ourselves arises from our being as yet so very unspiritual. We shall have it when we are more advanced. In all arts and sciences there are secrets which are known only to those who are adepts in them. So in spiritual science, which is the most excellent of all, inasmuch as it is purely supernatural, there are maxims the knowledge of which belongs only to the saints, who are doctors in this divine science. A St Francis of Assisi, a St Francis Borgia, were most eminent masters in humility. They esteemed themselves, not after a manner of speaking, but sincerely and from the bottom of their heart, the greatest sinners in the world. They were inwardly persuaded of that which their lips declared.

PURITY OF HEART

In what purity of heart consists
Purity of heart consists in having nothing therein which is, in however small a degree, opposed to God and the operation of his grace.

All the creatures there are in the world, the whole order of nature as well as of grace, and all the leadings of Providence, have been so disposed as to remove from our souls whatever is contrary to God. For never shall we attain unto God until we have corrected, cut off, and destroyed, either in this life or in the next, everything that is contrary to God.

How necessary purity of heart is to us
The first means towards the attainment of perfection is purity of heart; by it alone St Paul the Hermit, St Mary of Egypt, and so many other holy solitaries attained thereto. Next after purity of heart come the precepts and spiritual doctrine to be found in books; then direction and faithful cooperation with graces bestowed. This is the high road of perfection.

We must devote our whole care to the purifying of our heart, because there lies the root of all our evils.

To be able to conceive how requisite purity of heart is to us, it would be necessary fully to comprehend the natural corruption of the human heart. There is in us a very depth of malice, which we do not perceive, because we never seriously examine our own interior. If we did, we should find therein a multitude of desires and irregular appetites for the honors, the pleasures, and the comforts of the world unceasingly fermenting in our heart.

We are so full of false ideas and erroneous judgments, of disorderly affections, passions, and malice, that we should stand confounded at ourselves, could we see ourselves such as we are. Let us imagine a muddy well, from which water is continually being drawn: at first, what comes up is scarcely anything but mud; but by dint of drawing, the well is gradually cleansed, and the water becomes purer, until at last it is as clear as crystal. In like manner, by laboring incessantly to purge our soul, the ground of it becomes gradually cleared, and God manifests his presence by powerful and marvelous effects which he works in the soul, and through it, for the good of others.

When the heart is thoroughly cleansed, God fills the soul and all its powers, the memory, the understanding, and the will, with his holy presence and love. Thus purity of heart leads to union with God, and no one ordinarily attains thereto by other means.

The shortest and the surest way of attaining to perfection, is to study purity of heart rather than the exercise of virtues, because God is ready to bestow all manner of graces upon us, provided we put no obstacles in their way. Now it is by purifying our heart that we clear away everything which hinders the work of God. When all impediments are removed, it is inconceivable what wonderful effects God produces in the soul. St Ignatius used to say, that even the saints put great obstacles in the way of God's graces.

Without an abundant supply of grace, we shall never do any excellent acts of virtue; and we shall never obtain this abundant supply, till we have thoroughly purged our heart. But when once we have reached this perfect purity of heart, we shall practice those virtues, an opportunity for which is furnished us; and with respect to others, an opportunity of which may not occur, we shall possess the spirit, and so to say, the essence of them, which is what God principally requires; for it is very possible to perform an act of some particular virtue without possessing its spirit and essence.

Of all the exercises of the spiritual life, there is none against which the devil directs more opposition than the study of purity of heart. He will let us perform some exterior acts of virtue, accuse ourselves publicly of our faults, serve in the kitchen, visit the hospitals and prisons, because we sometimes content ourselves with all this, and it serves to flatter us and to prevent interior remorse of conscience; but he cannot endure that we should look into our own heart, examine its disorders, and apply ourselves to their correction. The heart itself recoils from nothing so much as this search and scrutiny, which makes it see and feel its own miseries. All the powers of our soul are disordered beyond measure, and we do not wish to know it, because the knowledge is humiliating to us.

The order to be observed in purity of heart, and the different degrees of purity
The order to be observed in cleansing the heart is, first, to note all venial sins, and correct them; secondly, to observe the disorderly movements of the heart, and amend them; thirdly, to keep watch over the thoughts, and regulate them; fourthly, to recognize the inspiration of God, his designs, his will, and encourage ourselves

to the accomplishment of them. All this must be done calmly, joining therewith a true devotion to our Lord, which comprises a lofty conception of his greatness, a profound reverence for his person and for everything belonging to him, as well as love and imitation of him.

There are four degrees of purity, and to these we may attain by a faithful cooperation with grace. The first is, to free ourselves from actual sins and the penalty due to them. The second, to get rid of our evil habits and disorderly affections. The third, to deliver ourselves from that original corruption which is called *fomes peccati*, the aliment of sin, which is in all the powers of our soul, and in all the members of our body, as is manifest in children, who have the inclination to evil before they yet have the power of actually committing it. The fourth, to shake off that weakness which is natural to us, as creatures taken out of nothingness, which is called *defectibility*.

The first degree is attained mainly by penance. The second, by mortification and the exercise of the other virtues. The third, by the sacraments, which operate within us the grace of our renewal. The fourth, by our union with God, who being our beginning and the source of our being, can alone strengthen us against the weaknesses to which our nothingness of itself draws us down.

A soul may attain to a degree of purity at which it has such complete dominion over its imagination and its powers, that they have no longer any exercise, except in the service of God. In this state it can will nothing, remember nothing, think of nothing, hear nothing, but what has to do with God; so that if in conversation, vain and frivolous discourse were held, it would have to withdraw into itself, for lack of ideas or images whereby to understand what was said, or to retain the remembrance of it.

OF THE GUIDANCE OF THE HOLY SPIRIT, AND DOCILITY THERETO

In what this docility consists
When a soul has given itself up to the leading of the Holy Spirit, he raises it little by little, and directs it. At first it knows not whither it is going; but gradually the interior light illuminates it, and enables it to behold all its own actions, and the governance of God therein,

so that it has scarcely aught else to do than to let God work in it and by it whatever he pleases; thus it makes wonderful progress.

We have a figure of the guidance of the Holy Spirit in that which God adopted in regard to the Israelites in their exodus from Egypt during their journeying in the wilderness towards the land of promise. He gave them as their guide a pillar of cloud by day, and a pillar of fire by night. They followed the movements of this pillar, and halted when it halted; they did not go before it, they only followed it, and never wandered from it. It is thus we ought to act with respect to the Holy Spirit.

The means of attaining this docility

The principal means by which we obtain this direction of the Holy Spirit are the following:

1. To obey faithfully God's will so far as we know it; much of it is hidden from us, for we are full of ignorance; but God will demand an account at our hands only of the knowledge he has given us; let us make good use of it, and he will give us more. Let us fulfill his designs so far as he has made them known to us, and he will manifest them to us more fully.

2. To renew often the good resolution of following in all things the will of God, and strengthen ourselves in this determination as much as possible.

3. To ask continually of the Holy Spirit this light and this strength to do the will of God, to bind ourselves to him, and remain his prisoners like St Paul, who said to the priests of Ephesus, "Being bound in the Spirit, I go to Jerusalem"; above all, in every important change of circumstances, to pray God to grant us the illumination of the Holy Spirit, and sincerely protest that we desire nothing else, but only to do his will. After which if he impart to us no fresh light, we may act as heretofore we have been accustomed to act, and as shall appear best for the time being.

   This is why at the commencement of important affairs, as the opening of the Law Courts, the assemblies of the clergy and councils, the assistance of the Holy Spirit is invoked by votive masses said in his honor.

4. Let us watch with care the different movements of our soul. By such attention we shall come gradually to perceive what is of

God and what is not. That which proceeds from God in a soul which is subjected to grace, is generally peaceable and calm. That which comes from the devil is violent, and brings with it trouble and anxiety.

Happy they whom God favors with this rare gift, like Jacob, of whom the wise man says: God gave him the knowledge of holy things. We ourselves, above all, have need of it, who, by the duty of our vocation, are obliged to mix in the world. This gift of knowledge is much more necessary to us than to solitaries and other religious, whose life is more retired and purely contemplative.

In order that intercourse with men may not be hurtful to us, in the functions which we exercise in their regard to gain them to God, we must observe that our life ought to be a mixture of action and contemplation, in such wise that the former may be animated, directed, and ordered by the latter; that among the exterior works of the active life, we may always enjoy the interior repose of the contemplative; and that our employment may not hinder our union with God, but rather serve to bind us more closely and more lovingly to him; making us embrace them in him by contemplation, and in our neighbor by action.

We shall enjoy this advantage, if we possess the gifts of the Holy Spirit, to such a degree as to be, to use a familiar expression, more than half filled with them. But meanwhile the best thing for us to do, after satisfying the requirements of obedience and charity, is to give ourselves to recollection and prayer, as also to reading and the other exercises of the contemplative life.

Let us take as our model Jesus Christ, who devoted thirty years to the contemplative life, and three or four only to that which is called mixed; and God himself, whose life, before time began, was purely contemplative, his sole occupation being the knowing and loving of himself. In time, indeed, he acts externally, but after such a manner, that action bears scarcely any proportion to contemplation; and in eternity, when time is ended, he will give himself still less to action, seeing that then he will no longer create new creatures.

To make much progress in perfection two things are necessary, one on the part of the master, the other on the part of the disciple. In the master, that he should be greatly enlightened with the gift of knowledge, as was St Ignatius; in the disciple, that he should have a will perfectly subject to grace, and a great courage, like St Francis Xavier.

It is a great misfortune for a soul towards which God has great designs, to fall into the hands of a director who is guided only by human prudence, and has more policy than unction.

An excellent means of acquiring the gift of knowledge is to study greatly purity of heart; to watch carefully over our own interior, to mark all its irregularities, and note its principal faults.

Such strictness will draw down the blessing of God, who will not fail in time to pour his lights into the soul, and will give it little by little the knowledge of itself, which is the most useful he can impart to us next to that of his own divine majesty.

This is the first study in the school of perfection. When we have applied ourselves to it constantly for some time, we begin to see clearly into our interior; and this we may do without difficulty, by means of the sudden lights which God communicates to the soul according to its state and present dispositions. At this point it is not far from contemplation, and enjoys, as it were, some pledges of the great gifts which God is about to confer upon it, provided it be faithful in corresponding with his designs. For God lays firm the foundation before he builds the edifice; and this foundation is the knowledge of ourselves and our own wretchedness, lest we should come afterwards to pride ourselves on the gifts of God. Now it is little to believe and know that of ourselves we are nothing and can do nothing. The most vicious believe and know this well enough. God would have us obtain an experimental and sensible knowledge of ourselves; and to this end he makes us keenly feel our wretchedness.

You will sometimes see persons who say they practice the prayer of simple regard, or take the divine perfections for the subject of their meditations, and yet are full of the grossest errors and imperfections, because they have attempted too high a flight before they have purified their heart. But tell them what you think of this, and they get angry, believing themselves already highly spiritual, and consider you but little enlightened in mystical theology; so that, after all, they must be sent back to the first elements of the spiritual life, that is to say, to keeping watch over their hearts, as at the very beginning, if they are to make any progress.

In vain do we practice so much spiritual reading, and consult so many books, in order to acquire the science of the interior life: the unction and the light which teaches come from above. A pure soul will learn more in one month by the infusion of grace, than others in several years by the labor of study.

More beyond all comparison is learnt by the practice of virtues, than by all the spiritual books and all the speculations in the world. It was to convince us of this truth that our Lord gave to mankind examples of virtue, before giving lessons in it and laying down precepts; *Coepit Jesus facere et docere*; and David said to God, "I have had understanding above ancients, because I have sought thy commandments." In this book it was that St Antony studied, in order to learn the science of the saints, and soar above the proud teaching of the philosophers. In this book it is that so many simple souls, without the study of letters, have acquired knowledge hidden from the learned of this world.

All our life long we ought to lay open our conscience to our superior and our spiritual father with great candor and simplicity, hiding from them none of the movements of our heart; so as to be willing, were it possible, to put our whole interior in their hands for their inspection. By the merit of this humility we shall obtain from God the gift of discernment of spirits, for the guidance of our own conduct and for the direction of others.

The vice which is opposed to the gift of knowledge is ignorance, or the want of that knowledge which we might and ought to have for our own guidance and that of others.

Our life is commonly spent in the three kinds of ignorance to which, as St Lawrence Justinian observes, persons who profess the spiritual life are subject....

The beatitude which answers to this gift is the third: "*Blessed are they that mourn*"; for the knowledge we receive from the Holy Spirit teaches us to know our faults and the vanity of earthly things, and shows us that we ought to expect from creatures only wretchedness and mourning.

The fruit of the Holy Spirit which corresponds therewith is that of faith, inasmuch as this gift perfects the knowledge we have gained of human actions and of creatures from the light of faith.

In the morning we ought to beg the assistance of the Holy Spirit for all the actions of the day, humbly acknowledging our ignorance and weakness, and protesting that we will follow his guidance with a full and entire submission of mind and heart.

Then at the beginning of every action we ought again to ask the light of the Holy Spirit to perform it well, and when concluded, beg pardon for the faults we may have committed while engaged in it. By this means we keep ourselves all the day long in a state of dependence upon God, who alone knows the particular circumstances in which we are to be placed, and therefore can guide us more surely on all occasions by his counsel than by all other lights, whether of faith or the other gifts, which are not so applicable to individual cases.

The vice that is opposed to the gift of piety is hardness of heart, which springs out of an ill-regulated love of ourselves; for this love makes us naturally sensible only to our own interests, so that nothing affects us except in reference to ourselves. We behold the offences done against God without tears, and the miseries of our neighbor without compassion; we are unwilling to incommode ourselves to oblige others; we cannot put up with their faults; we inveigh against them on the slightest ground, and harbor in our hearts feelings of bitterness and resentment, hatred and antipathy, against them.

On the other hand, the more charity or love of God a soul possesses, the more sensitive it is to the interests of God and those of its neighbor.

This hardness is worst in the great ones of the world, in rich misers and voluptuaries, and in those who never soften their hearts by exercises of piety and familiarity with spiritual things.

It is also often to be found amongst men of learning who do not join devotion to knowledge, and who, to disguise this fault from themselves, call it strength of mind; but the truly learned have been the most pious, as St Thomas, St Bonaventure, St Bernard....

It is a great misfortune when natural and acquired talents are more esteemed in religion than piety. You will sometimes see religious, and perhaps superiors, who will loudly declare that they attach much more value to a practical active mind than to all those petty devotions, which, say they, are all very well for women, but are unbecoming in a strong mind, meaning by strength of mind that hardness of heart which is so opposed to the spirit of piety. They ought to bear in mind that devotion is an act of religion, or a fruit of religion and of charity, and consequently that it is to be preferred to all the moral virtues, religion following immediately in order of dignity the theological virtues.

Of the gift of fortitude
Fortitude is a virtue which strengthens us against fear and dread of the difficulties, dangers, and toils which present themselves in the execution of our undertakings.

This the gift of fortitude admirably effects; for it is an habitual disposition which the Holy Spirit communicates to the soul and to the body both to do and to suffer extraordinary things; to undertake the most arduous actions; to expose ourselves to the most formidable dangers; to undergo the most toilsome labors; to endure the most grievous pains, and that with constancy and heroism.

This gift is exceedingly necessary on certain occasions, when we feel ourselves assailed with pressing temptations, to resist which we must resolve to lose our goods, our honor, or our life. It is then that the Holy Spirit powerfully assists with his counsel and strength a faithful soul, which, distrusting itself and convinced of its own weakness and nothingness, implores his succor and places all its confidence in him.

The gift of fortitude as respects the body renders those on whom God bestows it capable of performing deeds requiring miraculous strength, as David, Samson, and certain others of the Old Testament. We find in the lives of the saints that some, like St Dominic Loricatus, St Catherine of Siena, Father Gonzalez Silveira, have had this gift to enable them to practice prodigious mortifications beyond their natural strength.

But the gift of fortitude is chiefly bestowed to strengthen the mind, from which it banishes all human fears, imparting to the will and to the appetite a divine firmness which renders the soul intrepid.

It was by this spirit of fortitude that our Lord, in his Agony in the garden, overcame the dread of his Passion and death, and rising from prayer all on fire with zeal, said to his disciples, "Rise, let us go: behold, he is at hand that will betray me."

Of the gift of the fear of God
The gift of the fear of God is an habitual disposition which the Holy Spirit communicates to the soul to maintain it in a state of reverence before the majesty of God, and of dependence upon and submission to his will, causing it to fly from everything that can displease him.

This gift is the foundation and basis of all others, because the first step in the way of God is the avoidance of evil, which appertains to this gift. It is through fear that we attain to the sublime gift of wisdom. We begin to taste God when we begin to fear him, and wisdom in its turn perfects fear. It is the taste of God which renders the fear of God loving, pure, and detached from all self-interest.

The effects of this gift are to impart to the soul, first, a continual reserve, a holy trembling, a profound self-annihilation before God; secondly, an extreme horror of the least offence against him, and a constant resolution to avoid all occasions of displeasing him; thirdly, a humble confession when we have fallen into any fault; fourthly, a watchful care in checking the irregular inclinations of the appetite, and frequent self-observation, in order to investigate the state of our interior, and see what is passing within contrary to perfect fidelity in the service of God.

Never shall we attain to perfect inward purity until we so watch over all the movements of our heart and all our thoughts, that scarcely anything escapes us of which we may not be able to render account to God, and which does not tend to his glory; so that in the space of a week, for example, we should perform very few exterior or interior acts of which grace is not the principle; and if any exceptions occur, they should be owing simply to surprise, and last but for a few moments, our will being so closely united to God that it represses them the instant it perceives them.

It is seldom that we achieve a complete victory over our disorderly movements; scarcely ever do we so perfectly overcome any single one but there escapes or remains something, either through want of attention, or for lack of a sufficiently vigorous resistance. Thus one of the greatest graces which God bestows upon us in this life, and which we ought most to beg of him, is to be so watchful over our heart as that the least irregular movement shall not secretly arise in it without our perceiving it and immediately correcting it; for every day we are betrayed into a multitude of such which escape our observation.

As soon as we perceive we have committed a sin, we ought instantly to repent of it and make an act of contrition, for fear such sin should hinder subsequent graces; and this assuredly will be the result, if we fail in doing penance for it.

Some have no need of making a particular examination, because they no sooner commit the least fault than they are immediately reproved for it and made aware of it; for they walk always in the light of the Holy Spirit, who is their guide. Such persons are rare, and they make a particular examination, so to say, out of everything.

The spirit of fear may be carried to excess, and then it is prejudicial to the soul, and hinders those communications and effects which divine love would operate in it, if it were not thus shut up and chilled with fear.

The vice opposed to the gift of fear is a spirit of pride, independence, and license, which makes men unwilling to do anything but follow their own inclinations, and unable to endure any subjection, so that they sin without scruple, and make no account of slight faults, appear before God with little awe, commit many irreverences in his presence, despise his inspirations, neglect the occasions that offer themselves of practicing virtue, and live in a state of laxity and tepidity.

It is said that an idle thought, a careless word, any action performed without direct intention, is a small matter. This would be true, were we in a state purely natural; but supposing that we are raised, as indeed we are, to a supernatural state, which has been purchased for us by the precious Blood of the Son of God; supposing that on each moment of our life an eternity depends, and that the least of our actions merits the possession or the deprivation of a glory which, being eternal in its duration, is, in a manner, infinite—it must needs be confessed that every day, by our negligence and by our cowardice, we incur losses inconceivable for want of an abiding conversion of the heart to God. Let us be convinced, once for all, that the exterior actions to which we devote all our attention are nothing but the body, and that the intention and the interior constitute the soul.

Of the nature of the fruits of the Holy Spirit
When we have long exercised ourselves with fervor in the practice of virtues, we acquire a facility in producing acts of them. We no longer feel the repugnancies we experienced at first. We have no longer to combat and do violence to ourselves. We do with pleasure what before we did only with difficulty. The same thing happens to virtues as to trees. As the latter bear fruits which, when they are ripe, lose their sharpness, and are sweet and pleasant to the taste; so when the acts of the virtues have attained a certain maturity, we perform them with pleasure, and find in them a delicious flavor. At this stage, these acts of virtue inspired by the Holy Spirit are called fruits of the Holy Spirit; and certain virtues produce them in such perfection and sweetness, that they are called beatitudes, because

they cause the soul to be wholly filled with God. Now the more God possesses a soul, the more he sanctifies it; and the more holy it is, the nearer it approaches to that happy state in which nature being healed of its corruption, the virtues become as it were natural.

They who strive after perfection by the way of systematic practices and acts, without abandoning themselves completely to the guidance of the Holy Spirit, never have this sweetness and as it were ripeness of virtue; they always feel difficulty and repugnancies, they have always to combat, and are often vanquished, and commit faults: instead of which, they who proceed under the direction of the Holy Spirit, in the way of simple recollection, practice what is good with a fervor and a joy worthy of the Holy Spirit, and win glorious victories without a struggle, or if they have to combat, they do so with pleasure.

Whence it follows, that tepid souls have twice as much trouble in the practice of virtue as the fervent, who devote themselves to it in earnest and without reserve; because the latter possess the joy of the Holy Spirit, which renders everything easy to them; whereas the former have their passions to fight against, and experience the weaknesses and infirmities of nature, which counteract the sweetness of virtue, and render its acts difficult and imperfect.

Give a man the dominion of the world, with an authority the most absolute possible; let him possess all the riches, all the honors, all the pleasures that could be desired; impart to him the most perfect wisdom you can imagine; let him be another Solomon and more than Solomon, and be ignorant of nothing that the mind can know; add thereto the power of working miracles; let him stay the sun in its course, divide seas, raise the dead; let him be endued with divine power in as high a degree as you please, and let him, moreover, have the gift of prophecy, the discernment of spirits, the knowledge of the secrets of hearts. Yet I say that the least degree of holiness this man may possess, the least act of charity he may perform, is worth more than all; it brings him nearer to the Sovereign Good, and invests him with a being more excellent than all these other advantages would bestow upon him, if he had them. And this for two reasons.

First, because to partake of the holiness of God is to partake of that which is, so to say, most essential in him. The other attributes of God, as knowledge, power, may be communicated in such wise as to be natural to men; holiness alone can never be natural to them.

Secondly, because holiness and happiness are, as it were, two inseparable sisters, and God communicates himself and unites himself only to holy souls, and not to such as, without holiness, have knowledge, power, and all other perfections imaginable.

Of peace
It is peace that causes God to reign in the soul, and gives him the entire sovereignty of it. This it is that keeps the soul in that perfect dependence which it ought to have on God.

By sanctifying grace God forms to himself, as it were, a citadel in the soul, wherein he entrenches himself. By peace he makes a kind of sally and takes possession of all the faculties, fortifying them so strongly that creatures can no longer enter there to disturb them. God occupies all the interior: thus the saints are as united to God in action as in prayer, and events the most distressing never cause them any trouble.

Of patience and meekness
The property of the virtue of patience is to moderate excess of sadness; and the virtue of meekness allays the gusts of anger which rise impetuously to repel any present evil.

These two virtues combat and win the victory only by violent efforts, and that not without difficulty; but patience and meekness, which are the fruits of the Holy Spirit, reduce their enemies to obedience without combating, or if they combat, it is without labor, nay with pleasure. Patience beholds with joy objects calculated to produce sadness: thus martyrs rejoice at the threat of persecutions and the sight of tortures. When once peace is firmly established in the heart, meekness has no longer any trouble in regulating the movements of anger. The soul retains its equilibrium and never loses its tranquility. And this is the effect of the Holy Spirit, who, residing in it and possessing it in all its powers, banishes all objects of sadness, or prevents them from making any impression; so that the devil even stands in awe of such a soul, and does not venture to approach it.

Of the fruit of faith
Faith, so far as it is a fruit of the Holy Spirit, is a certain facility in believing everything that appertains to the belief of the faithful,

a constancy in adhering thereto, and an assurance of the truth of what we believe, without feeling those repugnancies and doubts, that darkness and dullness of mind, which we naturally experience in regard to matters of faith.

In order to do this there must be in the will a pious affection inclining the understanding to believe, without hesitation, the things proposed to it.

Of the fruits of modesty

Modesty, in so far as it is a virtue, is well known. It regulates all the movements of the body, the gestures, and the words. In so far as it is a fruit of the Holy Spirit, it does this easily and naturally; and, moreover, it composes all the interior movements of the soul, as in the presence of God.

Our mind is light and restless, always in action, fluttering on all sides, fastening on all sorts of objects, prattling unceasingly. Modesty checks it, moderates it, and settles the soul in a profound peace, which disposes it to become the habitation and the kingdom of God; thus the gift of the presence of God follows speedily on the fruit of modesty. The latter is to the former what the dew was to the manna; and the presence of God is a transcendent light, in which the soul beholds itself before God, and observes all its interior movements, everything that passes within it more clearly than we see colors at noonday.

Modesty is absolutely necessary to us; because immodesty, although in itself it seems to be a small thing, is notwithstanding of great importance on account of its consequences, and is no slight mark of a mind but little religious.

It often happens that when the Holy Spirit puts some good thought into our mind, the devil steals it away, playing off a cheat upon us, and suggesting in its stead another, which, although perhaps it be not in itself bad, nevertheless does us much harm, since it deprives us of that good impulse, and that peace resulting from the first thought, which came from God; so that we ought to be upon our guard, in order to confirm ourselves in the one and reject the other; and it is of the utmost importance that we should watch attentively over our thoughts, and test them thoroughly at their commencement, in their progress, and in their conclusion.

Of distinguishing between the operations of God and those of the devil.
Everything that destroys the peace and tranquility of the interior
proceeds from the devil. God has joined together happiness and
holiness in such wise that his graces not only sanctify the soul, but
also console it, and fill it with peace and sweetness. The suggestions
of the devil have the very contrary effect, either at once, or at least
in the end; the serpent is known by his tail, that is to say, by the
effects he produces, and the conclusion to which he leads.

All hypothetical or conditional propositions, calculated only to
cause trouble, come from the devil; as, for example, were God to
abandon me on such an occasion, what should I do? and the like.
We should make no reply to such propositions, nor allow the mind
to rest on such thoughts, which the enemy suggests to take from us
our confidence in God, and to cast us into disquietude and despondency. Let us trust in God, for he is faithful, and will never fail those
who, having wholly given themselves up to him, seek only to please
him in all things.

Secret illusions
It happens very often that when we feel some irregular movement
excited in our heart, we are unwilling to consent to the sin, but are
unwilling also resolutely to drive away the evil feeling. We reject the
sin which would be manifest in the eyes of men, and we allow the
interior irregularity which God sees, and which is displeasing to
him. For example, we have a feeling of bitterness against someone;
we are unwilling to consent to display this feeling towards him, but
we allow our heart to be filled with it, instead of ridding ourselves
of it at once. This is one of our most secret and most dangerous
illusions.

When we have a desire for anything, a thousand reasons occur
to us to give a color to our passion. We deceive ourselves when,
having formed some design from natural inclination, we seek for
some reason on the side of grace to lend it support. "I am going to
see so-and-so; I will also exhort him to make a retreat." Generally
speaking, this also comes from a bad principle; it is an invention of
self-love, which is ingenious in discovering such reasons.

It sometimes happens that when God gives us the light and the
inspiration of his grace to correct us of certain faults to which we
are subject, we turn our thoughts another way; we apply ourselves to
some other action of virtue, and practice a deception upon God, in

order to avoid the stings and reproaches of our conscience, escape the shame which the sight of our fault would cause us, and delude ourselves agreeably with the persuasion of our own virtue. But we shall never attain to this holy liberty, this largeness of heart, which we are seeking, unless we correct ourselves of the faults which God makes known to us.

Sometimes we do not sufficiently observe, that while meditating on the highest objects or engaged in the holiest occupations, our mind is not so completely engrossed therewith but that we are thinking at the same time of other idle things; and this is so much of our life that is lost, when it ought to be given to God.

In what the interior life consists

The interior life consists in two sorts of acts—viz., in thoughts and in affections. It is in this only that perfect souls differ from imperfect, and the blessed from those who are still living on earth. Our thoughts, says St Bernard, ought to be ever following after truth, and our affections ever abiding in the fervor of charity. In this manner, our mind and heart being closely applied to God, being fully possessed by God, in the very midst of exterior occupations we never lose sight of him, and are always engaged in the exercise of his love.

Good and bad religious differ from each other only in the nature of their thoughts, their judgments, and their affections. In this also consists the difference between angels and devils, and it is this that makes the former holy and blessed, and the latter wicked and miserable. Accordingly we ought to watch with extreme care over our interior, and pay continual attention to regulate our judgments according to truth, and to keep our affections in subordination to charity.

The essence of the spiritual and interior life consists in two things; on the one hand, in the operations of God in the soul, in the lights that illumine the understanding, and the inspirations that affect the will; on the other, in the cooperation of the soul with the lights and movements of grace. So that to hold communion with God, and to dispose ourselves to receive from him larger and more frequent communications, we must possess great purity of heart, great strength of mind, and observe a constant and inviolable fidelity in cooperating with God, and following the movement of his Spirit in whatever direction it may impel us.

One of the occupations of the interior life is the examining and ascertaining particularly three sorts of things in our interior. First, what comes from our own nature—our sins, our evil habits, our passions, our inclinations, our affections, our desires, our thoughts, our judgments, our sentiments; secondly, what comes from the devil—his temptations, his suggestions, his artifices, the illusions by which he tries to seduce us unless we are on our guard; thirdly, what comes from God—his lights, his inspirations, the movements of his grace, his designs in our regard, and the ways along which he desires to guide us. In all this we must examine and see how we conduct ourselves, and regulate our behavior by the Spirit of God.

We must carefully observe what it is that the Holy Spirit most leads us to, and in what we most resist him; at the beginning of our actions ask grace to perform them well, and mark even the slightest movements of our heart.

We ought not to devote all our time of recollection to prayer and reading, but employ a portion in examining the disposition of our heart, in ascertaining what passes there, and discovering what is of God, what is of nature, and what is of the devil; in conforming ourselves to the guidance of the Holy Spirit, and strengthening ourselves in the determination of doing everything and suffering everything for God.

How we ought to imitate the interior life of God
We ought to imitate the interior life of God in this, that he possesses within himself an infinite life, as well by the operation of the understanding, by which he is the principle of the Person of the Word, as by that of the will, by which he is the principle of the Person of the Holy Spirit. Moreover, he acts externally to himself, according to his good pleasure, by the production and government of the universe, without this exterior action causing any diminution or any change in his interior life; in such wise that in respect thereto he acts externally, as though he were not acting at all.

This is our model: in the first place, we ought to have within ourselves and for ourselves a most perfect life by a constant application of our understanding and will to God. Then we shall be able to go out of ourselves for the service of our neighbor without prejudice to our interior life, not giving ourselves up wholly to others, nor applying ourselves to exterior occupations, except by way of diversion, so to say: and thus our principal business will ever be the interior life…. "Do not give thyself up to thy neighbor," said St Bernard, "so as to be no longer thine own; possess thyself always; fill thyself with grace as a reservoir; then thou wilt be of use in communicating thereof to others. Be not like a canal, through which the water passes without staying therein."

This advice of St Bernard ought to be the rule of evangelical laborers. But often they do the very reverse. They pour themselves forth entirely; they exhaust themselves for others, and remain themselves dry. All the marrow of their soul, if one may use the expression, all the vigor of their mind, spends itself in their exterior actions. There remains scarcely anything for the interior.

Hence it follows, that unless they take care, they have just ground to fear that, instead of being raised to heaven, according to the excellence of their vocation, they will be of the number of those who will be detained the longest time in purgatory and placed in the lowest ranks in glory.

The exterior life of religious employed in the service of their neighbor is most imperfect, and even perilous, unless it be accompanied with the interior life; and they who are engaged in these kinds of offices of charity and zeal, unless they join thereto exercises of interior recollection, will never make any notable progress in perfection.

And first, they will never arrive at the perfection of the purgative life. It is true they will have at times some of its sentiments. They will do things that appear great in the eyes of the world. They will preach; they will labor in missions; they will traverse seas, and expose themselves to danger of death, and to the fatigues attendant on the longest journeys, for the salvation of their neighbor. But with all this they will never make much progress in the purgative life. The acts of virtue they perform will proceed partly from grace and partly from nature. They will never do such as are purely supernatural, and under specious pretexts self-love will always make them follow their own inclinations and do their own will. They will fall continually into their ordinary faults and imperfections, and will be in great danger of being lost; for as they are occupied in anything but discovering the irregularities of their heart, they never think of purging it; so that it is continually filling with sins and miseries, which gradually enfeeble the strength of the soul, and end at last in entirely stifling devotion and the Spirit of God.

Secondly, they will never attain to the perfection of the illuminative life, which consists in discovering in all things the will of God; for it is only interior men who can discern it in everything. My superiors, my rules, the duties of my state, may indeed direct me in regard to the exterior, and indicate to me what God desires me to do at such a time and in such a place; but they cannot teach me the way in which God wills that I should do it. I know, for instance, that it is God's will that I should pray when I hear the clock strike which calls me to prayer according to my rule; but the rule does not tell me what my comportment ought to be during my prayer. My superior will tell me what God wills that I should apply myself to; but he cannot teach me how I ought to apply myself.

In order to do the will of God well, it is not sufficient to know that it is God's will; for example, that I should forthwith sweep my room; I must also know with what thought he would have me occupy myself while performing this exterior act of humility which my rule prescribes, for God desires to regulate the interior of my actions as well as the exterior. I must fulfilll God's will in the manner as well as in the substance of the action. He desires to govern it even in the smallest details, and his providence extends to the direction of all my powers and all the movements of my heart; without this there will be a void in my actions; they will not be full of the will of God; I shall do what he demands of me only in part and by halves; the best will be wanting, which is the interior. Thus I shall incur great losses of grace and glory, losses that are irreparable; and I shall be the cause of others, whose salvation and perfection I am bound to promote, incurring the same.

Where, then, shall I be able to learn the will of God in regard to the manner of performing well those things which he desires me to do? It is in my own interior and in the depth of my own heart, that God gives the light of his grace, in order to enlighten my conduct. If I can enter into myself, listen attentively to him, and converse familiarly with him, I shall walk in his light, which will enable me to see what he desires of me, and the means of performing it, and the interior perfection which it is his will I should practice therein.

Thirdly, it is clear they will never attain to the perfection of the unitive life, since it consists in the interior union of the soul with God.

For the rest, whoever is resolved to lead an interior life, and to be really spiritual and a man of prayer, must expect that when he has reached a certain point, people will cry out against him; he will have adversaries, and other contradictions; but in the end God will give him peace, and will make everything turn out to his profit and the advancement of his soul.

As there are certain humors which cause the death of the body when they gain too much strength and are too abundant, so in the religious life, when action is carried to excess and is not moderated by prayer and recollection, it infallibly quenches the spirit.

And yet there will sometimes be found persons who, being occupied whole days and years in study and in the turmoil of exterior employments, will feel it difficult to devote a quarter of an hour a day to spiritual reading; and then how is it possible they should become interior men? Hence it is that we gain no fruit, because our ministrations are not animated by the Spirit of God, without which, with all our talents, we cannot attain the end we are aiming at, and are but as sounding brass or a tinkling cymbal.

An interior man will make more impression on hearts by a single word animated by the Spirit of God, than another by a whole discourse which has cost him much labor, and in which he has exhausted all his power of reasoning.

Peace is not found except in the interior life, and our dissatisfactions spring only from our not being interior men

Never shall we have peace until we are interior men and united to God. Repose of mind, joy, solid contentment, are found only in the interior world, in the kingdom of God which we possess within ourselves. The more deeply we enter therein, the more happy shall we be. Without this we shall always be in trouble and difficulty, always discontented, complaining, and murmuring; and if any temptation, any rough trial come upon us, we shall not overcome it.

1. By watching over our interior we gradually acquire a great knowledge of ourselves, and attain at last to the direction of the Holy Spirit; and at times God brings before us in an instant the state of our past life, just as we shall see it at the judgment. He makes us see all our sins, all our past youth; at other times he discloses to us the whole economy of the government of the universe: and this produces in the soul a perfect subjection to God.

2. They who have applied themselves for three or four years to watch over their interior, and have made some progress in this holy exercise, know already how to treat a multitude of cases with address and absence of all rash judgment; they penetrate, as it were naturally, the hearts of others, and discover

almost all their movements by the knowledge they possess of their own interior, and of the natural movements of their own heart.

3. Without performing extraordinary mortifications, or any of those exterior actions which might be the occasion of vanity to us, by simple attention in watching our own interior, we perform excellent acts of virtue and make prodigious advances in perfection; whereas, on the contrary, by neglecting our interior we incur incalculable losses.

4. This exercise may be practiced at every age, at all times, and in all places, in the midst of our exterior functions and in time of illness; and there is no business so embarrassing, which does not allow us to enter into ourselves from time to time, to observe the movements of our heart.

5. What exterior actions did St Paul the Hermit perform, and so many other holy solitaries and virgins? It is the merit of their interior life which raised them to the highest ranks of the blessed.

But, alas, we are so little enlightened, or so bewitched with all the brilliancy of exterior employments, that we understand not the excellence, nor the necessity, nor the merit of that life which is hidden from the eyes of men and known to God alone.

Such is often the end of the purely exterior life of those amongst us who are continually engaged in the tumult of action, abandoning the care of their interior under pretext of zeal and charity, because they labor for the service of their neighbor. But even should they not proceed to this extremity, it is still certain that by wasting themselves exteriorly, and giving scarcely any attention to the regulation of their interior in the exercise of their functions, they suffer incalculable losses of grace and merit. Their labors produce but very little fruit, not being animated by that strength and that vigor which come from the interior spirit, nor accompanied with the benedictions which God bestows on men of prayer and recollection. They do nothing purely for God, they seek themselves in everything, and always secretly mix up their own interest with the glory of God in their best undertakings.

Thus they pass their lives in this mixture of nature and grace, without once taking a single step forward towards perfection for ten or twenty years, the mind as distracted, the heart as hard, amidst all the exercises of Christian piety and the religious life, as if they had never enjoyed all these aids.

At last death comes; and then they open their eyes, they perceive their illusion and blindness, and tremble at approaching the dread tribunal of God.

The means of avoiding all these woes is to regulate our interior so well, and to keep watch over our heart so carefully, as to have ground for desiring, rather than fearing, to appear before our Sovereign Judge. This watchfulness it is that our Lord so much recommends to us in the Gospel, when he says so often, *Vigilate*, Watch.

We ought to join together action and contemplation in such a way as not to give ourselves more to the former than to the latter, endeavoring to excel as much in one as in the other. Otherwise, if we throw ourselves altogether into the exterior life, and give ourselves wholly to action, we shall undoubtedly remain at the lowest degrees of contemplation; that is to say, we shall practice only ordinary prayer, and perform the other exercises of piety in a low and imperfect manner.

We ought so to unite action and the exterior life with contemplation and the interior life, as to give ourselves to the former in the same proportion as we practice the latter. If we make much mental prayer, we ought to give ourselves much to action; if we have made but moderate progress in the interior life we ought to employ ourselves only moderately in the occupations of the exterior life; and if we are but little advanced in the ways of the interior, we ought to abstain altogether from what is exterior, unless obedience prescribes the contrary; otherwise we shall do no good to others and ruin ourselves.

We must be like the eagle, who soars into the air as soon as he has seized his prey. Thus we ought to retire for prayer after any active employment for our neighbor, and never intrude ourselves into such, unless obedience enjoins it.

Of the Person of the Word

In the God-Man three personal properties are to be considered, which are as it were the source and foundation of all his greatness:

he is the Son of God; he is the Image of his Father; he is his Word.

1. He is the Son of God properly and truly, because he proceeds from God the Father by way of generation, and is of the same nature as his principle. He is the Son of God in the most perfect manner possible. He is so necessarily, being necessarily begotten; and he has not only a portion of the substance of his Father, as the children of men, but the whole substance of God the Father, and the whole plenitude of his Divinity.
2. He is the Image of God the Father, because he represents him; and is his perfect image, because he is like unto him in everything, and bears in all things the nature and the substance of his original, which cannot belong to any created image.
3. He is the Word of God. We call the Word, the idea or mental portraiture which the understanding forms to itself of an object when it applies itself to the knowledge thereof. Thus God knowing himself and all possible creatures, the term of this knowledge is his Word, his image, and his Son. And as the understanding is of all the faculties the purest and the most detached from matter, it is not possible to conceive a purity more perfect than that of the generation of the Word, who is produced by the understanding of God the Father; thus by uniting himself to our nature he joins untreated purity to flesh; a prodigy which will be the admiration of the angels for all eternity.

We participate in these three qualities of Jesus Christ, and it is this that forms our true greatness. This is the foundation of the perfection after which we ought to strive.

1. Jesus Christ is the Son of God; we also are his children. He is his Son by nature, we are his children by adoption. We ought to live, as he lives, by the life of God, seeing that for this end he rendered us, like him, partakers of the divine nature.
2. Jesus Christ is the image of God the Father. We ought to be the copies of that image. It is our model. We ought to express in ourselves the features of his resemblance, his virtues, his mind, his interior life, and his exterior life.
3. Jesus Christ is the Word of God. We ought to be his echoes, and respond faithfully to all his graces. We must be the echoes of his doctrine, his sentiments, and his whole conduct.

The alliances of the sacred Humanity of Jesus Christ with the three Persons of the Holy Trinity
In the mystery of the Incarnation the sacred Humanity contracts admirable alliances with the three Persons of the Trinity.

1. With the Son: it is impossible to conceive a closer union than this. Nothing participates so truly in another as the Humanity participates in the Person of the Son, and as the Person of the Son reciprocally participates in the sacred Humanity. The connection of soul and body, and the intercommunion that subsists between these two parts of man, is not so close. Human nature is as much the nature of the Word as my nature is mine, although the two natures, the divine and the human, remain always distinct.
2. With the Father: because this divine union of the Word and the sacred Humanity is the Son of God by nature; and sonship is the first degree of relationship. The son is the heir of the father; he has a right to everything that the father possesses. Thus Jesus Christ, inasmuch as he is man, is heir of all the possessions of God. He is King. He is sovereign judge. Our adoration is due to his Person, his Soul, his Body, and his Blood.
3. With the Holy Spirit: because this divine Spirit, proceeding from the Son as well as from the Father, bears as close a relation to the Son as the Son bears to the Father, although the relation is different. We may say that Jesus Christ is the principle of the Holy Spirit and it is for this reason that the fullness of this divine Spirit was not given to the Church till after the coming of Jesus Christ into the world.

The great advantage of being a man of prayer
A man of prayer is attached to nothing; for he values neither talents, nor offices, nor honors, nor the friendship of influential persons, nor any other temporal advantages. He has no esteem or love except for the treasure he bears within himself, and which no external force can take from him. In comparison with this treasure he despises all else; and so that this only good be preserved to him, he is careless of losing everything beside. It is as if some connoisseur in precious stones had by him a false one, which, however, in common estimation, passed for being real; he would willingly give it to anyone who wanted it, because he knows it to be worth nothing, notwithstanding the high value set upon it by those who are

unskilled in the matter, and who judge of such things only by their appearance.

When a man has wholly given himself to God by a life of prayer, he is no longer pained either by calumnies or by anything that may befall him, however grievous. He is like men protected with armor of proof; whether the missile be snowball, or stone, or bullet, it matters not; it may strike them, but it cannot penetrate their armor; it does them no harm. In like manner, a man of prayer, when his reputation is assailed, examines his conscience, and if he finds himself guilty, confesses his fault and makes satisfaction to the party aggrieved. If he is innocent, he blesses God for the opportunity of suffering for Jesus Christ.

Advice on mental prayer in general

1. The spirit of devotion and prayer will never visit us until we have blotted out the ideas of our past life, the images and the memory of innumerable things which foster our self-love and vanity.
2. In prayer our only object ought to be, to perfect the will, and not merely to become more enlightened.
3. It is only our sins and our evil habits that prevent the will, in prayer, from flying instantly to its Sovereign Good and being enkindled with love. This obstacle removed, the will would soon be all on fire without any long exercise of the understanding.
4. Whatever has most impressed the mind out of prayer will not fail to return to us in prayer more readily than in our other actions. The reason of which is, that in the time of prayer the mind, being in a state of quiescence, is more disposed to receive disturbing impressions of this kind than during the excitement of other actions which occupy it more.
5. Before prayer it is necessary to regulate and dispose the mental powers: the imagination, by representing to it some place on which it may fix itself; the memory, by arranging the several points; the understanding and the will, by providing beforehand some special end of meditation, as the deep realization of some truth, exciting the affections towards some virtue, combating some vice.
6. One good method of prayer, according to the holy Bishop of Geneva, is to place ourselves silently in the presence of God,

and there without the active use of the understanding remain in the presence of God, as listening to him, although we do not deserve that he should speak to us. He will bestow this favor upon us when we shall have, in a manner, satisfied his justice for having neglected so many times to obey his inspirations.

7. Some in their prayer leave the sacred Humanity, and fly to the contemplation of the Divinity. Such a proceeding is generally rash and ill-advised; and if we examine such persons strictly, we shall find them full of imperfections, attachment to their own judgment, pride, and self-love, because they have not sufficiently applied themselves to acquiring self-knowledge and purity of heart before soaring so high. The safest path for them is to return to meditation on the mysteries of Jesus Christ, and the virtues, particularly mortification and humility.

8. Prayer presupposes a tranquil and recollected soul, which is neither agitated by violent passions, nor mastered by any irregular affection, nor burdened by too many occupations, nor embarrassed by cares; nor does God ordinarily communicate himself until we have been faithful in the exercise of prayer for some time, according to the method prescribed to beginners.

9. Everyone ought to adhere faithfully to the kind of prayer suited to his degree and state in the spiritual life. There are three sorts of prayer. Meditation, or discursive prayer, is suited to beginners who are in the purgative life; affective prayer to those who have made some progress and are in the illuminative life; contemplation and the prayer of union to the perfect who are in the unitive life.

OF CONTEMPLATION

There are two sorts of contemplation

1. We must distinguish between two kinds of contemplation, the ordinary and the extraordinary.
2. Ordinary contemplation is a supernatural habit, by which God raises the powers of the soul to sublime knowledge and illu-

minations, lofty sentiments, and spiritual tastes, when he no longer finds in the soul such sins, passions, affections, cares, as prevent the communications he would make to it.

3. They who possess this habit pray easily, and have, as it were, at their disposal the particular grace of the Holy Spirit necessary for the exercise of the theological virtues; so that they make acts of them whenever they will, after raising their heart to God to obtain his succor, which is always ready.

4. There is another higher kind of contemplation, which consists in raptures, ecstasies, visions, and other extraordinary effects. The former leads to this; and we make more progress in it in a short time than we do in meditation during many years—that is to say, we acquire more virtue, and that more speedily. By meditation, the soul walks afoot with labor; by contemplation, it flies without trouble. Thus St Teresa said, that when God had admitted her to this sort of prayer, all her difficulties ceased at once, and she experienced a powerful attraction towards acts of all the virtues, attended with a marvelous relish and sweetness.

They who possess this last gift of prayer commonly pray without knowing they are praying, or being aware of it; and it is then that their prayer is perfect.

In this sort of prayer we place ourselves in God's presence. We remain thus without making distinct or repeated acts, occupied either in a simple contemplation of God with awe and love, or in some pious sentiment which God inspires, and which lasts sometimes an hour, two hours, a day, two days, according to the disposition of the soul and the state of perfection and purity to which it has attained; in souls perfectly pure the presence of God becomes almost unceasing.

It is usually said that in this kind of prayer no acts are made. This is not strictly true, for some are always made, but in a manner more exalted, more simple, and as it were imperceptible. A complete suspension of all act is simple idleness of a very dangerous kind.

Of the gift of the Presence of God. The first step in contemplation
When, after a long cultivation of purity of heart, God would enter into a soul and manifest himself to it openly by the gift of his holy

presence, which is the first in order of his supernatural gifts, the soul finds itself so delighted with this new state, that it feels as if it had never known or loved God before. It is astounded at the blindness and stupidity of men; it condemns the indolence and languor in which we generally pass our lives; it deplores the losses it believes itself to have incurred by its slothfulness; it accounts the life it has hitherto led as not deserving the name of life, and that it is only just beginning to live.

In vain do we labor to have this sense of the presence of God unless he himself bestows it upon us. It is a pure gift of his mercy. But when we have received it, by that presence and in that presence we see God and the will of God in our actions, as we behold at one and the same time the light and the body which it enables us to see. This grace is the fruit of great purity of heart, and leads the soul to close union with God. He bestows it upon us, when, on our part, we do what we can and ought to do.

Were we fully possessed with God, we should be able to practice incessant prayer. It occasionally happens that some passion, or resentment, or vexation of mind, so possesses us, that we are altogether engrossed by it for two or three days together, and think of scarcely anything else. Not an hour in the day passes without our experiencing this ill feeling; and though we fancy we resist it, yet if God were to show us the real disposition of our heart, we should see that we had no desire to be free from it, and yielded it some sort of secret consent.

In like manner, if we had a tender devotion to our Lord, to the Holy Sacrament of the altar, we should think of him a thousand times a day. If our heart were wholly occupied with God, we should cherish an unceasing remembrance of him, and should experience no difficulty in realizing his presence. Everything would serve to raise us to him, and the least occasions would excite our fervor.

Let us be assured that our Lord and the Blessed Virgin behold us from the height of heaven, even with their bodily eyes, the perfection of their powers of vision compensating for the greatness of the distance. Thus we ought to perform all our actions as in their presence; and this is the means of attaining the most exalted sense of the presence of God, wherein the prophets Elias and Eliseus walked, and which made them say: "The Lord liveth, in whose sight

I stand"; a presence, the sense of which is more lively and more piercing than what we have by faith.

Contemplation is true wisdom. This it is the books of Wisdom, Ecclesiastes, and Ecclesiasticus recommend so much. They who dissuade others from it are guilty of a great error. There is no danger in it when we bring to it the requisite dispositions. True it is that there is danger of illusion in raptures and ecstasies, especially while grace is still weak, and the soul as yet unaccustomed to such things; but in contemplation there is no danger.

Meditation wearies and fatigues the mind, and its acts are of short duration; but those of contemplation, even such as is of a common order, last whole hours without labor and without weariness; and in the purest souls contemplation may easily continue several days together, in the very midst of the world and the engagements of business. In the state of glory, the first act made by a holy soul on beholding the beatific vision will last to all eternity without satiety or fatigue, ever the same and ever new. Now contemplation is a participation in the state of glory. It resembles it in its facility and duration. It injures neither health nor strength.

Contemplation opens a new world to the soul, with the beauty of which it is enraptured. St Teresa, when passing out of prayer, used to say that she came from a world incomparably more vast and beautiful than a thousand worlds such as this.

St Bernard, returning from converse with God, went back with regret to the society of men, and dreaded attachment to creatures as hell itself. That holy priest, John of Avila, on leaving the altar, could scarcely endure intercourse with the world.

In contemplation a pure soul discovers without labor, or any exertion of its powers, truths which throw it into ecstasy, and which, withdrawing it from all the operations of the senses, cause it to experience within itself a foretaste of paradise.

By contemplation we obtain a perfect knowledge of things human and temporal, supernatural and heavenly. The former we perceive to be so vile and contemptible as to be convinced that to set any value upon them is the greatest illusion possible, and that to attach our heart to them is the worst disorder we can fall into. We judge infallibly of the value of both one and the other, and distinguish between them as easily and with as much certainty as a man who understands coins, having several pieces before him, is able to pronounce, only by looking at them, or touching them, "This is good gold, and that is not."

Without contemplation we shall never make much progress in virtue, and shall never be fitted to make others advance therein. We shall never entirely rid ourselves of our weaknesses and imperfections. We shall remain always bound down to earth, and shall never rise much above mere natural feelings. We shall never be able to render to God a perfect service. But with it we shall effect more, both for ourselves and for others, in a month, than without it we should accomplish in ten years. It produces acts of great perfection, and such as are altogether pure from the alloy of nature; most sublime acts of the love of God, which we perform but very rarely without this gift; and, in fine, it perfects faith and all virtues, elevating them to the highest degree to which they are capable of rising.

If we have not received this excellent gift, it is dangerous to throw ourselves too much into active occupations of charity towards our neighbor. We ought to engage in them only experimentally, unless imposed upon us by obedience, otherwise we ought to occupy ourselves but little in external employments, the mind in such case having enough to do in acquiring self-knowledge, in purifying continually the natural acts and sentiments of the heart, and in regulating the interior, so that we may walk always in the presence of God.

What contemplation is
Contemplation is a perception of God or of divine things, simple, free, penetrating, certain, proceeding from love, and tending to love.

1. This perception is simple. In contemplation we do not exercise the reason, as in meditation.
2. It is free; because to produce it the soul must be liberated from the least sins, irregular affections, eagerness, and unprofitable and disquieting cares. Without this, the understanding is like a bird, tied by the feet, which cannot fly unless it be set at liberty.

3. It is clear and penetrating, not as in the state of glory, but as compared with the knowledge we have by faith, which is always obscure. In meditation we see things only confusedly, as it were from afar off, and in a dryer manner. Contemplation enables us to see them more distinctly, and as it were close at hand. It enables us to touch them, feel them, taste them, and have an inward experience of them. To meditate on hell, for instance, is to see a painted lion; to contemplate hell, is to see a living lion.

4. It is certain; because its objects are the supernatural truths which the divine light discloses to it; and when this disclosure is made immediately to the understanding, it is not liable to error. When it is made either through the senses or through the imagination, some illusion may at times mix with it.

5. It proceeds from love, and tends to love. It is the employment of the purest and the most perfect charity. Love is its principle, its exercise, and its term.

The gifts of the Holy Spirit which serve to contemplation are particularly those of understanding, wisdom, and knowledge, in regard to the intellect; and those of piety and fear, in regard to the will.

Of the properties and effects of contemplation
The properties and effects of contemplation are: elevation, suspension, admiration, raptures, and ecstasies.

1. Contemplation elevates the mind above its ordinary mode of action, and draws it supernaturally to sublime operations, whether with regard to God simply or any object relating to God. This elevation is produced either by the gift of wisdom or by that of knowledge; by the first, if contemplation is occupied with the perfections of God; by the second, if with some other object relating to him. The gift of understanding also contributes thereto, inasmuch as by its means the mind is enabled intimately to penetrate whatever appertains to wisdom or knowledge.

2. The mind thus elevated remains, as it were, suspended in the knowledge of the truth with which it is enraptured. This may be explained by comparing it to the flight of birds, which do not always continue mounting, but after raising themselves

aloft, keep themselves sometimes suspended in the air without vibration of their wings or any other apparent movement. In this state of suspension sometimes it is the understanding, sometimes the will that is most exercised, according as God communicates to the soul more light or more affection.

When it is said that the will is more exercised than the understanding, it is meant that its action is strongest and most sensible, and not that it acts alone, without the understanding acting at all, as some with little probability maintain. The will, then, in this condition is so penetrated, so inflamed with its object, that the action of the understanding is imperceptible. It is as if the will absorbed all the forces of the soul, so pre-occupied and possessed is it by the Spirit of God.

3. Suspension is followed by admiration; which may spring from two sources—viz., either the ignorance of the mind, or the greatness of the object.

4. Sometimes admiration is so strong that the mind no longer acts externally; and this is the cause of raptures and ecstasies. Rapture, properly so called, is a sudden transport of the powers of the soul, elevated in an instant by the Spirit of God. Ecstasy is the state and the repose in which the soul continues when thus elevated above itself. Some would have ecstasy to be that kind of transport which takes place gradually and gently, and is called by others the flight of the spirit.

Raptures are marks of imperfection, and of a certain remaining earthliness, when they happen to a soul simply because it is as yet unaccustomed to the objects which throw it into rapture; but when they proceed from the greatness and the extraordinary excellence of the light communicated by God, they are not marks of imperfection.

In first raptures the impression made by supernatural objects upon the soul and body is so powerful that we are unable to support it without being carried out of our senses; but in course of time the soul becomes accustomed to it, and gradually grows stronger, so that the impression produced by the divine communications it receives ceases to be attended with violent effects except when God, who is infinite in bounty, imparts some new and very extraordinary light; for on such occasions the soul will still fall into rapture, although it has become accustomed to those objects which heretofore produced that effect upon it.

In fine, when the soul, being perfectly strengthened and habituated to the most wonderful communications of grace, is no longer liable to be ravished out of itself it experiences the effects of rapture without being actually in a state of rapture. The impressions of grace are then purely spiritual, and act no longer on the body, as was the case when it was not perfectly subject to the spirit, and as pure as it is now become.

For it is a maxim of philosophers, that everything received into a subject is received therein according to the disposition of the subject. Thus, when the soul is still somewhat sensual, and the body not entirely purified, the operations of God, meeting with this obstacle, are more feeble, less sweet, and less perfect.

St Teresa said that after receiving graces of this sort, it is martyrdom to live among creatures; the soul, on returning to itself, feels more keenly than ever its exile and its miseries.

These wonderful effects of grace cannot be explained even by those who experience them, and much less by those who have no experience of them. Generally they fill the soul with so much sweetness and such solid contentment, that St Francis Xavier used to say that for the least of such consolations he would willingly have undertaken a second voyage to Japan, fearless of the toils he had endured in the first.

This is quite a different thing from those sweetnesses and tears of sensible devotion which God sometimes gives to beginners.

Whence we may see how great is the misery of spending our life in trifles and sensual satisfactions which deprive us of the favors of our Lord; and that there is incomparably more pleasure in serving God in self-abnegation than in remaining always attached to self and to creatures, and never arriving at union with God. This is to participate in the pain of loss which constitutes the eternal woe of hell.

God sometimes favors souls with such wonderful communications and such transporting sentiments concerning some of the objects of faith, that ever after the mere remembrance, the mere thought, the very name of them, is enough to throw them into ecstasies; as was the case with Blessed Giles of Assisi when he heard the word "Paradise" pronounced.

Raptures and ecstasies happen commonly rather to women and persons who are less actively employed than to others, because their life more disposes them thereto; and health, which is extremely affected by graces of this kind, is not so necessary in their case for the promotion of the glory of God. On the other hand, the devotion of apostolic men who have to labor for the salvation of souls is less sensible in its effects, more spiritual, and more solid. Generally speaking, God does not grant them the grace of ecstasies, unless it be that he desire thereby to give authority to their ministry, as is the case sometimes; witness St Vincent Ferrer and St Francis Xavier: and he communicates himself to them rather by the way of the understanding, which is capable of receiving lights of the highest order, than by that of the imagination, in which the divine lights are of a more sensible character, and their effects more externally manifested.

When a person falls into a state of suspended consciousness, in which the mind does not act, and receives no action on God's part, it is not an ecstasy, but a plain illusion of the devil, or a dangerous lethargy.

The connection between the soul and its senses is never interrupted, save in sleep, without much injury to health; for such disjunction is like the death of the senses; it is a commencement of that complete separation of the mind from the body which happens at death.

There is danger in desiring raptures and ecstasies, in wishing to have visions and revelations during such a state, and in hankering after other ways than those by which God is pleased to lead us: but there is no danger in asking for the gifts of the Holy Spirit and his guidance, solid virtues, and a high order of prayer.

Different divisions of the degrees of contemplation
The degrees of contemplation, according to some, are, first, recollection of all the powers of the mind; secondly, semi-rapture; thirdly, complete rapture; fourthly, ecstasy. But this division expresses not so much the essence of contemplation as its accidents; for sometimes a soul without rapture will be favored with a sublimer light, a clearer knowledge, a more excellent operation from God, than another who is favored with the most extraordinary raptures and ecstasies. The Blessed Virgin was more elevated in contemplation than all the angels and saints united; and yet she had no raptures. Our Lord enjoyed the beatific vision without ecstasy. The blessed in heaven will have a perfectly free use of all their senses.

Others distinguish the degrees of contemplation by different acts of the will, or by different states of fervent charity. Richard of

St Victor reckons four: (1) the wounds of love, *caritas vulnerans*; (2) the captivity of love, *caritas ligans*; (3) the languors of love, *caritas languens*; (4) the faintings of love, *caritas deficiens*. In the first, love pierces the heart and makes itself master of all the affections; in the second, it takes the mind captive and possesses itself of all the thoughts; in the third, it prevents the action of the external senses and the internal powers; in the fourth, it throws the soul into swoons and into a sort of death-like state by the boundless longings of its zeal, which it is unable to endure, as it perceives that all it does and all it can do is nothing, and that all it cannot do is infinite. Some mystical theologians add to this what they call the sepulcher of the soul, in which it is reduced, as it were, to dust and annihilated, afterwards to rise again and become a new creature in Jesus Christ, a creature wholly transformed into God.

The progress of these degrees is as follows:

1. When a person has applied himself for some time to the keeping of his own heart, the love of our Lord, and other such exercises, remaining the while faithful to God, so it is that he receives from heaven lights of a more abundant grace, which cause the soul to know its own state and its miseries; that what it has hitherto done for God is as nothing; that it owes everything to him, and that he merits that all hearts should burn with his love, and all beings be consumed in his service.

   At this sight the soul is filled with confusion; then, rousing itself, it abandons itself to love; and love, seeing it given up into its power, pierces it to the heart with its flaming arrows. It feels itself wounded, and the wound with which it is stricken causes it both pain and pleasure.

2. The heart being thus engaged, the mind can no longer think of anything but the beloved object. Love takes the thoughts captive, recalling them from their wanderings among creatures to attach them to God; so that they can no more be drawn away from him, save by compulsion. This, however, does not prevent a person still employing himself in indifferent matters.

   The merchant can attend to his commerce, the judge and the advocate to their suits of law, and married persons to the management of their family.

3. The soul now wounded and captive, continually receiving new impressions of divine love, does nothing but languish, and becomes incapable of any action which is not either of God or for God. If it sees or hears anything which has no reference to God, it is as if it saw or heard it not. In the two preceding degrees love makes itself master of the affections and the thoughts; in this it takes possession of the actions, permitting only such as are divine—that is to say, such as have God for their principle and end; and even in this state a person can act but very little, and is capable only of certain exercises conformable to his attraction.

4. The soul being in such wise wholly possessed by God, whatever it may do for his service, whatever it may suffer for his glory, it is never satisfied; it is ever desiring to do and suffer still more; thus putting no bounds to its desires, it loses itself in their immensity, and perceiving that there is an infinity of other things that might be done for God, but which it cannot do, it feels itself ready to faint away. Thus our Lord, although he did and suffered so much for the glory of God his Father, counted it all as little or nothing compared with what was due to him; and the martyrs, full of esteem and admiration for the Divine Majesty, could not satisfy their desires of glorifying a God so great and so worthy of love. This was also the disposition of those holy heroes who showed themselves insatiable of labors and sufferings.

Some change the order of these degrees, making the second that state of languor which follows a deep and extensive wound; and the third that of captivity, which takes place, they say, when the soul, no longer sensibly experiencing the operations of God, is, as it were, abandoned to itself and its enemies, amid disquietude and suffering, feeling itself on the point of offending God, but that it finds itself bound, as it were, and restrained by a secret power.

In that mystical death which, according to some theologians, takes place in the soul previous to deification, the person in this state suffers sensible pains even in his body, because the process is that of severing him from the corruption of his nature, his evil affections and bad habits, which, through their intimate connection with himself, cannot be torn away without the acutest pain. He must bear them courageously, and rejoice in the loss inflicted, seeing that he is but parting with his miseries to attain the sovereign good of this life.

Again, there is a state which, in mystical theology, is called that of burning love, in which the soul suffers a sort of fever, attended with fits and paroxysms, which even communicate themselves to the body and set it all on fire, causing revulsions, transports, and other marvelous effects—as was the case with St Catherine of Genoa, Blessed Stanislas, and numerous other saints.

Some make four degrees of contemplation in this wise
The first, they say, is when the soul, having attained great purity of heart, receives a new accession of the knowledge and love of our Lord by infused lights and extraordinary operations of grace.

The second, which some call the prayer of divine presence, is when the soul is ordinarily occupied with a simple attention to God; when it beholds itself before God with a profound awe for his adorable majesty and a holy horror of itself.

The third is a clearer and more penetrating knowledge of God, which enables the soul to see him in a manner more and more perfect; for God does nothing but give and take away, as if he were saying: "This is not yet it, it is something more."

In this state the soul may say with the Spouse: "Under the shadow of him whom I desired did I sit, such knowledge being, as it were, the shadow of God." There are souls which remain thus many years; and what they see of God creates such an ardent desire of beholding him as he is, that it seems as if they would quit the body to fly towards God. In this state the symptoms exhibited are like those of death; the limbs remain cold, stiff, motionless, destitute of feeling, like those of a corpse; and to such excess might this love proceed as to cause actual death. St Teresa, one Easter-day, fell into this state, and the effect was such as nearly to deprive her of life. And, indeed, there would be danger of death, unless an effort were made to dissipate the strength of this impression and distract the mind to some external object.

The fourth degree is called by mystical theologians the embrace of God, the chaste kiss of the Spouse. It is now that the soul is actually united to God as his Spouse. Some would have it, that when arrived at this degree it already loves God as perfectly as in the state of glory; but this is not so. So long as he is seen only through the medium of faith, and as in a glass, however vividly, he is never loved as much as he shall be hereafter in glory, where the blessed soul, being raised to the highest degree of contemplation, sees God face to face and as he is in himself.

Another division of the degrees of contemplation

Some reduce what concerns the essence of contemplation to four degrees. The first is the knowledge and the love of our Lord, together with those supernatural effects which devotion to him operates in pure souls. Many err in the way of the spiritual life, thinking to arrive at union with God and the sublimest order of prayer without attaching themselves to our Lord; yet he is the way, and it is through him that we are to go to God. We must become filled with the knowledge of his perfections and his mysteries, his doctrine, his Spirit, and his love, joining thereto the careful study of his purity of heart; in proportion as we advance in this path, we approach the Divinity.

The progress made within the extent of this degree consists, first, in a certain recollection of all the interior powers, attended in the beginning, not by any vivid lights, but by a sweet peace which keeps the soul ever tranquil. Secondly, in a secret feeling of the nearness and the presence of God, which causes the powers of the soul to be still more collected and drawn together in view of their union with God; in the same manner as several needles which have touched the magnet turn all in the same direction and join their points together to meet at their center. Thirdly, a presence of God more express and more formal than any hitherto experienced; not equal, however, to that enjoyed in the highest degrees, and one which lasts a greater or a less time according to the disposition and cooperation of the soul.

The second, which mystical theologians call the state of divine darkness, is when God strips the soul of all the experiences it had before, all its lights and affections, and all its spiritual sweetnesses; and thus stripping it, he thereby disposes it for more perfect lights and a purer and more ardent love, making it rise continually by the way of deprivation, ever giving, in order afterwards to take away and bestow upon it something better still.

When God places a soul in this state of mystical darkness, and strips it thus of its first lights, he enlarges its understanding and its will, rendering them capable of performing acts of eminent perfection.

To arrive at this degree, there is need of a generous virtue, a faithful correspondence with grace, a complete detachment from self, and an unreserved surrender of ourselves to God: and as we are exceedingly pusillanimous, there are but very few who have courage enough to reach this point, and fewer still who advance further, because men cannot make up their mind to strip themselves perfectly of creatures.

St Denis exhorts Timothy to separate himself completely from all created things, to strip himself of all affection for them, of the very thought and remembrance of them, of all imaginations and ideas regarding them, and to rise above the senses and the ordinary modes of knowledge and of action: to the end that, having arrived at this perfect void and nudity of spirit, he might enter within the ray of divine darkness and the luminous obscurity of the Divinity, to which no souls have access but such as are free and detached from everything that is not God. This mystical darkness is a participation in that which surrounds the throne of God in glory, and which was figured by the smoke and clouds wherein God appeared to Moses when he spoke with him on the mount.

The third is when God raises the soul to an extraordinary mode of action with regard to supernatural objects, communicating to it, through the medium of the imagination, lights and revelations which produce so powerful an impression upon it as to carry it out of itself. This it is that causes raptures and ecstasies, when the lights which the soul receives are so strong and so transporting as wholly to absorb it and abstract it from the senses and all exterior actions, to bring it into close application to the object manifested to it, which sometimes is of such a nature that all the powers of the soul combined are still too weak to endure or comprehend it. These raptures and ecstasies last as long as the operation of God continues, or as long as one operation is succeeded by others, or a single one by its strength and novelty arrests and captivates the soul.

In this state God is loved with a pure love, and acts of virtue are performed with great simplicity, acts which not being mixed with self-love or any of the impurities of nature, render more glory to God in a quarter of an hour than we ordinarily render to him in many years.

The fourth is when the soul acts no longer through the imagination, the medium through which raptures and ecstasies are caused, but is wonderfully enlightened by God by means of mental species or intellectual illuminations, independent of the imagination and of phantoms.

Then it is the pure spirit alone that acts, or, to speak more correctly, that receives the operation of God, and this divine operation does not prevent the exterior action of the senses.

This degree is described in the words of David in the second Book of Kings, where he says that God spoke to him as "the light of the morning, when the sun riseth, shineth in the morning without clouds, and as the grass springeth out of the earth by rain." The sun shining in the morning without clouds, denotes the operation of God in the soul, without admixture of sensible images and phantoms of the imagination.

Some say that souls that are raised to this degree are confirmed in grace. This at least is certain, that in it they exercise acts of virtue so pure and so perfect, that the honor rendered to God thereby, and the consequent increase of merit to the soul, are greater than we can conceive.

In this state God bestows, sometimes for a time, sometimes permanently, lights so penetrating, that without seeing with the bodily eyes those with whom we are in communication, we behold them with the eyes of the mind, and know what they would say before they open their mouth. We know what to answer on every occasion; and in all matters that come before us we receive supernatural lights to guide ourselves always and in all things by the Spirit of God.

This degree of divine union was the ordinary state of the Apostles, even in the midst of the world and their most important occupations. So also was it of St Ignatius from the very first year of his conversion, ever after an intellectual vision which he had while gazing at a stream along the banks of which he was walking while at Manresa. After this he was so enlightened in all the truths of faith, that he used to say that even were they not written in the Gospel, he would be ready to shed the last drop of his blood in their defense; and that if the Holy Scriptures were lost, nothing would be lost for him.

Opinion on the above divisions of the degrees of contemplation
Of all the above divisions of the degrees of contemplation, the truest is that which is formed from viewing the subject on the side of the understanding, and the different modes of knowing God and divine things: the first mode being by the lights received through the senses; the second, by such as come through the imagination and its phantoms; the third, by those which God himself communicates immediately to the understanding, without the ministry or the cooperation of the lower faculties.

These are, as it were, three sources of contemplation. The first corresponds with the first degree, in which the object of the soul's study is the love and knowledge of our Lord. The second corresponds with the second degree, which is called the divine darkness, in which progress is made towards the last by the way of deprivation; and with the third degree, in which souls are in a state of rapture and ecstasy. The third answers to the fourth degree, in which souls advance in the purest region of the spirit and in the highest perfection which it is possible to attain on earth.

Even in the lowest degrees of contemplation God communicates himself with so much sweetness, that a thousand years' enjoyment of all the pleasures of the world are nothing compared with the delight the soul experiences in God. The perfections and the joys it finds in him are so transporting to it, that it is, as it were, impossible for it to love anything but God, or to seek any satisfaction out of him.

The highest degrees are not attained until all sins have been remitted, not only as regards the guilt, but the penalty also; and if sins are still committed in the sublimest states (seeing there is no state so perfect as to exempt us from sin), they are but slight faults, faults of surprise and infirmity, which are bitterly lamented, and forgiven immediately.

As it is not possible to attain these highest degrees except through extraordinary purity of heart, so neither is it possible to abide therein without the utmost fidelity to grace. And as God is lavish of his liberality to a soul in such a state, so is the soul, on its part, bound to the strictest correspondence with God; otherwise he withdraws his graces, and the soul fails to persevere in the degree to which it had been raised.

From the time that a soul receives these extraordinary gifts from God, and especially when it has attained to the highest degree of contemplation, it is marvelous how detached it is from creatures; it ceases to be eager after anything whatever; nothing affects it save the love of God.

In these highest degrees of prayer, a person acts but very little from the formal motives of particular virtues. Since he is united to God by love, he does everything from the principle of love and under the direction of love, without troubling himself, generally speaking, with motives of the other virtues, which might distract the soul from its union with God.

When God bestows such grace upon a soul as to raise it to the highest degree of contemplation, he no longer refuses it anything; it commonly obtains everything it asks for. If it is requested to ask some favor of God, no sooner does it prepare to offer its petition, than it feels the Spirit of God carrying it away to the contemplation of admirable mysteries, in the midst of which it loses itself, thinking no more of the subject of its prayer, nor recollecting what it wished to ask; and yet God grants its request, and its desires are fulfilled without its bestowing any attention upon them. A soul that has attained to this point of perfection, may singly, by its prayers and merits before God, uphold a whole religious order or a whole kingdom.

The union of the soul with God differs in every one of these four degrees of contemplation, each having that which is peculiar to itself.

The first and the most excellent, to which all the exercises of the active and the contemplative life tend, is an habitual union, by which the principal powers of the soul remain continually united to God at all times, in all places, even amid the disturbance of exterior actions and the most urgent affairs, without causing a person to be more abstracted or less capable of acting externally.

The second kind of union with God is not as perfect, nor as general, nor as lasting; it is when the will is united to God, but not all the other powers, in such a way, however, that the imagination occasions no more trouble than in the first.

The third is when the will is united to God, but not in such a way but that it is sometimes distracted and harassed, or is in danger of being so, by the aberrations and roving propensities of the other faculties. This it is that happens to us so often at Mass: our will is really united to God, and yet the lightness of our imagination, sounds, and external objects striking on our senses, are an occasion of disturbance to us.

They who are subject to this weakness, not being as yet firmly settled in a state of interior recollection, run in pursuit of their imagination and their discursive thoughts with a view of checking them; but they do but fatigue themselves in vain, and the trouble they take serves only to make them lose the small degree of union they had with God, and to fill their soul with disquiet and excitement, which is a worse disorder than the first. St Teresa warns us of this, having herself experienced it.

In connection with this subject we may remark, that after Communion to exert ourselves to converse with our Lord by eliciting acts, is not the best mode of thanksgiving; and many give themselves a great deal of trouble in this way without much fruit. Then is the time for enjoying, not for seeking; for if it is true that acts of the virtues have no other end than to unite us to God, when once we have him within us, and when once we possess him, as we do in the Blessed Sacrament, what more do we seek? This should not prevent us from representing our miseries and our necessities to him, but without much inward discourse. At such a time, the better way is to remain recollected in his presence, and let him act in us according to his good pleasure, listen to him, receive what he gives us, keeping the mind always in a reverential attitude, and observing the other duties of interior recollection, neither allowing it its usual excursions, nor letting it fall into the inaction and the false repose of quietism.

We ought to seek to put ourselves in the same disposition which St Teresa speaks of being in: that great saint, seeking God alone in all things, and finding her repose only in God, did not even concern herself about the virtues where it was a question of God, his presence, and the enjoyment of him. She left off making acts of the virtues, that she might enjoy God when he vouchsafed to communicate himself to her; and in this there was no illusion: for what can we have without God? and if we have him, what virtues can we lack? It is to possess them all in an eminent degree and in a more excellent way than when we possess them formally, as theologians say, since they all tend only to unite us to God.

It sometimes happens to pure souls that, when they present themselves before our Lord in visiting the Blessed Sacrament, they experience immediately a transport of their spirit into the Heart of Jesus, where perhaps they remain for hours and whole days together.

Those who enjoy a certain union with God may be compared to children at their mother's breast; at times they cling more closely to it and press it more tightly. So there are souls which at times are more recollected in God and drink more deeply of him, according as the movement of grace draws them, and exterior occupations dispose them thereto.

In the various gifts and visits with which God favors souls, there is no fixed or definite order, so that one might say, for example: After such an operation such another will follow; or from such a degree of prayer you pass on to such another. St Teresa notices this, and says that the order she observes in enumerating the favors she received from God regards only herself, and denotes merely what she had herself experienced.

Motives that excite us to perfection

We must go on to perfection. The motives which excite us thereto are: (1) The great advantages it brings with it; peace of soul, perfect liberty of mind, the delights of the love of God, the abundance of the riches of grace. (2) The assurance of our salvation, which is not to be had save in the way of perfection; whereas in the practice of it salvation is morally certain.

There is great wisdom in making haste to acquire perfection, because then we are at rest for our whole life, and enjoy a solid satisfaction, that interior joy which the world knows not, nor can take away from those who possess it.

Wherein perfection consists, and what dispositions we ought to bring thereto

Perfection consists in the operations produced by interior grace, which proceeds from God alone; and as God is ever ready to operate in the soul according to his designs, all that a man who would become perfect has to do, is to remove the obstacles that stand in the way of the divine operation.

We remove them by cleansing the depths of the soul and making interior acts by which we seek God purely, to the exclusion of all the interests of the creature, convinced that nothing is worthy of consideration but God alone, nothing of importance but the accomplishment of his will, from whence his glory comes, and that all else is nothingness. In order to be in a state to form acts of such perfection, it is necessary to clear away all the impurities of the soul, render the will pliant to the movements of the Spirit of God, and cut off all desires of our own ease and natural gratification.

There are three principal kinds of impurity: the love of earthly things; the desire of being in favor with men; and illicit or excessive pleasures of the body.

In order to acquire holiness, three things are requisite: (1) to have a high idea of it and a great desire for it; (2) to use great diligence in the pursuit of it, which diligence, again, must have three characteristics: it must be not only fervent and persevering, but exclusive; (3) to be courageous in resisting the opposition we shall meet with in the prosecution of our design.

The foundation of the spiritual life consists in conceiving a great idea of God and of divine things, and a very low idea of all created things, and then regulating our life according to these two ideas.

Three sorts of dispositions are necessary in one who aspires after perfection. (1) Great watchfulness and close application in all things, keeping the eyes ever open for every opportunity of personal advancement. (2) Great courage in surmounting all difficulties and conquering himself whenever there is need. (3) Great perseverance in the study of perfection, so as never to relax his endeavors, never to grow weary, never to cease from watching and toiling to the end.

Of the practice of perfection

The whole practice of the spiritual life consists in two things: first, in watching continually over ourselves, on the one hand in order to do good, and on the other in order to avoid evil; secondly, in having the courage and strength both to do all the good and avoid all the evil we have a knowledge of.

Watching over ourselves includes three things. (1) Thinking almost continually of God, in order to prevent unprofitable thoughts. (2) Avoiding every kind of sin, and everything that can stain the soul. (3) Mortifying ourselves interiorly by resisting all our inclinations.

The order of the spiritual life demands that we should commence with the purification of our interior, correcting whatever is disordered therein. This is so necessary, that if we devote ourselves to the practice of virtue without having first done this, we shall mix therewith a thousand effects of self-love; we shall be always seeking ourselves in the holiest practices; and the good we may receive from God we shall appropriate in a spirit of ownership, and shall thus remain always novices.

There are four things of high excellence which it is necessary to practice in the spiritual life. (1) To purify our soul by continual examination and detestation of its vices. (2) To take no satisfaction save in God alone. (3) To live in the practice of great fidelity, not doing the least thing which may displease God. (4) To exercise ourselves continually in the presence of God and the love of our Lord, meditating without ceasing on his perfections and his mysteries.

Everyone who enters on the spiritual life must take pains to become filled with a threefold spirit, that of compunction, mortification, and prayer.

Compunction includes four or five excellent things: a serious and grave spirit, continual sorrow and inward moanings, profound humility, and devout solitude of heart.

Compunction has for its object three things in particular. (1) The vanity or miserable condition of man in this life, and the folly of the generality of Christians. (2) Our own sins and those of our neighbor. (3) The dolorous Passion of our Lord. These are the three motives which constrain devout souls, like gentle turtledoves, to fly from the vain joys of the world and the frivolities of life, that they may pass their days in continual plaints.

OF PURITY OF HEART

That the soul may be free to converse with God, it has need of being delivered from three sorts of hindrances: (1) from sins; (2) from passions; (3) from importunate distractions. These three sorts of hindrances are of very different degrees.

There are three degrees in true purity of heart. The first is to do nothing in which there is appearance of sin. The second is to attach the affections to nothing, either good or bad, which may interfere with perfect liberty of heart; but to study complete detachment from all created things. The third, never to perform an unprofitable act, or entertain any vain or petty thought, but always to be occupied in what promotes the glory of God. This is an excellent rule of life, which may be followed even in a state of dryness and interior suffering, affording, as it does, ample scope for the exercise of virtue, and an excellent test of our fidelity in the service of God.

The slightest faults and the least imperfections, when voluntary, inflict four evils on the soul: (1) they darken and blind it more and more; (2) they sully it; (3) they disturb and oppress it; (4) they diminish its strength and enfeeble it. The practice of virtue produces the four contrary effects.

The resolution to leave some fault, whatever it may be, uncorrected, although such resolution be tacit and not express, although it be glossed over by excuses and reasons plausible in appearance, prevents in the soul any powerful operations on the part of God, and hinders the effects of the Holy Eucharist.

One of the causes which most retards the progress we might make in perfection, which keeps the soul in its native littleness, and of which we are least aware, is allowing ourselves to be occupied with a thousand useless things. We ought to avoid all waste of time, and never do or think of anything which is not to the glory of God. For want of this we make very little progress, and attach our heart to a thousand objects which disturb and distract it in prayer. One of the greatest efforts of fervor is directed to watching over self, and avoiding everything unprofitable.

Until we combat as strenuously against the first disorderly movement of the heart as against sin itself, we shall never thoroughly correct our vices. And the reason that there is so little amendment in us is, that we fancy ourselves in the possession of virtue, notwithstanding the contrary movements of which we are sensible, not reflecting that such movements proceed from principles of sin which we take no pains to destroy. Thus we remain idle, under the pretext that the first movements are not in our own power, instead of laboring with all our might to tear up the root of them. It is impossible to say how much harm we do ourselves by this error and self-indulgence.

There are three sorts of dangerous poisons which flow insensibly to the heart: (1) that of the pleasure of vain-glory; (2) that of sensuality and immodest love; (3) that of anger and bitterness of spirit.

IN WHAT THE FAITHFUL SERVICE OF GOD CONSISTS

To serve God faithfully is to serve him: firstly, with exactness in all things, even the smallest; secondly, in simple faith, without the aid of consolations, or any large supply of interior lights; thirdly, without assurance that our services are agreeable to him, and without seeking for considerations calculated to give this assurance; fourthly, without a hope of recompense, or thought of our own interests, or solicitude whether we are furthering our own ends in promoting those of God; fifthly, contented with the little God gives us, though it be the lowest place in Paradise; just as a beggar asking alms at a gate, after leaving long waited, receives with joy a morsel of dry bread bestowed upon him.

IMPORTANT ADVICE FOR THE ADVANCEMENT OF SOULS

Here are some secrets which it is important to know in the spiritual life: the first is to remain constant, tranquil, and as it were balanced between God and nature, whenever there is question of passing from one motive of action to another; the second is, to enter into the things of God rather by a submissive love than by the force of reasoning; the third is, to give ourselves to interior recollection; the fourth is, not to soar higher until our interior is purified, striving after a mode of operation for which we have not yet received the required disposition; the fifth is, not to read mystical books without great precaution.

In the illuminative way, we must perfect more and more the ideas we have conceived of our Lord, in order that the will may operate thereupon more effectually.

In the spiritual life there are long nights to spend and wide deserts to traverse, which afford good exercise for patience and fidelity.

He who cannot endure something within himself, or who desires something external to himself, does not possess perfect resignation.

Among the interior virtues, there are three which we ought especially to endeavor to acquire—a true humility, a perfect disengagement from all things and from ourselves, and a perfect obedience or resignation to God.

OF HUMILITY

There is no solid virtue without humility. One who is truly humble must comport himself like a little child, or a public slave, or a convicted impostor; that is to say, he must behave with simplicity like a child, depend on all the world like a slave, take shame to himself like an impostor whose tricks have been discovered.

Humility and patience are, so to say, the shoulders of charity, inasmuch as they carry its burdens.

The root of humility is the knowledge of God; for it is impossible to know and feel our own vileness, except by reference to something great with which we may compare it. It is in vain that we think of the little that is in us; we shall never be any the more humble, unless we compare it with the infinite perfections of God. It is thus that savages who inhabit forests are insensible to the wretchedness of their condition, until they come to know the manner of life of civilized people, who dwell in towns in the midst of every sort of accommodation; and so a poor villager will never have any true idea of his poverty, until he has seen the mansions of the rich and the palaces of princes.

We may endure contempt from different motives: (1) from a sense of the vanity of human esteem, for in truth the honor and esteem of men is nothing but vanity; (2) from a motive of humility, because we deserve every kind of disgrace; (3) from a motive of fidelity, which constrains us to render to God what belongs to him, and to him alone belong honor and glory; (4) from a motive of love and gratitude, inasmuch as our Lord clothed himself with ignominies, and consecrated contempt and abjection in his adorable Person.

OF HOLY SIMPLICITY

True simplicity consists in having, like God, but one thought, and that thought must be to please God in all things. The vices opposed to simplicity throw us into a state of multiplicity.

These vices operate particularly in three ways. (1) In what regards our passions; to gratify them we multiply our thoughts and desires, acting not with the simple view of honoring God, but from various other motives. Hence spring our distrusts, our suspicions, dissimulations, concealments, subtle inventions, precautions, refinements, distinctions, etc. (2) In what regards others, about whom we have our judgments, interpretations, conjectures, inquiries, questionings, etc. (3) In what concerns reflections upon ourselves, for our own satisfaction: reflections on the past, on the present, on the future; on our good works, to take a pleasure in them; on our bad ones, to excuse them or waste useless regrets upon them; to form vain resolutions respecting the future. All this is opposed to true simplicity; but we close the gate to all such faults, when the mind is occupied only with the simple thought of pleasing God.

OF THE SPIRIT OF DEVOTION

The spirit of devotion is the mainspring of the spiritual life, and consists in keeping the heart always united to God or our Lord Jesus Christ. And when this is done effectually and without difficulty, everything else follows easily, as amendment of life, progress in virtue, forgetfulness of the things of the world, etc. So that to raise a soul to perfection in a short time two things are necessary.

The first is, to make it labor at knowing and correcting itself; the second, to fill it with ideas which excite it to devotion, and cause it to feel an interior relish for God.

When the soul has attained to this relish for God, it must endeavor to cherish it and render it enduring. To this end, it must despise the care of the body; it must discard all reflections on the life of others; it must give up a thousand little diversions which waste its time and retard its progress. Then also the virtues will introduce themselves sweetly and easily into the mind.

Let us therefore constantly endeavor to draw near unto God; to unite ourselves to him by our thoughts and affections, and allow nothing to divert us from him, unless it be such actions as appertain to his service, for which we must quit everything, even prayer and converse with God.

As soon as we find a void in our occupations, let us turn to the profitable employment of conversing with God in our own interior, or to Jesus Christ, in order to quicken devotion in us. The result will be, that our mind, being always occupied in some holy way, will give no admission to vices or a store of useless accomplishments; and will become noble and venerable in its own eyes and in those of others, breathing a perpetual odor of sanctity.

Of the three principal objects of our devotion, Jesus Christ, the Blessed Virgin, and St Joseph, we may say that what forms the glory and special luster of Jesus Christ in his mortal life is his humility and meekness; that of the Blessed Virgin, her purity; that of St Joseph, the wisdom of his conduct.

Three things are injurious to the spirit of devotion in some religious communities: (1) excess of unprofitable recreations; (2) a spirit of raillery; (3) particular friendships, and too great an intimacy between individuals.

In what the kingdom of God consists, and its advantages

God's kingdom is threefold: that of nature, that of grace, and that of glory. The first is connected with the second, and the second with the third.

The kingdom of grace is within us, and its end is a holy beatitude. For the beatitude of man results from his union with God, which is holiness.

This kingdom, as regards its exercise, consists in two things: (1) in the government of the King; (2) in the dependence of subjects: or, to use the language of Scripture, in the ways of God towards souls, and in the ways of souls towards God.

The ways of God towards souls are, justice and mercy, and a mixture of both one and the other. God has different kinds of wills. There are those of positive command and of simple permission. There are such as are evident and such as are hidden. He consoles and afflicts. He caresses and chastises. He inspires terror and excites confidence. He proceeds openly and as it were stealthily. He makes assaults and wins by sweetness, etc.

The ways of souls towards God are dependence, humility, resignation, abandonment of all care, mortification of self-love, purity of heart. The more we possess these holy dispositions, the more is the kingdom of God established in the soul.

The excellences of this kingdom are: the wisdom of the King, his power, his goodness; the nobility and dignity of his subjects; the peace, the security, the liberty, the goods, the pleasures they enjoy: wherein the kingdom of God has advantages infinitely above the kingdoms of the earth.

What a difference between the kingdom of grace and that of sin! Their rulers, their wars, their arms, their laws are different. They are both interior. Both one and the other are found within us; the one is founded on Adam, the other on Jesus Christ. They are based on the destruction the one of the other. St Paul sets this forth in an admirable manner. It is left to us to choose of which of these two kingdoms we would be the subjects. Salvation consists in withdrawing from that of sin and entering that of grace; and perfection in destroying within us the law of sin and the flesh, and in living according to the law of the spirit.

The Vows of Montmartre, 1534

PART II

JEAN-PIERRE DE CAUSSADE

1675-1751

THE SACRAMENT OF THE PRESENT MOMENT[1]

1. How God Speaks to Us and How We Must Listen to Him

God's Unchanging Word

God still speaks today as he spoke to our forefathers in days gone by, before there were either spiritual directors or methods of direction. The spiritual life was then a matter of immediate communication with God. It had not been reduced to a fine art nor was lofty and detailed guidance to it provided with a wealth of rules, instructions, and maxims. These may very well be necessary today. But it was not so in those early days, when people were more direct and unsophisticated. All they knew was that each moment brought its appointed task, faithfully to be accomplished. This was enough for the spiritually-minded of those days. All their attention was focused on the present, minute by minute; like the hand of a clock that marks the minutes of each hour covering the distance along which it has to travel. Constantly prompted by divine impulsion, they found themselves imperceptibly turned towards the next task that God had ready for them at each hour of the day.

Amazing Grace

Such were the hidden motives behind all Mary's behavior, lowliest and most obedient of creatures. Her reply to the angel, when she was content to say "Be it unto me according to thy word" (Luke 1:38), summed up the whole mystical teaching of her ancestors. Everything was reduced, as it is now, to the purest and simplest commitment to the will of God in whatever form it might present itself. That exalted and beautiful disposition which was the essence of Mary's soul shines out wonderfully in those simple words. How perfectly it accords with what our saviour wishes us to have unceasingly on our lips and in our heart—"Thy will be done"....

But what is the secret of how to find this treasure—this minute grain of mustard seed? There is none. It is available to us always, everywhere. Like God, every creature, whether friend or foe, pours it out generously, making it flow through every part of our bodies

[1] Selections from Jean-Pierre de Caussade, *The Sacrament of the Present Moment*, translated by Kitty Muggeridge, Harper & Row Publishers, San Francisco, 1981.

and souls to the very center of our being. Divine action cleanses the universe, pervading and flowing over all creatures. Wherever they are it pursues them. It precedes them, accompanies them, follows them. We have only to allow ourselves to be borne along on its tide....

2. How to Arrive at the State of Self-Surrender and How to Act Before Reaching It

God Living in Souls and Souls Living in God

There is a time when the soul lives in God and there is also a time when God lives in the soul. What is appropriate to one of these conditions is inappropriate to the other. When God lives in souls, they must surrender themselves totally to him. Whereas when souls live in God, they must explore carefully and scrupulously every means they can find which may lead them to their union with him. All their paths are clearly marked, their reading, values, and ideas. Their Guide is by their side, and when the time comes for them to speak for themselves all is clear. But when God lives in souls there is nothing of themselves left, save what comes from his inspiration. For them there are no plans, no longer any clearly marked paths. They are like a child whom one leads wherever one wills and who sees only what is pointed out to him. No more recommended reading for these souls. Frequently they are deprived of any spiritual direction. God leaves them with no other support than himself. They dwell in darkness, oblivion, rejection; suffer distress and misery without knowing from where or whence help will come. Calm and untroubled, they must wait for succor, their eyes turned towards heaven. And God, who seeks no purer aspirations in his loved ones than the total surrender of their whole selves, in order that they may exist by grace and divine action alone, himself replaces the books, ideas, self-assurance, advice, and wise guidance of which they are deprived....

Waiting on God

Everything in these solitary souls speaks to us of God. God gives their silence, quiet, oblivion, and isolation, their speech and their actions a certain virtue, which, unknown to themselves, affects others. And, just as they themselves are guided by the chance actions of innumerable creatures that are unwittingly influenced by the grace of God, they, too, guide and sustain many souls with whom they have no connection and no commitment to do so. It is God acting in unexpected and often mysterious ways. So that they are like Jesus, from whom escaped an unseen virtue with power to heal others. But with this difference that, more often than not, they are unconscious of any virtue escaping from them or even that they have cooperated in any way. It is like some mysterious balm whose unaccountable blessing is unconsciously felt....

Belonging Wholly to God
It is easy to conclude from all this that these committed souls are unable to take any interest in ambition, fashions, or other worldly matters, or in high society, important projects, or refinements of speech or behavior. This would assume that they are in control of their own lives, which in itself would preclude the state of surrender in which they find themselves. A state in which one discovers how to belong wholly to God through the complete and total assignment of all rights over oneself—over one's speech, actions, thoughts, and bearing; the employment of one's time and everything relating to it. There remains one single duty. It is to keep one's gaze fixed on the master one has chosen and to be constantly listening so as to understand and hear and immediately obey his will....

The Path of Pure Duty
So these souls are by their nature solitary, free, and detached from everything, in order that they may contentedly love the God who possesses them in peace and quiet, and faithfully fulfill their duty to the present moment according to his wishes. They do not allow themselves to question, turn back, or consider the consequences, the causes, or the reasons. It must suffice them simply to follow the path of pure duty as though there was nothing in the world but God and this pressing obligation. Thus, the present moment is like a desert in which simple souls see and rejoice only in God, being solely concerned to do what he asks of them. All the rest is left behind, forgotten and surrendered to him....

3. The Virtue and Practice of Surrendering Ourselves

Confined to the Present Moment
It is necessary to be disengaged from all we feel and do in order to walk with God in the duty of the present moment. All other avenues

are closed. We must confine ourselves to the present moment without taking thought for the one before or the one to come.... It is God who must decide what we shall do and when, and not ourselves. When we walk with God, his will directs us and must replace every other guidance....

God Revealed in the Present Moment

When God wishes to be the whole life of souls, and in a mysterious and secret way, to be himself their perfection, all individual ideas, understanding, endeavors, searching, or argument become a source of fantasy. And when, after several experiences of the folly of their own efforts, they finally recognize their futility, they discover that God has blocked every other avenue in order that they should walk with him alone.

Then, convinced of their nothingness, and that everything deriving from themselves is damaging, they surrender themselves to God so as to have nothing but him, from him, and through him. And so God becomes the source of life for these souls, not through ideas or enlightenment or reasoning—all that is but a fantasy to them now—but hidden in the operation and truth of his grace....

God Is Everywhere

Nevertheless, a preoccupation with God tells them unconsciously that all will be well provided they leave him to do what he will, and live by faith alone—like Jacob who said: "Surely the Lord is in this place and I knew it not" (Genesis 28:16). You are seeking God, dear sister, and he is everywhere. Everything proclaims him to you, everything reveals him to you, everything brings him to you. He is by your side, over you, around, and in you. Here is his dwelling and yet you still seek him. Ah! You are searching for God, the idea of God in his essential being. You seek perfection and it lies in everything that happens to you—your suffering, your actions, your impulses are the mysteries under which God reveals himself to you. But he will never disclose himself in the shape of that exalted image to which you so vainly cling....

4. Surrendering to God: The Wonders It Performs

A Divine Chain of Events

What profound truths lie hidden in this condition! How true that all suffering, every action, all the allurement of God's word, reveals him in a way which can only be described as the greatest of all mysteries! How true, therefore, that the holiest of lives is mysterious in its simplicity and humility. O, glorious celebration! Eternal bounty! God forever available, forever being received. Not in pomp or glory or radiance, but in infirmity, in foolishness, in nothingness. God chooses what human nature discards and human prudence neglects, out of which he works his wonders and reveals himself to all souls who believe that is where they will find him.... The only condition necessary for this state of self-surrender is the present moment in which the soul, light as a feather, fluid as water, innocent as a child, responds to every movement of grace like a floating balloon. Such souls are like molten metal filling whatever vessel God chooses to pour them into.

The Instinct of Faith

He directs our lives from these shadows so that, when the senses are scared, faith, taking everything in good part and for the best, is full of courage and confidence.

Since we know that divine action understands, directs, and creates everything apart from sin, we must love and worship all it does, welcoming it with open arms. In joy and confidence we must override everything in order to bring about the triumph of faith. That is the way to honor and acknowledge God.

To live by faith, then, is to live in joy, confidence, certainty, and trust in all there is to do and suffer each moment as ordained by God.

Nothing is more noble than a faithful heart that sees only life divine in the most grievous toil and peril.... For the instinct of faith is an uplifting of the heart and a reaching over and above everything that happens.

Living by faith and the instinct of faith are the same thing. It is joy in God's goodness and trust founded on the hope of his protection; a faith which delights in and accepts everything with good grace. It is an indifference and a readiness to face any situation or condition or person. Faith is never sad, sick, or in mortal sin. Faith always lives in God and his works even when they seem harmful and blind the senses. Scared, they suddenly cry out: "Wretch, you're lost! At the end of your tether!" And faith immediately replies yet louder: "Hold fast, march on, fear nothing."

Cherishing God and His Divine Order

And so God and his divine order must be cherished in all things, just as it is, without asking for anything more; whatever he may offer us is not our business but God's, and what he ordains is best. How simple is this perfect and total surrender of self to the word of God! And there, in continual self-forgetfulness to be forever occupied in loving and obeying him, untroubled by all those doubts and perplexities, reverses and anxieties, which attend the hope of his salvation and true perfection!...

5. Perfect Faith

The Trinity of Excellent Virtues

Perfect faith is faith, hope, and charity embodied in a single act uniting the heart to God and his purpose, becoming one single virtue, one uplifting of the heart to him in complete surrender. How otherwise can this divine unity, this spiritual essence, be expressed? How can its nature and meaning be truly conveyed? How the concept of three in one illumined? It is simply the fulfillment and enjoyment of God and his purpose. We see the beloved object, we worship him, we hope all things from him. We may call this perfect love, perfect hope, perfect faith: that trinity of mystical and theological virtues known simply as perfect faith. In this state of perfect faith nothing is more certain as far as God is concerned, and for the heart, nothing more uncertain. And in the union of the two, certainty of faith comes from God and from the doubting heart faith tempered by uncertainty and hope....

Surrendering to Divine Action

Let us not preach perfect faith or perfect love, suffering or blessings to all. These are not given to all, nor yet in the same way. But to every pure heart fearing God, let us talk of surrendering to divine action and make it clear to all that they will receive by this means that special state which has been chosen and ordained for them for all eternity....

Indeed ... God is only asking for your hearts. If you truly seek this treasure, this kingdom where God alone reigns, you will find it. Your heart, if it is totally surrendered to God, is itself that treasure, that very kingdom you long for and are seeking. When we long for

God and his will we rejoice in it and that rejoicing is the fulfillment of our longing. To love God is to long earnestly to do so....

Those with good intentions, therefore, have nothing to fear. They can only fall under that almighty hand which guides and supports them in all their shortcomings; which leads them towards the goal from which they are straying, and puts them back on the path they have lost....

Glad Self-Surrender

Self-surrender, trust, and faith, the universal means of accepting the state chosen by God's grace for each one is what I preach. To long to be the subject and instrument of divine action and to believe that it operates each moment and in all things in so far as it finds more or less good will—this is the faith I am preaching. Not a special state of grace or perfect love but a general state whereby each one of us may discover God, however he may reveal himself, and accept whatever transcendental state he has prepared for us....

Responding Faithfully to Grace

With divine action it is the same as it was with Jesus. Those who did not trust or respect him never benefited from the rewards he offered the world. Their ill will prevented them. Admittedly, all cannot hope for the same sublime state, the same gifts, or the same degree of excellence. But if everyone responded faithfully to grace, each one according to his own degree, everyone would be content, because all would attain that state of perfection and privilege corresponding to and satisfying their longing....

Love Always Prevails

As soon as their heart is willing, souls come under the influence of divine action, whose power over them depends on the extent to which they have surrendered themselves. Love is the way to this surrender. Love always prevails, is never denied. How can it be since it only asks for love in return for love? May not love long for what it gives? Divine action cares only for a willing heart and takes no account of any other faculty. Should it find a heart that is good, innocent, honest, simple, submissive, obedient, and respectful, that is all it looks for. It takes possession of that heart, controls all its faculties, and everything turns out so well for souls that they find themselves blessed in all things. Should what is deadly poison to other souls enter these, the antidote of their good intention never fails to counteract its effects. Should they come to the edge of an abyss, divine action turns them aside; if it lets them go, it holds them up; if they fall, it will catch them. After all, the faults of these souls are only faults of frailty and scarcely count. Love always knows how to turn them to advantage....

Grant Me a Pure Heart

May others, Lord, multiply their prayers and supplications. I ask but one thing. I offer up this prayer to you: "Grant me a pure heart!"....

O pure and willing heart! How right Jesus was to include you among the beatitudes....

You Are the Spring

O pure and willing heart! The only source of all spiritual states! It is to you that are given, and in you that blossom, the gifts of perfect faith, hope, trust, and love. It is on your branches that are grafted those flowers of the desert, those precious gifts only to be seen shining in souls that are completely detached, in which God has chosen to dwell to the exclusion of all others, as though in an empty house. You are the spring whence flow all the streams which refresh the spirit. Indeed, you may tell all souls "I am the source of true love!"....

6. With God the More We Seem to Lose, the More We Gain

Understanding Divine Action

Let us pursue our understanding of divine action further. What it appears to take from good will it replaces, as it were, *incognito*, never allowing good will to suffer any loss. It is as though someone let it be known that he was assisting a friend financially and, while continuing to do so, were to pretend, for the friend's benefit, to withdraw his help. The friend, not suspecting this strategy or understanding the mystery of love, would feel deeply hurt. But how mistaken he would be! What a reproach to his benefactor's generosity! However, once the mystery clarifies, God knows all the joy, tenderness, gratitude, love, embarrassment, and admiration that will fill his soul....

Listen to the Heart

However, to come back to these souls. Their heart may be said to be the interpreter of God's word. Listen to the heart, it interprets his will in everything that happens. For divine action secretly informs the heart of its purpose through the instincts rather than through the mind, indicating them either by chance happenings making the heart respond at random, or through necessity in which case there is no choice, or through impulses to which there is an instinctive response....

Wonderful Mystery of Love

How mysterious are the ways of divine action! To sanctify souls in the semblance of nothing but humiliation! This truly wonderful, divine, and exceptional sanctity can only grow out of humility! Nor do the fruits of such perfect faith ever perish for their husk is too dry and hard.

God's Secret Hiding Place

So may this seed germinate in your heart, God's secret hiding place, and through his mysterious virtue throw out branches, leaves, flowers and fruit which you cannot see but by which others will be nourished and enchanted. Give all who seek rest and refreshment in your shade fruits to their liking regardless of your own, and may each of your branches bear only the marks of grace. Be everything to all men and remain submissive and indifferent yourself....

7. The Mystery of God's Grace

The Mystery of the Perfected Soul

God's order, his pleasure, his will, his action, and grace, all these are one and the same. The purpose on earth of this divine power is perfection. It is formed, grows, and is accomplished secretly in souls without their knowledge....

To quench thirst it is necessary to drink. Reading books about it only makes it worse. Thus, when we long for sanctity, speculation only drives it further from our grasp. We must humbly accept all that God's order requires us to do and suffer. What he ordains for us each moment is what is most holy, best, and most divine for us....

Establishing Jesus in Our Heart

If the divine will ordains that reading is the duty to the present moment, reading achieves that mysterious purpose. If the divine will abandons reading for an act of contemplation, that duty will bring about a change of heart and then reading will be harmful and useless....

The mysterious growth of Jesus Christ in our heart is the accomplishment of God's purpose, the fruit of his grace and divine will. This fruit, as has been pointed out, forms, grows, and ripens in the succession of our duties to the present which are continually being replenished by God, so that obeying them is always the best we can do....

The will of God is the presence, the reality, and the virtue in all things, adjusting them to souls. Without God's direction all is void, emptiness, vanity, words, superficiality, death. The will of God is the salvation, sanity, and life of body and soul whatever else it may bring to either of them. Whether it be vexation and trouble for the mind, or sickness and death for the body, nevertheless that divine will remains all in all. Bread without the divine will is poison, with it true sustenance. Without the divine will reading only blinds and perplexes, with it it enlightens. The divine will is the wholeness, the good, and the true in all things. Like God, the universal Being, it is manifest in everything. It is not necessary to look to the benefits received by the mind and body to judge of their virtue. These are of no significance. It is the will of God that gives everything, whatever it may be, the power to form Jesus Christ in the center of our being. This will knows no limits.

The True and Only Virtue

Divine action does not distinguish between creatures, whether they are useless or useful. Without it everything is nothing, with it nothing is everything. Whether contemplation, meditation, prayer, inward silence, intuition, quietude, or activity are what we wish for ourselves, the best is God's purposes for us at the present moment....

8. The Sacrament of the Present Moment: The Soul's Part

Boundless Submission

"Sacrifice a just sacrifice and hope in the Lord" (Psalm 4:8, Vulgate) said the prophet.

That is to say that the sure and solid foundation of our spiritual life is to give ourselves to God and put ourselves entirely in his hands, body and soul. To forget ourselves completely so that he becomes our whole joy and his pleasure and glory, his being, our only good. To think of ourselves as objects sold and delivered, for God to do with what he likes.

With this foundation laid, souls have but to spend their entire existence rejoicing that God is God, surrendering themselves so completely that they are happy to obey his commands whatever they may be and without question.

God uses his creatures in two ways. Either he makes them act on their own initiative or he himself acts through them. The first requires a faithful fulfillment of his manifest wishes; the second, a meek and humble submission to his inspiration. Surrender of self achieves them both, being nothing more than a total commitment to the word of God within the present moment. It is not important for his creatures to know how they must do this or what the nature of the present moment is....

The Doctrine of Perfect Love

The doctrine of perfect love comes to us through God's action alone and not through our own efforts. God instructs the heart, not through ideas but through suffering and adversity. To know this is to understand that God is our only good. To achieve it, it is necessary to be indifferent to all material blessings, and to arrive at this point one must be deprived of them all....

Without the virtue of the divine will all creation is reduced to nothing, with it, it is brought into the realm of his kingdom where every moment is complete contentment in God alone, and a total surrender of all creatures to his order. It is the sacrament of the present moment.

Surrender and Assent

The practice of this excellent theology is so simple, so easy, and so accessible that it need only be wished for it to be had. This indifference, this love so perfect, so universal, is both active and passive, in so far as what we do through grace, and what grace accomplishes in us, requires nothing more than surrender and assent. In fact it is everything that God himself ordains and mystical theology expounds in a multitude of subtle concepts which it is often better for us not to know, since all that is required is oblivion and surrender.

Everything in the present moment tends to draw us away from the path of love and passive obedience. It requires heroic courage and self-surrender to hold firmly to a simple faith and to keep singing the same tune confidently while grace itself seems to be singing a different one in another key, giving us the impression that we have been misled and are lost....

The Reverse Side of the Tapestry
All goes well when God is, so to speak, both the author and the object of our faith, the one complementing and augmenting the other. It is like the right side of a beautiful tapestry being worked stitch by stitch on the reverse side. Neither the stitches nor the needle are visible, but, one by one, those stitches make a magnificent pattern that only becomes apparent when the work is completed and the right side exposed to the light of day; although while it is in progress there is no sign of its beauty and wonder....

Let God's Will Be Done
The more they work at their humble task, however lowly and obscure it may be outwardly, the more God adorns, embellishes, and enriches it with the colors he adds. "The Lord has made excellent he who is faithful to him" (Psalm 4:4, Vulgate)....

All saints become saints by fulfilling those duties themselves to which they have been called. It is not by the things they do, their nature or particular qualities that holiness must be judged. It is obeying those orders which sanctifies souls and enlightens, or purifies and humbles, them....

True Surrender
Duty to their state in life and to God's purpose is common to all saints; it is his general direction for them all. These souls live unnoticed in obscurity, avoiding the pitfalls of the world. This is not what makes them saints, but the more they surrender to God the more saintly they become....

It is mere idle curiosity to ask which of them is more saintly. Each one must follow his allotted path. Saintliness consists in submitting to the will of God, and all the perfection to be found in it....

The Third Duty Required of Souls
The first duty required of souls is self-discipline; the second is self-surrender and complete passivity; the third requires great humility, a humble and willing disposition, and a readiness to follow

the movement of grace which motivates everything if they simply respond willingly to all its guidance....

9. The Secret of Discovering God's Transcendent Will in the Present Moment

The Present Moment Holds Infinite Riches
Nothing is more reasonable, perfect, or divine than the will of God. No difference in time, place, or circumstance could add to its infinite worth, and if you have been granted the secret of how to discover it in every moment, you have found what is most precious and desirable....

The present moment holds infinite riches beyond your wildest dreams but you will only enjoy them to the extent of your faith and love. The more a soul loves, the more it longs, the more it hopes, the more it finds. The will of God is manifest in each moment, an immense ocean which the heart only fathoms in so far as it overflows with faith, trust, and love....

Recognizing God in the Most Trivial
Do not imagine that these souls judge things like those who judge them with their senses and who are unaware of the inestimable treasures they hold. He who recognizes a king in disguise treats him very differently from he who sees before him only the figure of an ordinary man and treats him accordingly. Likewise, souls who can recognize God in the most trivial, the most grievous, and the most mortifying things that happen to them in their lives, honor everything equally with delight and rejoicing, and welcome with open arms what others dread and avoid....

To discover God in the smallest and most ordinary things, as well as in the greatest, is to possess a rare and sublime faith. To find contentment in the present moment is to relish and adore the divine will in the succession of all the things to be done and suffered which make up the duty to the present moment....

Breath of the Holy Spirit
Faith is required for everything divine. If we live continually by faith we shall always be in touch with God, speaking to him face to face. In the same way as our thoughts and words are transmitted by air, so are God's conveyed by all we are given to do and suffer. Not only the

substance of his word will be manifest, but everything will be sanctified and perfected for us. In heaven this is glory, and on earth faith, with only a difference of degree, not of kind, between them....

Everything remarkable about the lives of the saints, their visions, their inner voices, is only a pale reflection of their continuing state of rapture which comes from the practice of their faith....

God's Instruments, Moment by Moment

The miracle of the saints lies in their life of continuing faith in all things. Without it, all the rest of their visions, and the voices they hear, would all fall short of that holiness which consists in the loving faith that makes them rejoice in God and see him in all things. This does not require miracles; they are only for the benefit of those who need such testimonies and signs. Faithful souls do not rely on them....

Wisdom of the Pure in Heart

In the course of time every truly wise concept is fulfilled by divine action. In the eyes of God everything has its own image which only wisdom can divine. If you were able to conceive all those not meant for you, the knowledge would get you nowhere. Divine action sees the word, the image in which you are to be made, the pattern it proposes, and what is most expedient for each one of us....

The wisdom of the pure in heart is to be contented with their lot, to keep on their way and never to overreach themselves. They are not curious about how God operates. They accept without question what he ordains for them, waiting only for each moment to reveal God's word, happy and contented in the knowledge that he speaks to the heart....

The Only Source of Perfection

When souls discover the divine purpose, they put aside all pious works, systems, books, ideas, spiritual advisers, in order to be alone under the sole guidance of God and his purpose which becomes the only source of perfection for them. They are in his hands as saints always have been, sure that he alone knows what is best for them....

The present moment is like an ambassador announcing the policy of God; the heart declares "Thy will be done," and souls, traveling at full speed, never stopping, spread the news far and wide. For them everything without exception is an instrument and means of sanctification, providing that the present moment is all that matters. It is no longer a question of supplication or silence, reticence or eloquence, reading or writing, ideas or apathy, neglect or study of spiritual books, affluence or destitution, sickness or health, life or death. All that matters is what the will of God ordains each moment....

God's Ineffable Will

If everything that happens to souls who have surrendered themselves to God is all that matters, it must be true that having everything there is nothing to complain of, and if they do complain, they are lacking in faith and living by their reason and their senses, which do not perceive the sufficiency of grace and can never be satisfied. According to the scriptures, to glorify the name of God is to recognize that he is holy, to adore and love him for everything he utters. Everything God does each moment tells us something significant, manifesting his purpose in so many words and sentences. His purpose is but one in itself, incomprehensible, unutterable; but its effects are countless and known by as many names. To glorify the name of God is to know, worship, and love that adorable, incomprehensible word which is his very essence....

Celestial Manna

Everything that happens each moment bears the stamp of God's will. How holy is that name! How right to worship it for its own sake! Can we look on him who bears it without infinite reverence? It is celestial manna falling from the sky, pouring down grace; it is the holy kingdom in the soul, it is the bread of angels consumed on earth as it is in heaven. No moment is trivial since each one contains a divine kingdom, and heavenly sustenance....

When God exists in all things, our enjoyment of his word is not of this earth, it is a delight in his gifts which are transmitted through many different channels. They do not in themselves sanctify us, but are instruments of the divine action which is able to communicate God's grace to the simple, and often does, in ways which seem contradictory....

The Bounty of the Present Moment

The mind, with all that goes with it, wishes to take the lead in spiritual matters. It must be reduced to nothing and subdued like a dangerous slave, whose simple heart, if he knew how to make use of it, could serve him to great advantage. It could also cause a great deal of damage if not properly controlled. When souls long for tangible action their heart is informed that God's purpose suffices. When they wish truly to renounce all worldly activity, it is informed that it is a measure they must neither accept nor reject, but must meekly comply with God's will, doing everything yet doing nothing, having nothing yet possessing all. Human activity, being substitute for fulfillment, leaves no room for the true fulfillment of divine purpose. But when divine action fulfils this purpose in earthly terms, it brings a true increase of holiness, innocence, purity, and disinterestedness....

10. The Secret of the Spiritual Life

God's Veiled Purpose
All creatures live by the hand of God. The senses can only grasp the work of man, but faith sees the work of divine action in everything. It sees that Jesus Christ lives in all things, extending his influence over the centuries so that the briefest moment and the tiniest atom contain a portion of that hidden life and its mysterious work. Jesus Christ, after his resurrection, surprised the disciples when he appeared before them in disguise, only to vanish as soon as he had declared himself. The same Jesus still lives and works among us, still surprises souls whose faith is not sufficiently pure and strong....

The Grace of Simplicity
I have more to fear from my own actions and my friends' than those of my enemies. There is no prudence to equal that of non-resistance to one's enemies, of opposing them simply by giving in. It is like sailing before the wind. One has only to sit still and let the galley slaves bring the vessel into port with all hands aboard. There is nothing more certain to resist the wiles of the flesh than simplicity; it effectively evades every trick without recognizing them or even being conscious of doing so. Divine action can make simple souls take exactly the right steps to surprise those who wish to surprise them, and even to profit by their attempts to do so....

The Magi Have Only to Follow Their Star
How can we resist the Almighty, whose ways are inscrutable? God champions their cause and they have no need to beware of intrigues, or to meet suspicion with suspicion by watching every move against

them. Their beloved relieves his children of all this anxiety. And, untroubled and safe, they leave all to him. Divine action delivers and exempts souls from all that sordid mistrust so necessary in human affairs. It may be all right for a Herod or the Pharisees, but the Magi have only to follow their star, and the infant Jesus only to lie in his mother's arms, and their enemies will do them more good than harm.

The Weapon of Gentle Yielding

The understanding of souls who are faithful to their duties, quietly obeying the inmost movement of grace, meek and humble in all things, is worth more than the most penetrating insight into mystery. If only we were able to perceive God's action in all the egotism and arrogance of humans we would have nothing but respect for them. Their chaos can never replace order whatever they do, and this uniting of God's action with his creatures through humility and meekness must never be abandoned; we must not look which way others are going but follow confidently our own, and thus by gentle yielding we break through forests and overturn mountains....

Let There Be Light

God's order is the whole wisdom of the pure of heart. They reverence it in those acts of defiance which the proud do to disparage it. The proud despise the meek in whose eyes they are nothing, seeing only God in all they do. The proud often imagine that humility is a sign that the meek fear them, when it is only a sign of their love and fear of God and his will which the meek see in the proud. No, poor fools, the meek are not afraid of you, they pity you. It is to God they are speaking when you imagine they are addressing you.... And so the more arrogant your tone, the more humble theirs....

11. The Dark Night of Faith

The Experience of Passive Saintliness

There is a kind of saintliness when divine communication is precise and clear as daylight. But there is also a passive saintliness communicated by God through faith from the impenetrable darkness which surrounds his throne, in terms that are confused and obscure. Those who find this way are often afraid, like the prophet, to follow it and afraid of running into danger when walking through that darkness. Have no fear, faithful souls! That is where your path lies, the way along which God is guiding you. There is nothing safer or more sure than the dark night of faith....

Verses in the Hymns of Night

When God speaks directly to us through life, he no longer appears as the way and the truth. If we seek him in darkness he is behind us, holding our hand, urging us on. But if we seek him face to face, he eludes us. In divine action there are secret and unforeseeable resources; unknown and marvelous ways of dealing with the cares, difficulties, troubles, failures, reverses, and anxieties of those who have lost all confidence in themselves. The more confused their situation, the better the charm works and the heart says, "All will be well!" All is in God's hands, there is nothing to fear. Fear itself, suspense, desolation, are verses in the hymns of night. We rejoice in not omitting a single syllable, for we know they all end in "Glory be to God!" Thus we find our way by losing it. The clouds themselves guide us, doubts assure us. The more troubled Isaac was about finding a sacrifice, the more Abraham relied on God for everything.

Jesus Lived and Lives Still

Jesus lives and works among us, throughout our lives, from the beginning of time to the end, which is but one day. He has lived and lives still. The life he began continues in his saints for ever....

The Book of Life

Teach me, Holy Spirit, to read this book of life! I will be your disciple, and, like an innocent child, believe what I cannot see. It is enough for me that my Lord is speaking. He says this, he declares that, he arranges words in this way. That is enough, I believe everything he has spoken....

All that we see is only vanity and lies. The truth is in God. What a vast difference there is between God's conception and our fantasies! How is it that, being continually reminded that everything that happens in the world is but a shadow, an image, the mystery of faith, we persist in relying only on our human faculties, and continue to interpret the merely temporal aspect of the unanswerable enigma of our existence?...

Faith Is the Light of Time

Faith is the light of time, it alone recognizes truth without seeing it, touches what it cannot feel, looks upon this world as though it did not exist, sees what is not apparent. It is the key to celestial treasures, the key to the unfathomable mystery and knowledge of God....

THE FIRE OF DIVINE LOVE[1]

The providential ordering of life

To avoid the anxieties which may be caused by either regret for the past or fear for the future, here in a few words is the rule to follow: the past must be left to God's measureless mercy, the future to his loving providence; and the present must be given wholly to his love through our fidelity to his grace.

Let us understand clearly that we shall not acquire true conformity to the will of God until we are perfectly resolved to serve him according to his will and pleasure, and not according to our own. In all things seek God alone and you will find him everywhere, but more so in those things in which you most of all renounce your own will.

Counsel on prayer

On the subject of prayer I have only two things to say. Begin it with an entire acquiescence in God's good pleasure, whether this be for your success or to try you with the cross of dryness, distractions, and helplessness.

But if you find it easy and full of consolation, then give thanks to God for this without attributing it to your own efforts or dwelling on the pleasure you gain from it yourself.

If your prayer does not go well, submit yourself to God, humble yourself, and go away contented and in peace even when there may have been some fault on your part, redoubling your trust and self-abandonment to his most holy will.

With these two points in mind, persevere, and sooner or later God will give you the grace to pray as you ought.

But never, never be discouraged, however helpless and unhappy you may feel.

Interior direction

We attain to God through the annihilation of self. Let us keep ourselves down so low that we disappear from our own sight.

---

[1] Selections from *The Fire of Divine Love: Readings from Jean-Pierre de Caussade*, edited by Robert Llewelyn, Triumph Books, Liguori, Missouri, 1995.

The more we banish from ourselves all that is not God, the more we shall be filled with God. The greatest good that we can do to our souls in this life is to fill them with God.

To lose oneself in one's nothingness is the surest means of finding oneself again in God. Let us practice then a simple remembrance of God, a profound forgetfulness of ourselves, and a humble and loving acquiescence in God's will. By this single practice we shall avoid all evil, and we shall make all things useful for us, and pleasing to God.

We must not distinguish between rest and work, either interior or exterior: it is all one when we keep ourselves in complete acquiescence and interior repose. It is good to note this.

How to deal with excessive fears

When fears for any fault we have committed become excessive, they obviously come from the devil. Instead of giving way to this dangerous illusion, we must repel it with the utmost steadfastness, letting these anxieties drop away from us, like a stone falling to the bottom of the sea, and never entertaining them voluntarily. If however by God's permission these feelings are stronger than our will, we must have recourse to the second remedy, which consists in letting ourselves be crucified unresistingly, since God permits it, just as the martyrs used to do, yielding themselves up to their executioners.

Temptations and inner sufferings

Violent temptations are in God's view great graces for a soul. They are an interior martyrdom. They are those great struggles and great victories which have made great saints.

The acute distress and cruel torment suffered by a soul when attacked by temptations are the sure sign that it never consents, at least with that full, entire, known, and deliberate consent which makes a mortal sin.

The majority of people who are not very far advanced in the ways of God and the interior life esteem only the operations of sweet and sensible grace. But it is certain that the most humiliating, distressing, and crucifying workings of grace are the most effective in purifying the soul and in uniting it intimately with God. And so the masters of the spiritual life agree in saying that we make greater progress by suffering than by action.

The intention in prayer

Inability to think or make acts during prayer must not sadden your soul. The best part of prayer, and indeed its essence is the wish to do it. Before God, desire counts for everything, in both good and evil.

As for direction of intention, the soul abandoned to God should not make too many acts, nor consider itself obliged to express them in words.

The best thing for it would be to rest content with feeling and knowing that it is acting for God's sake in simplicity of heart. Good interior acts are those which the heart makes itself, as by its own momentum, almost without thinking about them.

The virtue of self-abandonment

You do well to devote yourself vigorously and, as it were, uniquely to the excellent practice of a complete self-abandonment to the will of God. Therein lies for you the whole of perfection; it is the easiest road and leads soonest and more surely to a deep and unalterable peace; it is also a sure guarantee of the preservation of that peace in the depth of our soul through the most furious tempests.

The nature of pure love

It is true that even the purest love does not exclude from the soul the desire of its salvation and perfection, but it is equally incontestable that the nearer a soul approaches to perfect purity of love the more it turns its thoughts away from itself in order to fix them on the infinite goodness of God.

The divine goodness does not oblige us to repudiate the reward that it destines for us, but it has surely the right to be loved for itself without any backward glances at our own interests.

God arranges everything for our good

When I have done what I think before God I ought to do, the success of that enterprise will be what he chooses. I abandon that question entirely to him and with my whole heart, thanking him for everything in advance, desiring only in everything and everywhere his holy will, because I am convinced by faith and by many personal experiences that everything comes from God, and that he is powerful enough and a good enough Father to bring all issues to the best advantage of his dear children.

It is necessary to help ourselves

How can we doubt that God understands our interests much better than we do and that his dispositions of events in regard to us are advantageous even when we do not understand them? Would not a little wisdom be enough to determine us to allow ourselves to be led with docility by his Providence, though we cannot understand all the secret springs which God brings into play, or the particular ends he has in mind?

But, you will say, if it is enough to let us be passively guided, what becomes of the proverb: "Help yourself and God will help you"? I do not say that we must not act: no doubt we must help ourselves; to fold our arms and expect everything from heaven, whether in the order of nature or that of grace would be an absurd and sinful quietism. But while we are cooperating with God we must never cease to follow his direction and lean upon him.

Trusting God in all things

I do not understand your anxieties.... Why do you insist in tormenting yourself over the future, when your faith teaches you that the future is in the hands of a Father who is infinitely good, who loves you more than you love yourself, and who understands your interests far better than you? Have you forgotten that everything that happens is directed by the orders of divine Providence? But if we know this how can we hesitate to remain in a state of humble submission to all that God wishes or permits?

God's providence is over all

Remember our great principles:

1. That there is nothing so small or apparently trifling, even the fall of a leaf, that is not ordained or permitted by God.
2. That God is sufficiently wise, good, powerful, and merciful to turn the most seemingly disastrous events to the good and profit of those who are capable of adoring and humbly accepting all these manifestations of his divine and adorable will.

Let us be perfectly persuaded that God arranges everything for the best. Our fears, our fussiness, and our tendency to worry often make us imagine trials where there are none. Let us follow the leading of divine Providence one step at a time; as soon as we see what is asked of us, we also will desire it and nothing further. God knows far better than we, poor blind creatures that we are, what is good for us.

God's action in the depths of the soul

The mainspring of the whole spiritual life is goodwill, that is the sincere desire to be God's, fully and without reserve: you cannot, therefore, renew this holy desire too frequently in order to strengthen it and make it constant and efficacious in you.

The best way to drive off useless thoughts is not to combat them openly and still less to allow oneself to be troubled and disquieted by them, but just to let them drop, like a stone into the sea; little by little the habit of letting them drop makes this salutary practice quite easy.

The second way of thinking of nothing but God consists in a sort of general forgetfulness of everything, at which one arrives through the habit of letting drop our useless thoughts, so that, for some time, one may pass whole days without thinking, as it seems, of anything at all, as if one had become stupid.

The purgation of the will

This great emptiness of spirit of which I have spoken sometimes produces another emptiness which is more painful, namely emptiness of the will, so that one seems to have no feeling at all for the things of the world or even for God, being equally insensible to everything.

It is a second mystical death which must precede our happy resurrection to an entirely new life. We must esteem and cherish this double void, this double self-annihilation so hard to self-love and the spirit of pride, and accustom ourselves to this state in an interior spirit of holy joy.

Two governing principles

You are quite right in what you say, my dear daughter, and indeed the great maxim of Mother de Chantal was: "Not so many questions, so much learning and writing, but sound practice."

As regards souls that have acquired the habit of avoiding deliberate faults and faithfully fulfilling the duties of their state of life, all practical perfection may be reduced to this one principle: the exercise of a continual resignation to the manifestations of the will of God, a complete self-abandonment to all the exterior or interior dispositions of his Providence, whether in the present or in the future.

On the means of acquiring self-abandonment

Here, in a few words, is what you ought to do in order to attain promptly to pure love and perfect self-abandonment.

You must, first of all, ardently desire and energetically will it, whatever price you have to pay.

Secondly, you must firmly believe and say repeatedly to God that it is absolutely impossible for you to acquire by your own strength such perfect dispositions, but, also, that grace makes everything easy, that you hope to receive this grace from his mercy, and you must beg it of him in and through Jesus Christ.

Thirdly, you must gently and quietly humble yourself, whenever you have withdrawn yourself from the holy bondage of his will, without discouragement, but on the contrary protesting to God that you will await with confidence the moment at which it will please him to give you that decisive grace that will make you wholly die to yourself and live to him by a new life wholly hidden with Jesus Christ our Lord.

Fourthly, if you are docile to the inspirations of God's spirit, you will take care not to make your advancement depend on the warmth and sensible sweetness of your interior impressions. The divine Spirit will, on the contrary, make you esteem rather his almost imperceptible operations, for the more delicate and profound they are, the more divine they are and so much more removed from the impressions of the senses.

One belongs more totally to God then, because one tends to him and to union with him with all one's powers, and the whole extent of one's being, without particularizing any special point. For every being seeks its center.

All consists in loving well

Do not distress yourself so much at being so frequently at war with your wretched nature; heaven is worth all these battles. Perhaps they will shortly come to an end and you will achieve a complete victory. After all, they will pass, and rest will be eternal. Be at peace and let your humility always be mingled with confidence.

The prayer of divine repose

This is what I should reply with regard to the person in question: her prayer of recollection seems to me to proceed rather from her head than her heart. This is the inverse of what ought to be, for in order that this kind of prayer should bear fruit, it is necessary that the heart should be more applied to it than the intelligence.

It is, in fact, a prayer wholly of love: the heart, reposing sweetly in God, loves him without distinguishing clearly the subject of its love, or how this love is produced in it. The reality of the prayer is clearly shown by a certain ardor which is continually experienced in the heart, by a constant tendency toward the divine center of our being which continues without any clear intellectual perception, and by the overpowering attraction to which the soul yields without possibility of distraction. From this comes the great facility of this kind of prayer, which is a sweet repose for the heart and which continues without effort almost as long as one wishes.

Let us thoroughly persuade ourselves that God can be found everywhere without effort, because he is always present to those who seek him with their whole heart, though he may not always cause his divine presence to be felt. For instance, when you happen to be entirely unoccupied with created things so that you seem to be thinking of nothing and desiring nothing, you should know that then your soul is unconsciously occupied with God and in God.

Thus, the true presence of God is, to speak exactly, nothing but a sort of forgetfulness of creatures with a secret desire of finding God. It is in this that interior and exterior silence consists, so precious, so desirable, and so profitable: the true earthly paradise, where souls who love God enjoy already a foretaste of heavenly joy.

The test of solid virtue

If when we are ourselves exposed to various criticisms and unjust prejudice, we persevere in our line of conduct without change, following the guidance of Providence step by step, we are truly living by faith alone, with God alone in the midst of the quarrels and confusions with creatures.

In such a disposition of soul, external things cannot reach our interior life, and the peace which we enjoy can be troubled neither by their favors nor their contempt. This is what is called living the interior life, and a very interior life it is.

Until this independence of soul has been acquired the most apparently brilliant virtues are in reality very fragile, superficial, and liable to corruption by self-love, or to be upset by the slightest breath of inconstancy and contradiction.

Do not become attached to God's gifts

When, in the course of prayer, you experience certain attractions, such as a sweet repose of soul and heart in God, receive these gifts with humility and thanksgiving, but without becoming attached to them.

If you loved these consolations for their own sake, you would oblige God to deprive you of them, for when he calls us to prayer it is not in order to flatter our self-love and give us an occasion for self-complacency, but to dispose us to do his holy will and to teach us an ever-increasing conformity to that will in all things.

What has already happened will often happen again. What God may have refused you during prayer, he will give you when it is over, so as to make you realize that it is the pure effect of his grace and not the fruit of your own labor and industry.

The strength of peace to the soul

You should remember all your life that one of the principal causes of the small progress made by certain good people is that the devil continually fills their souls with disquiet, perplexities, and troubles, which render them incapable of serious, gentle, and constant application to the practice of virtue.

The great principle of the interior life lies in peace of the heart: it must be preserved with such care that the moment it is in danger everything else should be abandoned for its re-establishment.

Let God act

Your present method of prayer comes much more from grace than from yourself. You should, therefore, let grace act, and remain in an attitude of humble docility, calmly and simply keeping your interior gaze fixed on God and your own nothingness. God will then work great things in your soul without your knowing what is happening.

Beware of all curiosity on the subject, be content to know and feel the divine operation; trust yourself to him who is working in you and abandon yourself totally to him, that he may form you and shape you interiorly as he pleases.

Have no other fear in these happy moments but that of attaching yourself rather to his gifts and graces than to the Giver. Do not esteem or savor these graces except in so far as they inflame you with divine love and help you to acquire the solid virtues that please the divine Lover: self-abnegation, humility, patience, gentleness, obedience, charity, and the endurance of your neighbor.

Be sure that the devil is not the author of these favors, and that he will never be able to deceive you so long as you make your zest and sweetness serve toward the acquisition of the solid virtues that the Faith and the Gospel teach and prescribe to us.

Let God act; place no obstacle through your natural activity to his holy operation, and be faithful to him in the slightest things.

Living for God alone

The simplest ideas and those that lead to a spirit of holy childhood and filial confidence are always the best in prayer. How agreeable to God and how all-powerful with him are prayers that are at the same time simple, familiar, and respectful. How I wish for you the continuation of this simple and humble gift of prayer, which is the great treasure of the spiritual life!

Lord, have pity upon me

Everything good in you originates from God, everything evil, spoilt, and corrupt originates in yourself. Set aside then, nothingness and sin, evil habits and inclinations, abysmal weakness and wretchedness. These are your portion. These originate in, and unquestionably belong to, you.

Everything else—the body and its energies, the soul and its senses, the modicum of good you have performed is God's portion. It so manifestly belongs to him that you realize you cannot claim one whit of it as yours, nor feel one grain of complacency, without being guilty of theft and larceny against God.

At frequent intervals repeat interiorly: "Lord, have pity upon me; with you all things are possible." There is nothing better or more simple than this; nothing more is needed to call forth his powerful help. Hold powerfully to these practices and inclinations. God will do the rest without your perceiving it.

Confidence in God alone

Guard against discouragement, even though you witness the failure of your repeated resolutions to serve God. Your trust in God can never be pushed too far. Infinite goodness and mercy should induce trust as infinite.

If, having asked for grace, you have neither the impulse nor ability to look at the state of your soul, you must remain silent and at peace. Discouragement, so far from being evidence of pure intention, is a dangerous temptation; for progress is to be desired only to give pleasure to God and not to the self.

Remedies in sickness of soul

At present your soul's greatest failing is its perturbation, inquietude, and interior agitation. Thanks to God, its ills are not incurable; yet so long as they remain uncured, they can only be as disastrous to you as they have been grievous.

Interior agitation deprives the soul of the ability to listen to and obey the voice of the divine Spirit; to receive the delightful impress of his grace, and to busy itself with pious exercises and exterior duties.

A sick and agitated mind is in the same class as a fever-weakened body that can perform no serious work until healed of its complaint. As there is an analogy between the diseases of both, so, too, there are likenesses between the remedies to be applied.

Physical health can be restored only by a threefold prescription: rest, good food, and obedience to the doctor's orders. The like threefold prescription will bring back peace and health to a soul troubled and sick almost to death.

The first remedy

The first requirement for your cure is docility. Above all, base your virtue upon renunciation of your judgment and upon a humble and warm-hearted readiness to accept and perform everything your director deems pleasing to God.

If you are animated by the spirit of obedience, you will never allow yourself to be set back by any thought contrary to the direction you have received. Equally you will take good care to avoid the inclination to examine and question everything.

Yet if, despite yourself, thoughts antagonistic to obedience creep into your mind, you will cast them from you; or, better still, you will condemn them as dangerous temptations.

The second remedy

In the first place take care never to harbor voluntarily in your heart any thought calculated to grieve, disquiet, or dishearten it. From one point of view, such thoughts are more dangerous than impure temptations. Your need, then, is to allow them to pass you by, despising them and letting them fall like a stone into the sea.

You must resist them by concentrating your attention upon contrary reflections, and especially upon aspirations designed to this end. Yet while we are to put energy and generosity into our struggle, mildness, tranquility, and peace are as necessary. For unquiet grieving and vexatious restlessness will make the remedy worse than the disease.

In the second place you are to avoid purely human ardor, eagerness, and activity in all your efforts, whether exterior or interior. On the contrary you must make it your habit to walk and talk, to pray and read, softly and slowly, putting no strain upon yourself in anything, even though it be resistance to the most frightful temptations.

Remember that the best repudiation of such temptations is the grief they bring you. As long as your free will feels only horror and detestation for the end that these temptations hold out to the imagination, plainly it will give no consent to them.

Remain in peace in the midst of such temptations no less than in spiritual ordeals.

The third remedy
We come now to the remedy for the weakness evinced by a troubled soul as a result of the fever that afflicts it. For such a soul a strengthening diet is necessary.

Let good books be read and this reading be done in a low voice with frequent pauses, less to bring to it the reflections of the intelligence than to allow the mind to digest what it reads. This apt saying of Fénelon's should not be forgotten: "Words we read are but the leavings, while the relish we have in them is the juice upon which our soul is fed and fattened." We need to do with spiritual food what the greedy and the sensual do with ragouts, sweetmeats, and liqueurs, which they still taste and savor, even after they have swallowed them.

At all times shun the pursuit of consolation through vain talk with fellow human beings. This is one of the essentials for those passing through spiritual ordeals. God, who sends us these for our good, wishes us to endure them without seeking consolations other than his own, and ordains that he himself shall determine the juncture at which these consolations shall be bestowed upon us. Each according to his ability and inclination must devote himself to interior prayer, and this with neither strife nor violence, and keep himself quietly in God's holy presence, turning to him from time to time with some interior act of adoration, repentance, trust, and love.

Abandonment to be embraced not feared

When we have reached the lowest depths of our nothingness, we can have no kind of trust in ourselves, nor in any way rely upon our works; for in these are to be found only wretchedness, self-love, and corruption.

Such complete distrust and utter scorn of the self is the one source from which originate these delightful consolations of souls wholly surrendered to God—their unalterable peace, their blessed joy, and their unshakeable trust in none by God.

Ah, would that you knew the gift of God, the reward and the merit and the power and the peace, the blessed assurance of salvation that are hidden in this abandonment; then would you soon be rid of all your fears and anxieties!

You imagine yourself lost as soon as you think of surrendering yourself, notwithstanding that there is no more certain path to salvation than that which leads through complete and perfect self-abandonment.

Faith in Christ alone

But, you will say, I could believe myself warranted in practicing this self-abandonment and ridding myself of my fears only if, living a saintly life, I had performed many good works. You delude yourself, dear Sister.

Such a remark on your part can be prompted only by your unhappy self-love that would completely rely on yourself, whereas your duty is to put your trust in God alone and in the infinite merits of Jesus Christ.

The last and costly step

I am stressing this point strongly, because I have been taught by experience that it is here that souls in your state offer their last resistance to grace and the final leap that may free them from the self—a leap that is as difficult as it is necessary.

Objections answered

What of the question of my salvation? you ask. Can it be that you still do not know the surest guarantee of that, too, is by dwelling only on God, to place the whole burden of that also upon him?

Yet is it not a duty to commune with and to be watchful over the self? Why yes, upon your entrance to God's service when your need is for detachment from the world, withdrawal from exterior things, and correction of bad habits previously formed. But afterwards you are to forget self and think only of God.

In your case your one desire is to remain buried in yourself and in what you imagine to be your spiritual interests. To deprive you of this last wretched recourse to self-love, God ordains that you find in yourself only a hot-bed of doubts and fears, grieves and uncertainties, disquietude and defeat.

Such is God's way of saying to you: Do but forget yourself and you shall find in me peace, tranquility, interior joy, and a firm assurance of your salvation. I and I alone am the God of salvation, you by yourself can effect only your perdition.

You may argue further that in this self-forgetfulness you will not even perceive your faults and imperfections, much less correct them. Error, illusion, and ignorance are never so clearly perceived as in the clear sight or presence of God. These are like a sun shining interiorly, that, freeing us from the dread of perpetual self-examination, at a stroke reveals to us all we need to know. Equally it serves to consume gradually, as a fire consumes straw, our every fault and imperfection.

A warning against preoccupation with self

Surrender all things to God and in him you shall find all things more abundantly. So shall you rid yourself once and for all of that wretched retrospection, fear, perturbation, and anxiety, to which those calculating souls are condemned who would love God only out of love for themselves and who seek their salvation and perfection less to please God and to glorify him than to serve their own interest and eternal welfare.

Yet, you will say, God ordains that we should yearn for salvation and eternal happiness. Undoubtedly; but that yearning must accord with his desire and decree. Now this is God's decree: God created us only to serve his own glory and to fulfill his own purpose. Yet, since also he is infinitely merciful, he willed that his creature should gain his own ends and his eternal welfare by accomplishing God's will.

Precisely the opposite is true in that unhappy self-love which seeks itself in all that it does: first and foremost we think of our own spiritual and eternal interests; thus preoccupied, we relegate to second place that which has to do with the glory of God.

What are we about when we are for ever preoccupied with ourselves? We might well be saying: I should be lost did I not constantly think of my interior needs and did I not as constantly ask how I stand with you and what is to become of me. These must be my ceaseless preoccupation. I can only think occasionally of those things that tend to your glory and gratification.

In the Holy Scripture the divine Savior has answered clearly and precisely brides of his who use such language: "He that loveth his life shall lose it: and he that hateth his life in this world keepeth it to life eternal."

The harmfulness of indiscriminate zeal

I order you never to speak of God or any holy thing except in a spirit of meekness and humility, and in a manner at once loving and gracious. In such speech be always restrained and encouraging; never bitter and harsh, since this is likely to chill and rebuff those who hear you. For although your talk be only of what is in the Gospel and the best kind of books, I judge that, in the state in which you are now, that talk can take so clumsy a form that nothing but evil results from it.

Truth consists in relating things exactly. It is distorted immediately it is stated extremely or applied unsuitably. Your peevish mood is like a blackened glass which, unless you make allowance for it, prevents you from seeing things and describing them to others in their true colors.

Be always on your guard against this distressing tendency; cherish thoughts and sentiments that counteract such peevishness; assure yourself and make it your delight to assure others of the infinite goodness of God and the trust we should have in him; let your behavior give them an example of virtue that is neither stiff nor embarrassing to others; take special care never to make harsh announcements to your sisters. When you can find nothing gentle to say, keep quiet, leaving the burden of such pronouncements to others who will find it easier than you to be rightly strict, avoiding too great leniency and too great severity alike.

At all times severity is as blamable as strictness is laudable: it serves only to antagonize minds instead of convincing them, and to embitter hearts instead of winning them. That true gentleness which has God's approval is as calculated to frustrate evil and forward good, as excessive harshness is to make good difficult and evil obdurate. The one builds; the other destroys.

A most dangerous temptation

Just now you are victim of one of the most dangerous temptations that can assail a well-intentioned soul—the temptation of discouragement. I adjure you to offer every resistance in your power.

Trust in God, and be sure he will complete the work he has begun in you.

Your vain fears for the future come from the devil. Think only of the present; leave the future to Providence. A well-employed present assures the future.

We grow into deeper freedom

Can a soul wholly given up to a pursuit of recollection, to a conflict with self, and the acceptance of many constraints both interior and exterior—can such a soul be expected to appear playfully gay and pleasantly amusing? Indeed, if any do appear so, I gravely doubt whether any interior change has taken place.

Yet are there not, you ask, those whose intense interior life goes with much exterior graciousness? True, but only after long practice that has in a measure made interior recollection natural to them. At the outset they were as you are, my dear Sister. They have said nothing, but have gone their way, till God has at last brought them to that spiritual state known as the freedom of God's children.

You will reach it just as they, have no doubt about that. A day will come when your recollection will be free and unforced, mild and pleasingly gentle. Then you too will make others approve of and rejoice in you because of the exterior peace which the full love of God and your neighbor makes abundantly manifest in you.

Yet you cannot attain this either quickly or at once. For it comes of virtue assiduously practiced and of an interior life which, at the beginning, must needs be somewhat forced and difficult. All this will come naturally at the end, however.

Once you have attained this, you can resume your gaiety of manner and unreservedness, since both will then be changed and made spiritual by the blessed workings of grace, whereas at an earlier stage these would certainly do harm.

Over-eagerness a stumbling block

The inclination God gives you to surrender your soul wholly to him and to live, despite the mind's vagaries and the rebellion of the flesh, a wholly interior life, is a grace whose value I wish God would make known to you as he has made it known to me.

Why, then, in spite of the inclination of all your pious reading, are you able to get no farther than the threshold of the interior life? I see plainly that this is the reason, my dear Sister: you have frustrated this inclination by unrestrained desires, by over-eagerness, and human activities which are displeasing to God and obstructive to the gentle workings of grace.

Further, the reason is that in your behavior is a secret and scarcely perceptible presumption that causes you to put too high a value on your own work and efforts. Without taking much account of it, you acted as if you claimed to do all the work yourself and even to do more than God wished.

Uneasiness, foolish fears, and depression

While I find no trace of deliberate sin in your behavior, I do find a multitude of faults and imperfections which will do you much harm unless you attempt a drastic cure. These include anxieties, vain fears, dejection, weariness, and discouragement that are half deliberate, or at least not sufficiently resisted, and that constantly disturb in you that interior peace upon the need for which I have been insisting.

What are you to do to prevent them? First, never cling to them voluntarily; secondly, neither endure nor resist them with violent effort since that merely strengthens them. Allow them to drop as a stone drops into water; think of other things; as St Francis de Sales says, talk to God of other things; take shelter in your refuge—the interior silence of respect and submission, of trust and complete self-abandonment.

Green wood for the burning

When you throw on the fire a dry piece of wood for kindling, the flames catch it first of all and then burn it gently and quietly. But if the wood is still green, the flames envelop it for a moment merely, then the heat of the fire coming into contact with the moist green inner wood makes it sweat and hiss, moves and twists it noisily this way and that, until as a result the wood is dry and in a fit state to kindle. Then the flames again envelop it, set it alight and silently and effortlessly consume it.

There you have a parable of the action and operation of the divine love upon souls which are yet full of imperfections and self-love's evil inclinations. These must be purged, purified, and refined—which cannot be done without causing them vexation and suffering. Liken yourself, then, to that green wood upon which the divine love acts before it is able to kindle and consume it.

We must allow God to work in this way
In prayer there can be a gentle and pleasurable peace. But that peace can be also bitter and barren and even sorrowful. God can effect more in our soul by the latter than by the former liable as it is to the activities of self-love.

Thus, self-abandonment is necessary in this matter as in all others. Leave him to act; he knows our need better than we.

We have but one thing to fear: that we voluntarily allow ourselves to go astray. To avoid the risk of this we have only to wish exactly what God wills at every hour, at every moment, and in every happening of the day. The surest, swiftest, and, I venture to say, the sole way of perfection lies in that. Everything else is liable to illusion, pride, and self-love.

To conclude: gently and without too much effort learn to refrain from those lengthy reasonings with which your mind is busied during prayer, and incline rather to loving aspirations, to simple rest and delight in God.

This, however, need not prevent you from dwelling for a little time on good thoughts when their nature is sweet, simple, and peaceful, and when they seem to be spontaneous.

The importance of the fixing of the heart on God
The fact that your thoughts wander is in your case only one more of God's ordeals, providing an opportunity for suffering and humiliation, an exercise in patience and an evidence of merit; while the grief that it occasions you is proof of the desire you have to be ever concerned with God.

Now, God sees this desire and in his sight desires, whether good or bad, are the equivalent of acts. Suffer then, humbly and patiently, all these mental distractions, and take good care not to be worried about them or to investigate anxiously the source from which they come.

Holy and profitable idleness

The exhaustion and sense of emptiness you feel in longing to increase and attempting to repeat your interior acts do not surprise me. These come of withstanding God's work and acting alone as if you wished to forestall grace and perform more than God wishes. This is merely human activity.

Be content to withdraw peacefully into your soul, staying there as if in a prison in which it pleases God to keep you captive, and making no further attempts to escape. That holy and profitable idleness spoken of by the saints is thus acquired, and those vast tasks accomplished that need no work for their accomplishment.

It is only self-love that grows weary and despondent in doing nothing, seeing nothing, and understanding nothing. Yet let self-love grumble to its heart's content. Its very weariness and despondency will rid us of it in the end. By cutting it short of food we shall make it die of hunger—a death to be desired indeed! With all my heart I long for it in your case as I long for it in mine.

The tree is known by its fruits

One of the commonest experiences known to souls who have not yet had much experience in the interior ways is the fear you have told me of. I refer to the fear of wasting time in the prayer that is a simple dwelling in the presence of God.

Such souls can easily be reassured, and so can you. All you need to do is to remember the divine Master's precept: the tree is known by its fruits. What produces only good effects can be nothing else but good. Now, your own experience tells you that since you have adopted this manner of prayer, you have greatly benefited interiorly. You have, then, but to thank God for the favor he has done you in substituting, as he has, the peaceful action of grace for the feverishness of your human activity.

Prayer of the heart

Your soul's inclination is very simple and what is simple is best. It turns straight to God, and so you must follow it unfailingly and gently, without effort or eagerness either to keep it or recapture it when your perception of it is gone, otherwise you would be claiming God's gifts as your own.

Distractions and dryness are fairly frequent in this type of prayer. Yet these endured with patience and self-abandonment are themselves excellent prayers. Moreover, though these distractions and aridity be painful, they do not hinder that sustained desire to pray that is found in the depths of the heart. Heartfelt prayer is no other than this.

Resolutions are rarely used in this kind of prayer. Yet much more good comes of it than of resolutions made during meditation.

Two kinds of interior peace

There are two kinds of interior peace: the one is sensible, sweet, and delightful; while, as it does not depend upon ourselves, it is by no means indispensable. The other is almost unperceived and is to be found in the depths of the heart and the most secret recesses of the soul.

Usually it is dry and savorless and it can be possessed during the greatest tribulations. Intense recollection is necessary before it can be recognized; you might imagine that it was buried at the bottom of an abyss. It is the peace in which God dwells and which he himself calls into being that he may dwell in it as in his own element. There in the depths of our hearts he performs his unperceived and marvelous works. These are recognized only in their effects: thus it is through God's beneficent influence that we find ourselves in a state of steadfastness amid grief, violent upheavals, great difficulties, and unforeseen afflictions.

If you discover this bare peace and tranquil sadness in yourself it remains but to thank God for it: no more is necessary for your spiritual advancement. Cherish it as the most precious of gifts. Slowly increasing, it will one day be your most precious delight. Conflict and victory must precede that day.

True recollection

True recollection lies in the calm that you enjoy in solitude, and in the tranquility of a mind and heart that are emptied of all created things and are less and less preoccupied. God deprives you of it at prayer time, because you are then too full of desires and eagerness.

Stay then during prayers just as you are during solitude; I require no more concentration and eagerness from you. Keep perfectly quiet and meditative, relinquishing all desire of created things. Then will you dwell with God, though you neither know, feel, nor understand how this can be.

Spiritual progress must be in God's time

I must desire my advancement and perfection only so far as God wishes it and by the means that he wishes. Such a desire can only be calm and peaceful, even when it is full of vehemence and fervor.

But there is another desire for our perfection that springs from pride and an immoderate love of our own excellence. This does not depend upon God: consequently it is restless and forever agitated.

Our need to surrender our soul to the first of these and our need to put all our energy into defeating the second are equally great.

All desire for our advancement, therefore, however holy it appears, must be curbed the moment eagerness, restlessness, or perturbation enters into it. Such results can only come from the devil, since all that comes from God leaves us tranquil interiorly.

Let your hope be in God

The words that you say interiorly time after time—Lord, who are able to do all things, have compassion on me—make the best and simplest prayer that you can offer. No more is needed to secure his powerful help. Make this your steadfast practice.

The use of ordeals

Do you not know that utter dying to self, to live only in God and for God, can only take place by degrees, through a persistent fidelity in making the sacrifice of the intelligence, of the will, of all the passions and caprices, of our feelings and affections; finally and above all, the sacrifice that comes in a complete submission in all trials, in unceasing interior vicissitudes, and in states, sometimes painful indeed, through which God makes us pass in order to change us completely into him?

The acceptance of weakness in suffering

To suffer in sweetness and in peace and without offering any resistance is to suffer in the right way, even though you do not then make any vigorous acts of acceptance. The submissive heart offers these, without taking thought, in the humility and simplicity of its passive acquiescence. Know further, dear Sister, that you are to thank God, as though for a grace, for what you suffer meanly and weakly, that is to say, without much courage. At such times you feel overcome by your ills, upon the verge of giving way to them, inclined to grumble about them and to yield to the rebelliousness of your human nature.

Indeed, this is true grace and a great grace at that, since to suffer this is to suffer with humility and with lowliness of spirit.

If, instead, you feel a measure of courage, a measure of strength and conscious resignation, your heart is puffed up by these, and you become, yourself unaware, full of trust in yourself, interiorly proud and presumptuous. In such a state as yours, however, we draw near to God, altogether weak, humiliated, and disconcerted at having suffered so feebly. This truth is sure and comforting, essentially interior, and little known.

Domestic trials

I admit ... there is nothing more difficult than to maintain perfect equanimity and unswerving patience in the midst of domestic vexations and in our contact with people of a different disposition living with us. The continuity of these annoyances makes us, in a measure, powerless at times to preserve our self-control.

Yet if at one moment we fall, we rise the next. The fall is a weakness, the rising again a virtue. If we avoid a fall, we resume our serenity, knowing no vexation. Slowly God gives all things to those who can wait for them patiently. But your own desires are impetuous and you seek to be perfect all at once. We must try by degrees to modulate the turbulence and agitation of those desires that battle in our heart and threaten to break it. Now, if we are unable wholly to prevent them clashing, let us at least try to endure the affliction gently and humbly, and not set out to aggravate it by tormenting ourselves for being tormented.

The phantoms of the mind

Could you not check both your fears and your tears, since you have so often discovered that in all that keenly affects your heart you have been liable to indulge in delusions, and to imagine non-existent terrors?

If you find it impossible to prevent these deplorable vagaries of your imagination, seek at least to profit by them in making them a subject for interior sacrifices and an opportunity for manifesting complete self-abandonment to every decree of divine Providence, whatever it be.

I agree with you: I, too, have never desired—still less have I implored—either difficulties or consolations. Those sent by Providence suffice and we have no need to desire them or secure them ourselves. Our need is to expect and to prepare for them. In this way we shall have more strength and courage with which to encounter and endure them, as we must when God sends them.

This is one of my most cherished practices, which avails me both in this life and the next. I make offering to God in advance of every sacrifice, the idea of which has entered my mind without my seeking it.

When, on the other hand, he sends us consolations, whether spiritual or temporal, we must accept them with simplicity, gratitude, and thanksgiving, but without over-eagerness or excessive delight; for all joy that is not joy in God can only tend to inflame self-love.

Dependence on God alone

Interior tribulations are, as you say, the most torturing. Equally they are the most meritorious and the most purifying; while once these purifications and interior detachments are effected, life is all the sweeter because of them. It is then the easier to achieve full self-abandonment, and filial trust in God alone through Jesus Christ.

The reflections made by you upon this subject are in truth just and reasonable, though all too humanly inspired. Our need is in every case to get back from them to self-abandonment and to hope placed solely in divine Providence.

Depend then solely upon God who is for ever unchanging, who knows our needs better than we do, and who supplies them unfailingly like the good Father he is. Yet he has often to deal with children so blind that they know not what they ask. In the very prayers that seem to them the most righteous and most reasonable they find delusion in that they seek to foresee a future that belongs to God alone.

The fear of temptation

It is an illusion to have too great a fear of spiritual conflict under the pitiable pretext that by avoiding a struggle you will avoid the danger of committing faults. Blush for your cowardice. When you find yourself face to face with contradiction or humiliation, tell yourself that the moment has come to prove to God the sincerity of your love. Trust yourself to his goodness and to the power of his grace: such trust will assure you victory.

Even when you chance to fall into this fault or that, the harm done is negligible compared with the gain you will make, whether by the efforts in the fight, or by the merit secured in the victory, or even by the humiliation caused by your minor reverses.

Now if your temptations are purely interior, and if it is through your thoughts and your feelings that you fear to be led astray, rid yourself likewise of this fear. Do not so much as directly struggle with these interior impulses; let them die down; struggle against them indirectly by means of recollection and the thought of God.

This distrust which leads you to flee temptation ordained by God calls down upon you others, still more dangerous, of which you are unaware. Let your eyes, then, be opened; recognize that all these thoughts that discourage, trouble, and weaken you can come only from the devil.

I adjure you not to allow yourself to be caught in this snare, nor to let yourself look on this rebellion of your human passions as a sign of God's estrangement. No, dear daughter; it is, on the other hand, a greater grace than you imagine. By making you to perceive your weakness, it leads you to expect nothing save from God, and to rely on no one save him. God alone must suffice the soul who knows him.

The good fruits of temptation

It could almost be said, dear Sister, that you have never pondered the numerous texts in the sacred Scriptures by which the Holy Spirit gives us to understand the necessity of temptations and the valuable results they produce in souls who never allow themselves to despond.

Do you not know that they have been compared with the furnace in which clay receives its hardness and gold its gleam? Or that they are presented as a cause for rejoicing, a sign of God's regard, a lesson indispensable if knowledge of God is to be acquired?

Did you remember these comforting truths, how could you allow yourself to be overcome by melancholy? I declare to you in our Lord's name that you have no cause to fear. Do you but wish it, you can unite yourself as much as, and more than, you did in your moments of greatest fervor.

To this end you have one thing to do: endure your soul's painful state in peace and silence, with unswerving patience and utter resignation, even as you would endure a fever or other physical sickness.

From time to time you need to tell yourself what you would tell someone sick when you exhort her to bear with her sickness in patience. You would put it to her that in giving way to impatience or complaining she would merely succeed in aggravating or protracting her illness. So you must put it to yourself.

Self-love the cause of excessive fear

You fear, you say, lest your past infidelities should prevent God's operation in your soul. No, dear Sister, it is not your past infidelities, any more than your present wretchedness, helplessness, and darkness, that should excite your fears. It is your lack of submission, your voluntary vexation in times of spiritual poverty, darkness, and helplessness, that alone can obstruct the divine operations. Poverty, darkness, and helplessness, provided they are unaccompanied by such fears, can, on the contrary, only facilitate the divine action. You have, then, nothing to fear save your fears themselves.

Now, if you wish to know what you are to do during these interior upheavals, I am going to tell you: you must remain in peaceful expectancy, silent submission, and complete self-abandonment to the divine will, just as you take shelter and wait for a storm to pass, leaving God to calm the raging elements. Interior storms, tranquilly endured, effect the greatest good in the soul.

Your excessive fears upon the subject of past confessions are one more result of self-love, which wishes to be reassured in everything. God, on the other hand, wishes us to be deprived of that complete certainty. You are then, generously to make sacrifice of this certainty to the sovereign Master.

Despite these mistakes, due to your inexperience, by God's grace I find in your soul—and I rejoice at it—the two conditions essential to the divine operation: a steadfast resolution to belong unreservedly to God and a firm and constant determination to avoid the slightest deliberate faults. Persevere in that frame of mind, taking more precautions than you have done hitherto against the promptings of self-love. So shall you see the kingdom of God established within you.

The last stage to perfect union

You are experiencing a dearth of grace and strength, only because at the moment God wishes no more of you. But at no time do you have a dearth of blessed desires, since you feel so much grief at your inability to give effect to them. Remain, then, in peace in your great spiritual poverty, for it is a true treasure when we know how to accept it out of love for God.

I perceive clearly that you have never understood the true poverty and nakedness of spirit by which God succeeds in detaching us from ourselves and from our own works, the more thoroughly to purify and simplify us. This complete despoliation, which leaves us only acts of pure faith and pure love, is the last stage to perfect union. It is a true death to self, a most secret, torturing, and hardly endurable death; yet a death soon rewarded with a resurrection, after which we love only for God and in God, through Jesus Christ and with Jesus Christ.

Judge your blindness from this: you are grieved by what is the surest guarantee of your spiritual advancement. After a soul has climbed the first rungs of the ladder of perfection it can make little progress except by ways of despoliation and spiritual darkness, and the way of self-obliteration and death to all created things including the spiritual.

It is only in such a state that it is able to unite itself perfectly with God, in whom is nothing we can either feel, know, or experience.

Foolish fears and fancies

You are well aware that in themselves your fears are but futile fancies. Now, if it pleases God that you shall be unable to rid yourself of them completely, you have nothing to do but to drop them from you as a stone drops into water. Take no further notice of flies that come and go, buzzing in your ear. Ignore them and cultivate patience.

It is indeed surprising after all you have said and read, that you should revert once again to the interior changes and vicissitudes that you experience. This is rather as if you believed yourself obliged to note every atmospheric variation, and had to let me know that a rainy period followed a few fine days, or that a wild winter had succeeded a beautiful autumn. Such is God's established order; such are the vicissitudes of life in which all things change.

Instead of all these violent and strenuous acts that you believe yourself obliged to make, it would be far better at such times to dwell, as I have said, in the presence of God, in an interior silence of respect and humility, of submission and self-abandonment. Self-love, however, yearns always for conscious delight, That, nevertheless, cannot be, and God does not wish it. Let us then renounce it with a good grace.

It crosses your mind, I know, that you are deceiving everybody. It must be enough for you to know that you do not wish to mislead them. If it crossed your mind to kill yourself or to hurl yourself from a great height you would at once exclaim: "I am perfectly aware that I do not want to do this—away with such follies!"

They are but so many more buzzing flies. Let us put up with them patiently. When they have flown away others will come, and these, too, we must suffer likewise in patience and resignation.

On falling again and again
The account you have given me of your misfortunes and, in particular, of your faults and interior rebelliousness, has left me most sympathetic. Yet when it comes to a cure, I have no other than that which I have pointed out to you: each time you have new evidence of your wretchedness, humiliate yourself, make offering of it all to God, and cultivate patience.

If you once more relapse, do not be vexed and perturbed the second time as you were the first, but still more deeply humiliate yourself and, above all, do not fail to make offering to God of the interior grief and confusion caused by this rebelliousness and those faults arising from your weakness.

If you be guilty of fresh faults, with the same confidence come again to God and endure as patiently as possible the further remorse of conscience and rebellious inner grief. And let this be your invariable practice.

Be sure that as long as you do this, and as long as you struggle with yourself in this way, scarcely anything will be lost; in fact much will be gained as the result of the involuntary interior rebelliousness which you suffer.

Whatever the fault that escapes you, provided that you consistently seek to recollect yourself and to come back to God, in the way that has just been explained to you, it is impossible for you to fail to make good progress. If once and for all you learn to humiliate yourself sincerely for your slightest faults by sweetly and peacefully allowing your trust in God to pick you up again straightaway, you will provide yourself with a good and assured remedy for the past, and a potent and efficacious safeguard for the future.

In times of deep suffering
Be of good courage … and do not imagine yourself to be estranged from God. On the contrary, you have never been nearer to him.

Remember our Lord's agony in the Garden of Olives, and you will realize that bitterness of heart and anguish of spirit are not incompatible with perfect submission. These are the outcries of suffering nature, and signs of the difficulty of the sacrifice.

Do nothing, then, against God's decree, nor utter one word of complaint or lamentation. In this lies that perfect submission which is born of love, and of the purest love at that. At such junctures, would that you could do nothing and say nothing, but dwell in a humble silence of respect, faith, adoration, submission, self-abandonment, and sacrifice: then you have discovered the great secret of sanctifying all your sufferings, and even of turning them into great sweetness.

You must strive for this state and seek to make it habitual, but when you have failed in it, you must be careful not to fall into grief or discouragement, returning rather to that great silence in peaceful and tranquil humility.

For the rest, rely with an unswerving trust on the help of grace, which can never be denied you.

Giving the devil his chance
At no time take heed of those diabolical thoughts that would lead you to say: "I am for ever the same, for ever as lacking in recollection, as prone to distraction, as impatient and imperfect."

All this vexes you interiorly, burdens your heart, and leads you to a melancholy distrust and discouragement, and so plays the devil's game. By this feigned humility and this regret for your faults he rejoices to deprive us of the strength we need to shun, and atone for, those faults in the future.

Bitterness spoils everything; sweetness, on the other hand, can cure everything. Be, then, greatly tolerant of yourself, gently return to God; gently repent, showing neither exterior nor interior anxiety, but cultivating peacefulness of spirit.

This one practice, carried out with thoroughness, will, as time goes on, secure your interior calm, and will enable you to advance farther on God's way than all your agitation can ever do. When we feel a measure of gentleness and of peace in our hearts, we take pleasure in returning to that way, and willingly carrying out that practice, doing so consistently, easily, and almost without taking thought.

Hope in God alone
The absence of hope grieves you more than any other trial. Let me, with God's grace, try to cure you of this ill.

You want to find a little help in yourself and your good works? That is precisely what God does not wish; that is what he cannot tolerate in souls that aspire to perfection.

What! rely upon self, count upon your good works—what a wretched survival of self-love, pride, and perversity! It is to rid chosen souls of these that God makes them pass through a desolating state of poverty, wretchedness, and spiritual nakedness. He wishes slowly to destroy all the trust and reliance they have in themselves, to deprive them of all their resources, so that he may be their sole support, their sole trust, their one hope, their one resource!

How accursed is that hope which unreflectingly you thus seek in yourself? How glad I am that God destroys, confounds, and obliterates that cursed hope by means of this state of poverty and wretchedness! When all trust, all hope, all earthly and created aids have been taken from us, we shall have no more aid, we shall have no more trust, we shall have no more hope save in God alone.

This is the right hope, the right trust known to the saints, a hope and a trust based solely upon the mercy of God and the merits of Jesus Christ. But you will have this hope only after God has destroyed in you the last clinging roots of your trust in self. This may come to pass only if God keeps you for a while yet in entire spiritual poverty.

Think only on God's mercy
Yet, you will say, of what use to us are good works if they are not to inspire us with trust? Their use is to secure us the grace of a still more complete distrust in ourselves and a still greater trust in none but God. This is the sole use the saints made of them.

To what, indeed, do our works amount? They are so spoilt and so corrupted by our self-love that if God judged us rigorously, we should deserve more punishment than reward. Give no further thought, then, to your good works as a means of enjoying tranquility at death: merely fix your eyes on the mercy of God, the merits of Jesus Christ, the intercession of the saints, and the prayers of righteous souls.

Turn then away from everything—everything that might give you occasion to rely upon yourself, or even in the smallest measure to place your trust in your own good works.

The remarks you make to others—or rather the remarks God gives you to make—in the time of your greatest spiritual aridity do not surprise me at all. It is God's usual attitude, determined by the fact that his wish is to console others, the while he keeps you in desolation and self-abandonment. At such times you speak what God gives you to speak, leaving you dead to all feeling in yourself but alive in the feeling you have for others. I see no manner of hypocrisy in this.

Perseverance in darkness

You see nothing in your present state. In the midst of this obscure night, go forward, then, by the light of blind obedience. It is a safe guide that has never yet led anyone astray, and whose guidance is more sure and more speedy than that of even the most perfect acts of self-abandonment.

Such acts are indeed excellent, though it is possible that you may sometimes find yourself unable to perform them. On such occasions you will be able to put yourself in a still more perfect state, which consists in dwelling in the interior silence of respect, adoration, and submission, of which I have written so much.

Such silence tells God more than all your formal acts. Moreover, it knows no return to self-complacency and is without consolations perceptible to the senses. Here you have the true mystical death, which must necessarily precede the supernatural life of grace.

Unless God perceives in you this second death—death to spiritual consolation—you will not attain to this wholly spiritual and interior life for which you long so fervently.

Spiritual consolations are in fact so sweet that, were not God to detach us from them by the violence of spiritual ordeals, we should become even more attached to them than to any worldly pleasure, and this would be a supreme stumbling-block to perfect union.

Take courage in realizing that those things that today constitute your sorrow and your martyrdom will in a day to come be your greatest delight. When will that blessed time be? God alone knows; it will be when it pleases him.

A hurtful and dangerous temptation

The terrors caused by your old faults are the most dangerous and hurtful of your temptations. Hence I order you to reject all such advances of the devil, as we reject the temptations of blasphemy and impurity. Think only of the present and shut yourself up in the will of God, leaving all else to his Providence and mercy.

115

Your stupidity and insensibility are emphatically not punishments for some hidden sin, as the devil would have you think, so that your interior peace may be troubled. They are pure graces, which have indeed a bitter taste, and yet have had good effects already, and in the future will have still more. Who says so? I—on God's behalf—assure you that it is so.

Trials to be suffered until relieved

The difficulties in your soul's lower part when your grieves are most poignant can never destroy your peace of spirit, as long as your submission to God is complete. This is known as possessing the solid and undoubted peace of God.

The painful awareness of our nothingness

The vivid awareness you feel of your nothingness in God's sight is one of the most salutary operations of the grace of the Holy Spirit. I know how thoroughly painful this operation can be; the poor soul appears to be on the brink of utter obliteration, whereas it is only nearer to true life.

Indeed the deeper we are plunged into our nothingness, the nearer we are to truth, since our very essence is of that nothingness from which we have been drawn out by the Lord's pure goodness. We ought, then, to dwell in that unbrokenly, and thus, by our voluntary self-obliteration, render continual homage to the grandeur and infinite nature of our Creator. Such sacrifice is a holocaust in which self-love is utterly consumed in the fire of divine love.

When this sorrowful, yet blessed, hour has come, we have nothing to do but imitate Jesus Christ on the cross: we must commend our soul to God, surrender ourselves still more completely to all that it pleases the sovereign Master to do with this poor creature, and remain in that agony as long as his good pleasure ordains.

Let us be of good courage, dear daughter: let us assent to everything with the blessed abasement of spirit of Jesus Christ crucified. From all this our strength must come. Let us make a habit of saying, when such anguish besets us: "Indeed, Lord, I desire all that you desire, in Jesus Christ and through Jesus Christ!" In such company as his, how could we be afraid? In the most violent temptations a simple abasement at the feet of the Savior-God will make all things calm: he will render you victorious; while, with his strength, he will enable your weakness to triumph over all the tempter's cunning.

A good foundation for humility

May God be blessed ... for the notable graces which it has pleased him to accord you! Your chief care henceforth must be to guard these precious gifts with watchful humility.

Your experience of the peace of God during prayer comes, without a doubt, from the Holy Spirit. Take care lest, by a most ill-advised multiplication of your religious acts, you emerge from that simplicity which is the more fruitful the nearer it approaches the infinite simplicity of God. This way of knowing union with him through a complete effacement of the self is based upon the great principle that our Almighty and all-good God gives his children ... what he knows will be most fitting for them, and that the whole of perfection lies in the heart's steadfast clinging to his adorable will.

To be in no way astonished at our wretchedness is a good foundation for humility based upon self-knowledge: while to feel that wretchedness keenly and constantly, and yet to be untroubled by it, is a very great grace from which spring distrust of self and true and perfect trust in God. Your devotion to the sacred Heart of Jesus and the practices you have adopted in regard to it are true spiritual treasure that suffices to enrich both you and your dear daughters. The more you draw upon this treasure, the more there remains for you to draw, inexhaustible as it is.

A spirit of gentleness and moderation in government is a noble gift from heaven; government is the more effectual and salutary for this spirit. When we fall let us humiliate ourselves, pick ourselves up, and continue our way in peace. That way is at all times to ponder upon the true self which is God—God in whom we must plunge and lose ourselves, rather as we shall find ourselves plunged and lost in heaven, in the everlasting duration of eternity's great day. Amen! Amen!

St Ignatius and his first companions

PRAYER FROM THE HEART[1]

WHAT DO WE REALLY MEAN BY THIS PRAYER?

This prayer most necessarily springs from the heart, otherwise no merit at all can be found in it or any other prayer. We call it fully heart-charged to distinguish it from vocal prayer, in which the heart expresses itself through the mouth, and from prayer of affection, in which the heart expresses itself with interior speech, pronounced interiorly as it would be pronounced aloud if we wanted others to hear what we are saying in our hearts. In exact terms, this fully heart-charged prayer is carried out in the heart by unsigned acts, which are unexpressed even interiorly, but truly practiced in the depths of the heart; or ... by simple, unexamined, direct acts; or again, by an effective and actual turning of the heart towards God and every person loved by God.

Let us give an example to better establish and make understood a truth that depends upon a clear understanding of all that we have to say here. A mother who tenderly loves her son, in looking at him or thinking of him, even for a long time, will have actual love for him in her heart during all this time, in actuality not shown by signed, expressed acts, which she can't make, but by simple direct acts really practiced in her heart, or, if you wish, by the same continual act pro-longed during the whole time she looks at him or thinks of him. All this is carried out so actually and so freely for every object for which the heart has affection that if this object is evil, we really sin the whole time we spend paying attention to it or entertaining it with the heart's simple dispositions; it is in no way disavowed, but desired and consented to by these simple tendencies of the heart to which we voluntarily adhere. Thus we sin not by signed acts expressed interiorly which we are careful to avoid; rather, we want to be able to hide these interior secret iniquities from ourselves; but neverthe-less we sin by acts truly carried out in the heart or by a subsisting, persevering act, one and the same, which bears the stamp of even more passion, malice, and perversity of the heart.

---

[1] Selections from Jean-Pierre Caussade, S.J., *A Treatise on Prayer from the Heart: A Christian Mystical Tradition Recovered for All,* translated, edited, and introduced by Robert M. McKeon, The Institute of Jesuit Sources, St Louis, 1998. Used with per-mission: © The Institute of Jesuit Sources, St Louis, MO. All rights reserved.

How are these notions applied to this topic?
Nothing is easier, for it doesn't require more to be worthy than to be unworthy; God doesn't have a fuller awareness of the evil practiced in the heart by these direct unsigned acts than the good accomplished in prayer by simple acts of the same kind; God tends more to reward than to punish. Draw this conclusion: before God, all acts executed only in the heart are as much for good as they are for evil, except in a directly opposite way....

Isn't grace stronger, or at least more effective, than the passions?
Since grace gives us real power to overcome them, then why aren't we able to do good in the heart by means of this grace, just as we are able to do evil by means of nature's perversities? Did the saints pursue the love of God, crosses, and humiliations less than sinners do the love of the world, their pleasures, and their fame?

How can we do this prayer and assure ourselves that we are doing it?
Most virtuous people—and even sinners, once deeply moved—could very easily do it, at least intermittently, if they knew this prayer well; for if, in the course of their meditation, reading, vocal prayer, and so forth, they feel the heart touched in a holy way by some kind of pious stirring, the fear of God, love, regret for the past, or the desire to do better in the future, then what prevents them from yielding to these simple stirrings, from resting in them to give themselves the leisure to penetrate right down to the bottom of their souls; and then, if necessary, after renewed stimulation of similar feelings, what prevents them again from halting, from yielding in the same manner, trying to hold onto all these simple but edifying impressions as long as possible?

What good or what advantage comes from it?
We could give space to the sweet impressions of grace that we too often choke off or interrupt with our many inner agitations or our usual inner routines.

We could continue prayer longer and more easily. With the help of grace, we could do what divine Providence has done with food for the body, and find flavor and pleasure in prayer. Thus, we ourselves could transform prayer, the most necessary thing in the world, into something easy and agreeable.

But how do we recognize these simple, unexamined, and unperceived direct acts of the heart, to assure ourselves that we are really doing this kind of prayer?

If we let ourselves be a little self-attentive, these unexamined and consequently unperceived acts are in themselves in a sense felt, as the philosophers have said. It is only by feeling and awareness, as the Schoolmen say, that we know our soul, its workings, and its ways of acting which are revealed in these acts. We recognize so well, in spite of ourselves, these simple acts when unreservedly practiced for evil. For if in giving alms or in practicing some other virtue, there arises in my heart a simple movement of vanity or self-satisfaction that I do not immediately reject, because I have allowed myself to be led by its pernicious sweetness, right away I feel that I am doing evil and that this unsigned act of the heart fully spoils the good deed. Those who have some tenderness of conscience don't fail to accuse themselves of this simple movement, as well as of its duration, although they had only adhered to it in their hearts.

Now I am beginning to understand a bit what a fully heart-charged prayer is; it is, you say, a prayer from the heart and of the whole heart, because God clearly sees all that goes on in the heart.

He wants only the heart. It is from the heart, as he himself says, that both good and evil come; all the goodness and malice of ours acts have no other source. Furthermore, the ensuing acts, which differ from the simple acts of giving assent, in themselves add exactly nothing, as theologians assert.

But do you want to reduce every prayer to this kind?

Not at all, as you see, for we need the others to do this one well. Indeed, how could the heart produce pious movements and good desires, much less sustain itself in them, if it isn't moved, touched, and excited? How, without special grace, will it be moved unless by meditation, reading, by various reflected-upon and discursive acts that ought to place the heart in motion, in action, and reheat it when it finds itself cooled off?

Then why speak so much about the acts of this kind of prayer if it presupposes the others as first prompters? Because the prompter prayers do not at all presuppose these prayers from the heart, and because too often one engages in them without the heart entering into them in the least, even though such engagement is essential. On this we must insist here.

We want to draw many people from a very common and very harmful error, namely, believing that they aren't praying or meditating well unless they incessantly make reflections and acts expressed interiorly or exteriorly. In some this gives birth to excessive eagerness that troubles them rather than filling them with the peace in which God abides and works, as Scriptures tells us. In others this error gives birth to distaste, boredom, and discouragement in prayer the instant they feel the cessation of what the majority calls acts, although the unsigned acts about which we are speaking still subsist in the heart, which was moved and touched, and can easily continue to subsist there if we knew well how to recognize them, to rest there with them, to entertain them with simple attention, and to be content with them, because they properly constitute and are the best kind of prayer. Even acts represented and expressed interiorly are nothing before God except by virtue of these direct unsigned acts, because acts take birth in the heart before they can be represented in any way.

Without an exact understanding of these direct unsigned acts about which we are talking, we couldn't reach a good understanding of the different ways in which the ancient and modern authors speak about fully heart-charged prayer. Of all the kinds of prayer, it is: a) the most perfect because it is the simplest; b) the most natural for the human heart, for which it is the pure language; c) the most efficacious in itself since it alone, to speak exactly, redresses the heart and turns it to God; d) the most powerful with respect to God because it goes straight to God's heart free from and beyond all expressions.

These are the interior sighs of which St Paul speaks, the groans ineffable even to him who sends them heavenward without words, neither spoken exteriorly nor interiorly, words being too weak to express the simple language of the heart. All human beings agree with this. After they have tried to witness mutually their gratitude or friendship, they add, "I wish you could see the feelings in my heart." But God sees what humans can neither see nor express as they wish. He hears whatever we say, even in the very preparing of our hearts: "Your ears hear the preparing of their heart," in the words of the prophet; that is to say, he hears the very first movement of a heart which stirs itself to form a simple desire....

HUMILITY HAS TO PRECEDE THIS PRAYER AND IS EXCELLENTLY PRACTICED WHILE DOING IT

How little experience do those have who fear vanity from this prayer, either for themselves or for others. With the most magnificent words, let us praise it as much as we want to. Because it is essentially the most humiliating and annihilating of all prayers, it can precisely be called:

- sublime in the eyes of God but not in the eyes of men, according to what they ordinarily understand;
- sublime in the same sense as the incomparable knowledge of Jesus Christ, "*supereminentem scientiam Iesu Christi*" ("the surpassing knowledge of Jesus Christ"), in the words of St Paul when he explains so magnificently the knowledge of the cross, which ultimately is no more than the practical understanding of the sufferings and humiliations of the God-man, where very few people need to fear vanity and much less to find it;
- sublime, not because it puffs up the spirit as human knowledge does, as St Paul tells us, but rather because it brings it low, humiliates it, and annihilates it by the simple regard of the grand totality that is God and the nothingness of the creature;
- sublime, not because it lifts and enhances the learned and the great geniuses, but rather because it obscures and engulfs us in the holy shadows of faith where we have only a vague, general, and confused notion of God, without form or images or illustrious views, and where in truth we feel that we love, but without knowing how, as St Teresa says, because the object is incomprehensible and will be better understood only insofar as it appears more incomprehensible;
- sublime, finally, not from the beautiful ideas and the grand knowledge by which we are enriched, but rather ... because we are impoverished of all natural light, all resulting magnificent knowledge, beautiful thoughts, and rich ideas in order to be fully poor in spirit.

This poverty is nakedness of spirit. Do these obscurities, shadows, and inexplicabilities naturally have what serves to awaken and entertain pride rather than to crush and annihilate it? If someone still doubts, I send him to his own proper experience, for whoever prays can, without changing his usual way and easily without risk, make several attempts during these attentive pauses that we shall further explain in greater detail.

Why do writers who speak of [this prayer] warn us to guard against vanity?
First of all, pride is so natural and so well rooted in us that there is nothing so sanctifying or so humbling that can keep pride from easily slipping in. We can swell up from humiliation, even interiorly glorify ourselves over it, vainly delight in it, and so pride ourselves on having reached the abysses of humiliation and of the practice of humility. Secondly, if in seeking out this kind of prayer, we were following the false ideas that even certain pious people have of it, or the vain desire of some imagined elevation or other, then it is sufficient for us to become either incapable of this prayer and lose attraction for it or fall into illusions.

What difference ... do [we] find between this prayer and the so extraordinary and sublime prayer of most saints?
Concerning the extraordinary, as we have already said, this prayer is not accompanied by extraordinary gifts, as is the prayer of the saints: visions, revelations, ravishments, ecstasies, and so forth. About the sublimity of this prayer and that of the saints, we must think about it along the lines of what we have been saying and understand it differently from that prayer. Certain vain spirits who were chasing after sublimity sought after this way of praying; but, once they found nothing in it or less than what they had imagined, they quickly abandoned it and, irritated at having been fooled by their vain pretensions, thereafter spoke of it only with contempt, describing it as pure imagination. Such is the lofty effect of these high, sublime, but false ideas that these vain spirits have put into their own heads, perhaps even following the opinion of some so-called spirituals, who in the same way think and proclaim these ideas instead of saying that here we find the prayer of the humble and that prayer that makes those that practice it humble.

Furthermore, there is the same difference between the prayer of the good souls of whom I speak and the prayer of the saints of whom you speak, as there is between all the virtues possessed by the latter in an eminent degree, and by the former in a very low or inferior degree; the same difference that is found between the usual patience of average Christians who try, as we say, to make necessity into a virtue and the extraordinary and fully heroic patience of the saints, who go so far as to place their joy in the cross, in humiliations—to such an extent, indeed, as to seek those as eagerly as the worldly seek pleasures and honors. Finally, to get back to my point, there is the same difference as between those who, at their eyes' least glint at God, annihilate themselves and lose themselves in God by the force of being immersed again and again into the immense bosom of the divinity, and those who fix their eyes on God and rest in his presence.

Why did [we] add that of all the prayers this one is the most humbling?
First of all, it is the prayer of the weak, whom God pushes on unceasingly and holds by the hand like small children; strong and courageous souls, says St Teresa, don't need this to make them progress in virtue. Secondly, in the other kinds of prayer, we act with grace on our own initiative: we think, we reflect, we reason, we become attached—in a word, we appear—to act by means of all the powers of our own soul. Insofar as we believe we have succeeded in our actions, we feel very pleased and very satisfied with ourselves. In St Francis de Sales' view, our miserable satisfactions do not add up to God's satisfaction. In contrast to the other kinds of prayer where our mind and will are tied to their usual ways of working, the Holy Spirit works and does all within us in such a profound and hidden way that we hardly perceive our minds freely cooperating, because they do so with direct but unreflected and unperceived acts....Thus we are inclined to believe that we have done nothing: we fear having been idle, we complain to our directors, we consult and often harass them; and if, at other times, especially in the beginnings, these interior actions manifest themselves very sensibly, we feel very good, although at the same time we realize that they do not spring from our own resources, since they are something so strange and so commanding that it is impossible to attribute them to ourselves, as St Teresa says. Thus, with God we can without doubt delight in them but not boast about them, any more than can a poor person who has just received lavish alms.

Hence, in everything that they do, say, or think, people who are accustomed to this prayer discover well and perceive what comes from their own depths and what is foreign and borrowed. By virtue of this they come to a conviction of heart so intimate and so habitual that, without effort and from an unquestionable inner feeling which wards off every reflection, they immediately ascribe to God every good deed. Why? They almost never have those first movements of vain complacency that, without cease, besiege and harass most devout people in whom, according to their own avowal, these vain complacencies often spoil and corrupt all the good that they appropriate to themselves, revealing abundant secret self-love that is as natural and maybe as frequent as breathing, were it not for special grace and extraordinary vigilance.

How are this profound humility and total mistrust of one's self above all inherent in this holy recollection?
First it happens in a simple thought or, rather, in a simple sentiment of that sovereign Majesty which absorbs and engulfs all. Then we see ourselves or, rather, feel ourselves like a mere dot in that immensity, or like a small worm crawling on several grains of dust. Therefore, human beings are no more than mere shadows of beings; everything seems annihilated before him who is and so calls himself. Expressing this same sentiment, King David called out that, even without knowing it, he had been reduced to nothing. Why? This happens much less by distinct ideas than by a hidden and obscure sentiment, almost like printing on paper in a very short time and in the obscurity of a printing shop all that is wanted, which we then read in daylight. Likewise, not during the obscurity of this prayer but afterwards in various occasions, these sentiments and confused ideas develop through knowledge of and insights into the present time in the minds of people who, it must be added, are simple and without instruction.

By the way, from this we can infer the source from which the saints drew with such facility, promptitude, and abundance the most admirable of all that they left us in their divine writings, which only follow and reveal the plenitude that they received in prayer. This plenitude, however, was usually neither the matter nor the subject of their writings, contrary to what a not inconsiderable number of people imagine.

Second, on other occasions this divine recollection takes place in the deep abyss of our misery, weakness, powerlessness for any good, and perversion and corruption of heart that render each of us capable of the same disorders, excesses, and abominations, from which spring contempt, hate, and holy horror of ourselves, a mistrust so strong and so pressing that we actually seem drawn to all kinds of crimes and about to commit them. From this there arises, not in the mind but in the heart, that conviction so rare and at the same time so inherent in this holy recollection that a wise person only needs a touch of this deep and humble self-knowledge. This conviction suffices to judge that the person out of whom similar sentiments well forth has drawn them from this prayer and walks without doubt in this path of great self-denial. So also it very often suffices—after perceiving in another a slight wisp of pride, self-sufficiency, self-esteem, or a certain air of vanity even in talking about spiritual matters, or perceiving a scoffing, fault-finding, and carping mind—to judge not only fully the contrary but, furthermore, that such a person is incapable of this prayer.

Until I see persons of this kind work with all their force to fight off these failings, which, as light as we want to suppose them, are directly opposed to this prayer of simplicity, I would willingly give a name still more humbling if the expression I have in mind, fully consecrated as it is by the Scriptures, would not repel all those who have never discovered the lowly feelings that we draw out of ourselves in the exercise of this prayer. The king-prophet understood it well when he said to God, "I have become before you like a beast of burden, and it is on account of this that I remain always in your presence."

Therefore, this prayer is truly the prayer of small folk and the humble, whom it renders always smaller and humbler, incessantly diminishing them both before God and themselves. This virtue alone so greatly reveals the presence of the spirit of Jesus Christ that the Church has constantly determined the different degrees of prayer primarily by this solid humility of heart that I understand, not as consisting only in a blind submission of the spirit to all its decisions, but as more, namely, a perfect submission in all and everywhere, always avoiding anything that can possibly offend and displease God.

THE ADVANTAGE OF THIS PRAYER

Is this prayer necessary?

In general, prayer is necessary to obtain grace, without which there is no salvation; but no kind of prayer in particular is necessary, except in a certain sense prayer from the heart, because the heart should animate every prayer. Without the heart, mental prayer would merely be pure mental entertainment and vocal prayer only the empty sounding of words. Just as God took to task his chosen nation when he said through one of his prophets, "These people glorify me with their lips, but their heart is far from me." Consequently, purely heart-charged prayer, which is made by acts not at all signed but simply carried out in the depths of the heart during prayer of recollection, silence, and rest in God—this prayer, I say, without end, stressing their utility and importance in proportion to their salutary effects.

An example

Among the many that have come to my attention, I shall cite only two very useful thoughts, so it seems to me. Speaking one day with one of those great sinners whose conversion had such very happy results, I asked him, "At the time of your conversion, what was your chief inclination?" "The love of solitude," he replied. But here is precisely the same inclination that I discovered afterwards in St Teresa, who at the time of her second conversion said, "But what do you do above all during solitude? Read a lot, meditate without stop, make reflection upon reflection, prayer upon prayer?—Not at all. I often read, but very little; as for meditation, I didn't know how to do it, which greatly afflicted me; often I couldn't even pray in any way at all, which seemed unsupportable to me, for I was wanting to be meditating always, always praying." Well then, I affirm, there the heart's secret desires pray incessantly for you even during your longest dry periods; God sees these hidden desires even when you do not notice them and hears them even in the continual preparation of your heart, which God hears very well without words either vocal or silent.

This heart, once deeply touched, only requires from time to time simple reflection on two or three words to put itself into pious motion and to continue in it. Recall the story of the publican. In your solitude do something like what he did in the back of the temple: "Lord," he cried out from time to time, "have mercy on this sinner." But just like you, without repeating incessantly the same words, he was trying to preserve the same sentiments and secret impressions as long as he could. This attitude visibly appears from the humble posture of his body so unpretentiously described in the Gospel, and in turn it clearly represents to us the humble posture of his soul, all confused interiorly, humiliated, and sighing before God. Thus he returns converted and sanctified.

The representative of all the sinners of the world, the Savior himself, who humbly prostrated himself in the garden before his

Father, seems to have wanted to give us the model of this simple prayer, because all the evangelists agree in so expressly drawing to our attention that he is always repeating the same words: "*Eundem sermonem dicens*" ("Speaking the same words"), and without doubt he did so after very long intervals, since on the one hand his words were so short and on the other hand his prayer lasted so long.

We should endeavor to pray like the publican and like Jesus Christ himself, especially in reciting what he has taught us, since just one of his entreaties: "*Fiat voluntas tua*" ("Let thy will be done") sufficed for such a long prayer. This is what that pious widow of whom St Teresa speaks almost literally practiced. She sometimes spent whole hours reciting a few *Paters* (Our Father). And by the way, this is all that can ordinarily be done by most of the simple but innocent and virtuous souls who are raised in the country or in hamlets. Can we even require of them or teach them anything else? Also God often makes up for whatever they lack by impressions so secret that many of these good souls remain for whole hours in their churches without boredom, without disgust, and with a modest, respectful, and attentive demeanor that edifies and touches bystanders. Then ask them what they said to God. They will answer you, with tears in their eyes, that they don't know how to pray and never have been able to learn how. Good God! What are they doing there for such a long time and what secret charm holds them with such a great taste of piety and of so much peace and sweetness that they can hardly tear themselves away from the holy place? Yes, I dare to affirm, in the company of many holy country parish priests, that they are doing this heart-charged prayer, this prayer of faith, of the presence of God, this prayer of simplicity.

Many of our learned hardly understand it and will never understand it as long as in following the heights and sublimity of their intelligences they evaluate it with those high and sublime ideas that they forge at will. Instead, they should look at it as the prayer of the small and humble, and to find it themselves by walking arm in arm with the humble in simplicity of heart according to the usual expression of the Scriptures. Simplicity of heart so pregnant with the taste of God that, even in the Old Testament, the prophets never tired of repeating to the great kings of that time these short words: "If you walk before the Lord in simplicity of heart, if you look for him with simplicity of heart, you can expect all kinds of good things and graces."

What other fruit should we draw from these examples and reflections?

At the least the purely heart-charged prayer of simple recollection cuts away the superfluity of our meditations, readings, and vocal prayers to substitute assets, that is to say, attention of the heart, savor of the heart, peace and rest of the heart, which many people hardly think of.

Among many good Christians and people of virtue, this prayer abolishes a double illusion as nefarious as it is crude: illusion in the excessive earnestness of some, illusion in the pitiful discouragement of others, because they all think alike, convinced that they never meditate well, pray well, or read with fruit unless they are in perpetual agitation, piling up reflection upon reflection, prayer upon prayer, reading upon reading. In this way they pass their whole life without ever wanting to learn from simple souls the great secret of knowing from time to time to restrain themselves a little in peace and in silence, attentive before God, not even when he seeks by some interior inclinations to draw them to this saintly and loving rest, which is the end and principal fruit of prayer, according to St Bonaventure's opinion. On the one hand, we only seek God to find him, to be united to him, and to rest in him who is the center of the heart and the unique object of its true rest, as St Augustine says; on the other hand, all of our holiness on earth consists in this holy union of heart, as in heaven all our happiness will consist in perfect union and eternal rest.

Alas! If with a little more distrust of ourselves, of our own skills, and of our customary undertakings, and if with a little more confidence in God and abandonment to the Holy Spirit—whom the Church calls the finger of the right hand of the celestial Father, because he engraves all that pleases him in our hearts—if with this double awareness we were willing to try to practice, to proceed gently, and to make short attentive pauses during all our exercises of piety, confessors and preachers would not have so many reasons to berate us without end for the little fruit that we harvest from our prayers, spiritual readings, Masses, Communions, and especially from vocal prayer, which, not being animated by the heart, lacks this interior spirit and remains as if it was without effect and without soul.

ATTENTIVE PAUSES: WHAT, HOW, AND WHY?

As for going slowly and gently word by word, either spoken or interior, all masters well acquainted with prayer teach the following about it:

Go slowly and gently to avoid, they say, every harmful effort and every struggle of the mind. Prayer, they add, which causes a headache can hardly be good, because on the whole prayer should be the work of a heart that speaks with respectful freedom and filial confidence to him whom Jesus Christ orders us to address as Father at the very start of our prayer.

What we usually reckon as fervor, far from being in the heart or in the mind, is merely a flush of the blood or imagination: purely natural acts so apt to trouble the Holy Spirit's actions that one of the major concerns of those who are progressing consists in working to destroy this natural activity, which, if it opposes the gentle peace of the Spirit of God, is a great imperfection, one which we ought to tolerate only at the beginning....

Why is it necessary to make these small and frequent pauses about which we are speaking?
I have just hinted at it: it is to listen to God after having spoken to him in different ways in the depths of the heart.

Sometimes he speaks with those kinds of interior words that we hear in the depths of the soul, says St Teresa, as if someone pronounced them out loud in our ears; but here there isn't any question of such kinds of words, since we are speaking only of something that arrives during our commonplace recollection.

God speaks in intuitions and inspirations; it is therefore necessary to stop to receive them.

He speaks while acting, for in God, to speak and to do what he wants are the same. Therefore, it is necessary to stop from time to time to make space for the impressions that God wants to imprint on our hearts and wills, which in an incomprehensible way he moves, turns, and fashions as he wishes, as long as no obstacle at all is found, much more easily than the most skillful craftsman would know how to mold a piece of soft wax as he wishes.

God speaks in giving what we ask for, as the rich answer the poor by giving alms. Therefore, imitate those poor persons who, far from only crying and wailing without interruption, stop from time to time, hold out and open their hands to receive alms. Likewise, let us stop now and then, suspend our interior cries, give time for our desires and for our confidence to expand well, and open our hearts into which God, acting just as softly as he does discourse, secretly, will by his divine infusion pour the graces fervently hoped for and patiently awaited....

Are these pauses done, as some think, by a suspension of our interior acts? Those who view them this way imagine something absolutely impossible, for, as the Scholastic philosophers and theologians say, our acts, specifically in this case the interior operations of our soul, are states of being one way at one time and another at another time. In other words, if you wish, just as our acts with respect to the soul are like shape with respect to the body, so our soul can no more be without any activity than our body can be without any shape; but just as a body can well have at one time one shape and at another time another shape—what was a square becoming round, thus losing one shape to receive another—likewise can our soul at one time be in a state with certain acts, at another time with certain other acts, dropping certain thoughts, certain feelings, in order to take up others, even contrary ones. Having established that interior pauses cannot be mere suspension of our acts, I will now explain how interior pauses can be done.

As we have already hinted, these attentive pauses are made precisely by a unique suspension of the acts, which we call usual, formal, explicit, and deliberate, in order to better apply ourselves to the interior and to what goes on there. This kind of suspension happens when, thinking that we are about to hear a beautiful voice or an agreeable symphony, we each during this expectation suspend our thoughts, deliberations, and interior motions in order to be more attentive to what we are hoping to hear. Indeed, suspension and expectation would be in themselves evil if the awaited thing were also evil. Therefore, acts occur during this attentive suspension or, to speak more exactly, during the suspension itself. The awaiting itself is truly an act belonging to the kind that the bishop of Meaux calls direct, deliberate, and in a sense unperceived; that is to say, perceived not by explicit deliberation but only by awareness itself, which we find imperceptibly in the soul as we do in hundreds of purely natural cases.

Even the supernatural and divine suspension of which St Teresa speaks, which avoids the word "rapture," which astonishes us—even this suspension in rapture doesn't happen without acts, for God at that time suspends the powers of the soul and its usual operations only in order to lift the soul up and to make it perform acts even of a superior order, fully supernatural and divine. Concerning this, it is most fitting to underscore the misunderstanding and contempt of some writers who mix all at the same time, mixing both the fully divine suspension, of which St Teresa speaks, with what we are speaking of, and the most ordinary recollection with the extraordinary. In order to combat simple recollection, these writers have taken it upon themselves to argue that accordingly we want to carry ordinary souls to a kind of prayer and suspension so rare that St Teresa herself confesses to have never experienced it for longer than half an hour. After this, they add, the souls of fairly common virtue will claim to be able to remain in the same state for entire hours on end, although in simple recollection there is nothing of that sort. However, these books do not fail to leave strong impressions and to engender strange presuppositions against the truth....

These pauses should be more or less long depending on each one's capacities, since beginners, who don't yet have the habit or facility to know how to hold themselves peacefully and silently attentive before God, have to make them fairly short; but as they advance, the pauses become, as naturally could be expected, easier and longer, either by virtue of acquired dispositions or of a small beginning of an ensuing attraction.

These pauses should last as long as we feel a good sentiment in our hearts, whether excited by a pious reflection or an affective act or any small interior attraction. When these interior movements appear, we gently try to stimulate them with the same affections or with other similar ones that likewise always lead to new attentive pauses; we continue in the same fashion until the end of prayer.

As it necessarily follows from the above, we should place ourselves in silence and remain there as if eavesdropping every time and as long as we feel either a desire to love and to unite ourselves with God or a sweet rest in his presence, a simple taste for piety or simply a great interior calm, a certain peace that we aren't in the habit of experiencing. The risen Jesus Christ always gave his disciples this peace when he approached them: "*Pax vobis*" ("Peace be with you"). This profound calm of our passions shows, so says blessed John of the Cross, that God in his way puts both peace and love at the bottom of our hearts.

But what if after various attempts at attentive pauses, I don't feel anything like that at all?

Then it is necessary to do what God reveals in the Scriptures: bear up as we wait for the Lord. We must say to ourselves, as King David did in similar cases, "With expectation I have waited for the Lord." We must do what is done with respect to temporal favors in the courts of princes, where, no matter how little we hope, we do not at all grow weary of waiting. We must do what Jesus Christ taught us in the parable of the man who at midnight comes to wake up his friend and ask him for three loaves of bread. First he is refused and waits in vain, but finally his noisy dunning and his redoubled efforts obtain for him what he seemed to have asked for in vain and waited for over a long interval. Finally, at this point we should imitate what most of the poor do. Tired and weary of having often waited at the door of the rich, they still do not fail to return there again with the hope of a favorable moment; finally, owing to the force of new lamentations and repeated expectations, they come to obtain what was refused to others who were less courageous in practicing patience while waiting.

But what if during the pauses I am exposed to all sorts of distractions and even to bad thoughts?

Since the most abominable distractions and thoughts are involuntary, as I suppose, they don't harm you any more during these pauses than during the remainder of your prayer or during any of your other prayers. On the contrary, patiently suffering them constitutes a great subject of merit, for then, so say our masters, we are doing the prayer of patience.

But still, if after a considerable time I have done my prayers with these attentive pauses without ever experiencing at all what you have spoken of, then haven't I wasted a lot of time, especially the most precious time, that devoted to prayer?

No, no, it is anything but lost time; it may be your best time spent in prayer. Why?

Just as fully as God sees the heinous intention of a scoundrel who waits hour after hour to catch his prey, doesn't he likewise see the good intention of your attentive pauses to hear him better in silence and be better disposed to receive his illuminations, impressions, and operations at the very moment he wants? Therefore, it takes just as much to be worthy as to be unworthy.

Doesn't God continue to see all the diverse acts practiced, although unsigned, during these attentive and silent pauses?

He sees acts of keen faith, for I wouldn't have been careful to remain thus in attentive silence if I didn't firmly believe that God is everywhere, that he is looking at me, that he penetrates right to the actual preparation of my heart, and that he is strong and good enough to answer with the graces that he knows that I most need.

He sees acts of desire and hope that form the essence of prayer, for we wait only insofar as we desire and hope.

He sees acts of a great mistrust of oneself and entire confidence in God, in that I stop my usual operations only because I count much more on those of God.

He sees acts of the greatest humility, when we want to remain in the presence of God, according to the expression of the prophet-king, like a beast of burden to whom silence is more appropriate than words before the supreme Majesty of God.

He sees acts of resignation and perfect abandonment, because I am ready for all, willing to see my request denied or granted, to see myself rejected or heard as it pleases my God, before whom I remain firm in spite of all the inner distractions and dryness that occur during these now very painful pauses and very boring awaitings.

But what if during these attentive pauses I don't any longer think about all the above acts?
Never mind, you are in reality practicing them and that's enough: your eager awaiting embraces all of them. When a sinner commits a crime, usually he is exactly concerned only with satisfying his passion, but not at all with his ingratitude, nor with the abuse of grace, nor with contempt for God's words, promises, and threats, nor even with the blood of Jesus Christ, nor with the so many breaches of duty for which books and preachers upbraid him endlessly. Why? Because, as theologians tell us, all these evils are contained in his free act of doing wrong. Consequently, he is presumed to will them all efficaciously and actually. In virtue of this principle, you are willing all the good acts of which I was speaking, because they are all enclosed in your voluntary, silent, attentive, eager, humble, and always resigned pauses.

PURITY OF CONSCIENCE

What is purity of conscience? Why and how should we acquire it?
It consists in a firm disposition of the heart never to want to consent to the least offense against God through deliberate purpose. This habitual disposition can subsist very well alongside many other contrary ones that, however, are forthwith given up.

This disposition is needed to succeed well at attentive pauses in prayer. Why?

When it is simply a question of acquiring active recollection by means of ordinary grace, won't grace be more effective insofar as we are more faithful to want to avoid even the least sin that could soil the conscience?

If it is a case of infused recollection, how dare we expect this special grace from God as long as we have for him so little love and so little filial fear that we fear offending him merely from self-love, that is to say, being concerned whether the offense will lead to our downfall, and not at all whether it will merely displease him without putting at risk our salvation?

We can acquire bit by bit this purity of conscience by following the recommendations of spiritual writings and directors, but especially by paying great attention to all our interior agitations, so that the continuous perception of our own weaknesses leads us to have recourse to God at every occasion of a fall and to repent and humiliate ourselves after the least failings.

How must we repent and humble ourselves?
This repentance must be neither worrisome nor turbulent but moderate and peaceful; for, as St Francis de Sales says, "Mustn't we even at the bitter end from the pain of our sins find peace there?"

This interior humiliation must likewise be exempt from bustle, sorrow, resentment against oneself; for not only do agitations unsettle the soul and solve nothing, they are likewise new faults often more dangerous than the initial ones. Why? Because they arise from vexed self-love and pride scandalized at seeing ourselves still so imperfect. Therefore, St Francis de Sales continues, drop all that sorrowful, anxious, and resentful humility that consequently is full of pride; learn to accept yourself just as you must accept your neighbor; with the same charity, practice kindness towards yourself just as you do towards others, by correcting yourself without anger, bitterness, and spite. This brings you back to God with the same confidence as if nothing has happened to you. This is the great secret for quickly acquiring great purity of conscience and, in the meanwhile, perfect knowledge of yourself and deep humility of heart founded on frequently experiencing our pitiable weakness. In this way, all things turn to the advantage of people of goodwill.

Isn't it rash and presumptuous to expect such prompt forgiveness of our daily and frequent faults?
Here is what *The Spiritual Combat,* a book greatly esteemed, especially by St Francis de Sales, says: "I assume that you have fallen not many times, but one hundred times in one day, not inadvertently but with full knowledge, not into small faults but into very grievous ones. After you have asked forgiveness for them and have been humiliated by them for the last time, just as for the first time, without wasting any time, return to God and to yourself and take up your occupations and habitual exercises, with the same confidence as if you hadn't at all failed." Model yourself on the example of a wise traveler who is as courageous in spirit as he is weak in body. If he happens to fall, he gets up right away and continues his journey without wasting time uselessly lamenting; if, several paces later, he again falls, he thinks only of getting up again and always courageously continuing his journey in spite of his many repeated falls; finally he completes his journey, although later than others.

Can we justify such conduct for the path of salvation and perfection?
Because we are always duty-bound to return necessarily to God, is it possible for us to do so too quickly? Furthermore, such eagerness reveals a good will in spite of its great weakness and a proper confidence in God, because only in him can we expect goodness such that it always covers the multitude and enormity of our sins. To behave otherwise is wicked distrust of God's mercifulness. We would have a hard heart little responsive to the mischief of having displeased him or the evil shame of a conceited soul. Such a soul so often cannot bring itself to acknowledge its infidelities and ingratitudes, or such love of freedom that, instead of looking at these frequent reversals as encouragements to do better, we avoid binding ourselves and refuse to commit ourselves to anything. What does this lead to? We become further separated from God and weaker and weaker; we fall more often, more seriously, and make our renewal more difficult.

Ah, if some spiritual people understood this maxim well, we wouldn't at times see them after a relapse so conceitedly distressed and demolished that they even abandon their exercises of piety and dare not, so they say, present themselves before God after such infidelities. Moreover, they flatter themselves for this as if such feelings came from real affliction and true humility. The truly spiritual have very different feelings and act very differently. Strongly imbued with their nothingness, with both their misery and their weakness, they are neither discouraged nor devastated nor even surprised by their relapses. From them they learn to know themselves better, to humble themselves always more and more profoundly, to mistrust themselves, and even to despair of themselves fully, in order to place their confidence exclusively in God alone and to wait for no more than his goodness.

Distinguish well the faults always worthy of our regret from those having fortunate consequences, as does the Church when in speaking of the fall of the first man it exclaims, "O fortunate fault"—fortunate not in itself but "for having merited such a redeemer." Likewise, to view in a better light our poorly understood pain and humility after our relapses, let us right away screw up our courage and hope by keeping in mind that God is strong and merciful enough to give us even in the middle of our relapses the precious treasure of true humility. With its total mistrust in ourselves and perfect confidence in God, which are like the two poles of the spiritual life, humility forms the foundation and guardian of all the virtues.

Also, when a soul has progressed to this point, God lavishes his gifts and favors upon it. Why? He no longer risks that we will purloin any of his glory by appropriating anything to ourselves. Therefore, we understand from our own experience that beautiful maxim of a great servant of God that a well-known affliction is better than an angelic virtue which we appropriate to ourselves by vain complacency. For this reason God sometimes leaves in very elevated souls some faults well below their elevated path with the purpose of having them exercise at the same time both humility and charity towards others.

These blemishes are not found in them as in the imperfect who foster or tolerate their cherished faults, but rather these faults are hated, detested, and unremittingly fought off. Because the attachments of the heart uniquely define its orientation, these cherished souls do not displease God as the imperfect do. By God's permission there remains only weakness, the pure misery of our nature, so apt to keep these souls, in spite of their elevation, always interiorly humble and often even exteriorly so.

In them, these involuntary faults receive admirable compensation as the soul acquires heroic virtues, but always accompanied with the most profound humility that develops under the aegis of these same faults which they themselves never succeed in correcting. This admirable divine guidance should alone render us more reserved in our judgments about people whose interior is unknown to us and often disguised under appearances so deceptive that it ought to be enough for us to have seen or heard cited only one example to persuade us to suspend at the very least the wickedness of rash judgments and, even more, of our ill-advised conversations.

PURITY OF HEART, MIND, AND ACTION

What is purity of heart? Why and how should we acquire it?
The heart is free from every attachment: not only from evil ones but even from those that we call innocent, because in truth these never can be fully innocent, since the heart, which is only made for God, leaves room for creatures. But how will a heart thus divided—and usually most unequally—succeed at these pauses needed to enter fully into this prayer? Let us recall what we have written. This prayer is a sweet rest of the mind and heart in God, as we have said. But how can a heart that is accustomed to letting its thoughts and affections rest on the objects to which it is attached really rest in God unless it has killed its initial attachments, in order to carry itself to God and rest there as it did formerly on its deeply cherished attachment? Purity of heart is taste for God. But how can a heart that dotes on sensible goods and the pleasures of the senses, such as honor, esteem, reputation, idleness, and commerce with the worldly, taste God unless it purifies itself of its terrestrial, carnal, human predilections? Purity of heart is a gaze fixed on God. But how can this gaze of pure faith be sustained through the thick clouds of ideas and sensible images, when even one attachment fills the mind and the imagination?

Purity of heart is recollection in God. But how can we gather our powers, thoughts, desires, and emotions into God if it only takes one foreign object to hold them as if tied and chained or to call them back to itself by the same charms by which it knew how to capture our heart in the first place? Finally, purity of heart is an interior silence of respect, admiration, and love. But how can we enter or remain in this deep interior silence in the middle of the noises and clamors of thousands of pressing desires, so many anxious hopes and afflicting fears, with a heart that sighs without end, almost in spite of itself, for any object but God?

Look at a worldly lover who is interiorly preoccupied with the beauty that he idolizes. Won't he find in this interior pursuit sweet rest for his heart, enjoyment as delightful as it is sinful? This unfortunate recollection, which lets him only think of his idol, seems to absorb all the faculties of his soul and reveals quite a continuity in the inner gaze fixedly attached to his idol. Doesn't he fall into a deep interior silence that suspends any other sentiment in order to give place only to an outburst of love? During the course of prayer, this is more or less the holy and blessed state of those who are truly detached and fully occupied with their divine object. Such is a rough image of these most holy and most meritorious dispositions in which any can have shares proportional to their degree of purity and love.

But here is something rather surprising, at least to me. When it is merely a question of a heart possessed by profane love, we easily understand all its evil dispositions and even the vocabulary especially designed to express them. But what happens when there is question of a heart given over to the impressions of divine love? Then all the holy dispositions become incomprehensible; all these expressions become too mystical even for some pious persons. Consequently, do they really believe that this love, which is stronger than death and hell, has lost all of its strength and past rule over hearts; or that there are no longer those who can feel these movements; or that these movements, even though they are less sensible and less palpable than those of worldly love, are less real and less true?

If the degree of facility to enter into this prayer and to do it well is in general proportional to the degree of purity of the heart, what hope is there for those who have hardly any facility?

At the very minimum they must have the least, the lowest degree, which is the sincere desire to acquire it, to work on it, and to use varied means, even this prayer in particular, which is one of the most efficacious means. God would delight in this goodwill of those who at present don't know how to do better. Then if, in reward for this goodwill, God lets himself be felt and tasted from time to time in a soul, even if only for a few instances during this holy recollection, ah, how this soul will soon make great progress in this detachment. Why? Our hearts are so made for God that, when once we savor him, everything else seems insipid. This impression of the taste of God in a heart is a secret charm that makes it turn incessantly towards God, almost as the needle of a compass turns without ceasing to the rising sun.

God, says St Augustine, brings about in the order of grace this second wonder by pouring into the soul this celestial delight, which surpasses every earthly consolation and gives us the strength to triumph. Now the onset of purity and unattachment in a heart produces in its turn a new taste, a new attraction, and a new facility for recollection. Such rapidity in the progress of both occurs—that is to say, in the progress of purity of heart facilitating recollection and in that of recollection increasing unattachment—that directors themselves are surprised at it, especially in the case of people hitherto so weak that they didn't have the courage to overcome anything or the fortitude to detach themselves from the least trifle.

What is purity of mind? Why and how should we acquire it?
It consists in conquering a certain aimlessness of the mind that naturally drifts about considering anything that pleases it, even when nothing wrong is involved; and at the very least it consists in having acquired enough sway over the mind in order to stop and temper its natural activity to run unceasingly after all the vain images of sensible objects, just as children run after butterflies.

Why is purity of mind absolutely necessary? If the mind in this way accustoms itself to dissipating itself vainly by continual running about, how will it enter into itself, especially during times of interior prayer, which, more than any other kind, requires a tranquil mind, since it is the prayer of recollection itself?

How can a mind that is always flitting and wandering about all those agreeable or entertaining objects turn its inner gaze to fix it either on God or on the incomprehensible objects of faith? Furthermore, even when it can do so for several instants, won't the many different ideas and flattering images, which come continually and in swarms to display themselves in its imagination, be with regard to the mind like a cloud of dust lifted up by a whirlwind around a traveler, who will no longer know where he is going or where he is or even see himself? Therefore, it is necessary to resist continually the natural aimlessness of the mind and to curb continually its natural activity by never permitting it to look willingly at itself and to stray with vain or useless thoughts and, even worse, to hold onto them, to feed on them, and to live on them. Therefore, it is necessary to look at all these merely useless or frivolous thoughts in the same way as good people look at truly evil ones in order to behave likewise as soon as we are aware of them.

Isn't this purity as explained the most difficult of all?
It certainly is, but grace makes easy what appears impossible to man. Once we have tasted God and God's peace within us, this enticing taste calls us without cease with a gentleness that easily leads us to forget everything else; and this same enticement gives us an aversion to creatures: we think no more of them except reluctantly. Then, what freedom of mind we have in being attentive only to God and celestial matters. But to arrive at this bit by bit, here is what it behooves you to do:

By recourse to recollection itself, we must work at weakening and destroying our unfortunate predilections. Just as for all most compelling thoughts, the most difficult to divert come solely from our predilections; but in proportion to their weakening, we feel less hesitancy in withdrawing the mind and thought from what we have already started to leave in heart and affection.

Since it is principally by the pleasure of the heart and vain delights that the mind fixes its interior attention on the objects from which these agreeable feelings come to it, as soon as we feel natural pleasure, we must no longer pause to taste these feelings, to savor them, as we would do if they were heinous pleasure; and at the occasion of the least joy from either good news or happy success or an advantageous event, we must right away withdraw from it, wean the heart from it, and sidetrack it by giving the heart its true object, which is God, in order to accustom ourselves to take pleasure, to rejoice only in God. For the same reason we must do the same thing with regard to other strong feelings arising in the soul, such as hope, fear, sadness, affliction, and the like, for fear that our spirit will absorb all these thoughts.

As for other less stimulating thoughts, which are really only useless or frivolous, we must either drop them like a stone into water or without hesitation let them rush by like garbage floating in the middle of a torrent that sweeps it away; but if inadvertently we let ourselves be led astray, right away we must gently and without effort call back our mind from its least detour, either by simply remembering God, by elevating the heart to God, or by recalling pious thoughts prepared in advance and well calculated to turn our minds back to God when necessary.

Doesn't the innocent freedom of pondering its own thoughts, cherishing its ideas, nourishing itself with its own reflections give the mind its most treasured delights? Consequently, isn't abandoning all of these the severest subjugation of the mind, and perhaps the most crucifying interior abnegation and interior death?

Exactly for this reason we must be on watch all the more against the surprises of self-love, which so jealously gives free rein to its thoughts, which constitute the food and life of the mind, whose activity cannot be confined within the proper limits of the purely necessary. Hence, we find so many paths leading to detrimental, excessive preoccupations, such as: a) under the pretext that we must think about what we ought to do and say, how futilely and unnecessarily we ruminate and reflect, even though the time we waste in deliberation and introspection over the least things would often have been long enough to accomplish them? b) under the pretext of scrutiny and introspection after some speeches, conversations, or the affairs that we have already dealt with, no matter what were the circumstances, time, or place, we will not fail to examine, exactly recall, words spoken or frivolously blurted out, and thus immediately open the gates to a crowd of very futile reflections. Usually these only serve to incite vain joys, melancholies, fears, or even vainer hopes; but in turn all these only increase without end the dispersion of the mind and overthrow interior peace by carrying anxiety and trouble right into the depths of the soul; c) under the pretext of thinking of however many necessary things, or of what we think are necessary but for which we aren't able to know whether they will happen all at once, or even, perhaps, whether one alone will happen how, during the time when we are reflecting, we let rise up in the soul a state of confusion, a chaos of thoughts and reflections that agitate, worry, upset the whole interior and so overwhelm the mind that it no longer knows how to call itself back to God or to itself or to that with which it should begin; d) under the pretext of spiritual progress, how often and vainly do we reflect and plan worthless projects upon which self-love ruminates all the more uselessly, because this wastes the present time and is fruitless for the future, a future that will not turn out as we expect, for we shall find ourselves in other circumstances; e) finally, under the pretext of foreseeing what can happen, in order not to tempt Providence, as it is said, how long do we spend in turning over thought upon thought, reflection upon reflection, and plan upon plan? We wear ourselves out with anxious forethoughts, with distressing solicitudes, with fully futile precautions, since when the time comes, things have changed or we ourselves have changed our minds and feelings. We take up new measures often contrary to those very ones that we previously had and so needlessly imagined and so vainly determined.

But the great remedy for all these harmful and endless miseries of the human mind would be to tell yourself according to the occasions: Such and such a thing has happened; what good is it for me to continue busying myself with it? For what is left over to undertake, do, or say, God will provide. "To each day suffices its tribulation"; don't tomorrow and the following days bring with them their own graces? Let us think only of profiting from the present moment as God gives it to us, and leave the past to his mercy, the future to his providence. Cast upon his paternal bosom all our worries and all our solicitudes, because he takes care of us, says St Peter. Do what Jesus Christ recommended to St Teresa, to St Catherine of Siena, and to many others, when he said, "My daughter think of me and I will think of you." Let us practice what still today so many good souls do who, in similar encounters, with a simple renewing of abandonment and confidence in God, know in an instant where to remedy everything: "Lord, I hope that at the time and place you will give me the grace, thought, impulse, and facility to undertake or execute such or such things which so inopportunely come to present themselves to my mind. I abandon them all to you with their outcomes, with the intention of only paying attention to you and of waiting for all to happen at the pace of your wise and sweet providence." It is in virtue of this double sacrifice and of this continual preparation of mind and heart that this loving providence, always attentive to their needs and to their style of acting, disposes in the favor of these good souls and arranges right down to the least details apparently accidental opportunities and the most favorable encounters. Moreover, by frequent experiences of these happy arrangements, their confidence and abandonment continually increase. Happy, therefore, are those who, to be more recollected in God and more fit for this prayer, know how to constantly banish every useless pursuit from their minds, in order to retain only what is absolutely necessary both with regard to the present time, which is so fleeting—and that is little enough at this point—but especially with regard to the future, which has yet to unfold and may perhaps never unfold for us.

What is purity of action? Why and how should we acquire it?

It consists, not in the substance of our actions, but in the purity of the motives that propel us to act. This purity boils down to acting precisely only for the love of God or according to God's plan and perspectives.

If we lack this, our conduct will never be anything but purely natural, generally infected by the corruption of nature, and consequently completely filled with sins or coarse imperfections. Now the readiness to practice a prayer that unites us to God more intimately than any other necessarily supposes in the soul a degree of purity in every facet proportional to its degree of union with the God of total purity.

This purity of action is primarily acquired by three means:

Purity of conscience in heart and mind leads to it. Why? Insofar as we make it a point to avoid all that might displease God, attach ourselves only to God, and occupy ourselves only with God, don't we inevitably find ourselves fully disposed to act only for God or according to God's perspectives?

Purity of action is acquired by continual vigilance in the beginning of our actions and especially as they unfold. I say in the beginning, because if these actions are so agreeable and in conformity with the inclinations of nature, right away they are carried forward by their own motion through the sole attraction of pleasure or interest. But to prevent the will from being immediately drawn by the force of natural motions that flatter and captivate it, how much mastery and how much vigilance should we not have over ourselves?

I said, especially in the unfolding of our actions. Although at first we may have had the strength to renounce every flattering enticement of the senses or of self-love in order to follow in everything only the views of the faith with pure intention, if then we forget to keep careful watch over ourselves, the real satisfaction either with the good that we are experiencing or with the advantages that we discover as we enjoy what we are doing inevitably exerts greater and greater pull. Thus the heart weakens bit by bit, and our natural inclinations, although mortified by early sacrifices, wake up and regain their ascendancy.

But soon self-love, cunningly and almost unnoticed by us, slides in its self-seeking views and substitutes them for the good motives with which our actions were taken up and begun. Wherefore there occurs—who knows on how many occasions?—what St Paul said, that after having started with the mind, we finish with the body; that is to say, with base, worldly, ambitious, sensual, or self-serving views that cause us to lose or to corrupt all the purity and merit of an infinite number of undertakings and actions of piety, charity, zeal, justice, and love for order and the public good, reaching right into the most holy ministries and sacred functions.

How do we acquire the perfection of this purity?
We acquire it by trying on every occasion to act not only according to the divine ordering of things but even more so with the sole intention of pleasing God. The excellence of this pure motive, which is stripped of every advantage, even the spiritual, enhances our least actions so much before God that even only one such pleases him more and is of greater merit than a hundred others, even the greatest, although praiseworthy and holy but done with inferior motivation.

That is why someone who accomplishes little in a state of life that affords little opportunity for accomplishments, at least such as appear great in the eyes of the world, or one who must labor under restrictive circumstances can nonetheless become more holy and lay up greater stores for eternity than can others who, in far superior states of life, in quite different circumstances and professions, might accomplish many things, even important things, but would not act out of love, or out of pure love. This is the case because it is the degree of our love and its purity that confer value on everything. The truth of this statement can humiliate some while consoling and encouraging others.

What kind of impurity of action should be most feared, especially for spiritually minded people?
Vanity, whether outward or inward. In most of our actions, outward vanity directs its attention and biases to what will be said and thought by such or such a person whose esteem and approval are most cherished and most precious, because we make into an idol a certain reputation that, if we don't renounce it once for all, will become, as St Teresa says, like a worm that attacks the roots of a plant, imperceptibly gnaws at them, destroys them, and causes the plant's fruit and leaves to fall. On the contrary, once we know how to trample underfoot all that others consider esteem, praise, and approval, and how to be satisfied with pleasing only God, then we will find ourselves in one of the most valuable stages of the spiritual

life, one that places us in a state ready to delight in God not only during prayer but also in every occasion and in every place.

Inward vanity appears to me even more ominous, not just because it also is evil, but because it is much more covert. First of all, it consists in puffed-up self-esteem, which causes us to prefer ourselves to others, to measure ourselves, and incessantly to compare ourselves with them. It gives birth to contempt and scorn, then envy and jealousy. Second, it is a swollen self-confidence that unnoticeably leads us to rely much more on our own enlightenment, resolutions, and forces than on the grace of God. We count much more on a foundation of virtue or acquired merit than on the pure mercy of God, although often we assert the contrary and are truly persuaded of it. Third, it is an almost continuous rekindling of secret self-satisfaction through which, without reflection, we attribute to ourselves all the good we accomplish and all we do for God, for salvation, and for perfection. But, as all our masters say, is there anything more against the spirit of God and of this holy prayer than these smoke screens of vanity which give birth to such a profound hidden pride that we begin to recognize it only insofar as we begin to be cured of it?

Why haven't you said anything about exterior mortification, which by common assent so greatly helps prayer?
Because no one overlooks its usefulness. All spiritual books recommend it, all preachers preach it; but in a brief work, we must stick to the essentials. But I do know that the author of *The Spiritual Combat* and all our other masters teach that exterior mortification is only a means for acquiring interior mortification, which truly constitutes real holiness and real perfection. But how could the persistent attempt to acquire these four kinds of purity not finally achieve complete interior abnegation? This abnegation will leave nothing to be sacrificed in our conscience, heart, or mind, not even the least desire or most trifling thought; it operates by interior principles rendering the senses and all our nature powerless to be vainly self-satisfied with anything at all.

Moreover, isn't it interior mortification that carries us outward, animates us, and purifies us of all the stains of so many instances of vain contentedness, hidden pride, and secret overconfidence? Without it, all we esteem so much in exterior mortification has slight value, because we can too often meet in the uncircumcised heart all the liveliness of unrestrained desires and the violence of unmortified passions. This formerly led St Francis de Sales to say about a man as distinguished by his merits as by his profession, "I would never have thought that with such exterior mortification he would have so little in his interior."

Even more so, doesn't interior mortification have two additional advantages? First, we can pursue it as far as we want without having to fear exceeding or over-stepping the limits of discretion. Second, because it strives without respite to extinguish all the passions in the heart, the enemy no longer finds a handhold for his temptations, not even for the least figment of one, because they can only come from self-love residing in itself or in one of its offspring, unhappy fruit of the accursed stock of Adam.

Why not at least speak of peace of soul, since most authors lay it down as the foundation of the prayer of simple rest in God and of all the interior life?
I admit that they are correct and that we will never build anything solid except on the unshakable foundation of this peace. First, without doubt the spirit of God lives and functions only in peace. Second, a soul lacking this peace is like a body lacking health; just as disease, in weakening bodily forces, renders them unable to take care of the needs of the body, so likewise all that troubles the health of the soul renders it feeble, listless, totally sick, and almost unable to function spiritually. This explains why St Francis de Sales so often repeated in his works that other than sin nothing is more pernicious for the soul than agitation, grief, worry, and gloom, which are the soul's true diseases. Once more I acknowledge all of this, but by not speaking of it directly, perhaps I am accomplishing more by teaching the practice of the four kinds of purity. These are the infallible means of coming to such a solid, profound, infallible, and well-established peace that henceforth the soul can no longer be troubled by the following: harassing remorse that comes only from impurity of conscience or inattention to its promptings; the cruel tyranny of our attachments, which have no other source than the impurity of a heart that lets itself be captivated by the lures of material goods; the violence of the passions, which initially arise in the impurity of a mind delivered up to the wandering of its thoughts; the pressing desire of pleasing men or the vain fear of displeasing them; these come only from a lack of purity in the motives of our actions.

Might you have some recommendations for those who, by means of their attentive pauses, have for a little while begun to really enter into the simplicity of this prayer, and for those who are well advanced, and even for those who by their fidelity have made great progress in it?

I have, so it seems to me, fairly important advice, but perhaps it will appear so only to those who are interested, or perhaps to each according to his path in life, as we shall see in the following chapter.

EMPTINESS OF MIND, THE IMPOTENCY THAT FOLLOWS, AND THE EXTRAORDINARY REBELLIONS OF THE PASSIONS

What do you mean by emptiness of the mind?

The expression "emptiness" almost explains itself: it is a mind empty, as it seems to itself, of every thought of either God or of the world. Whereas to purify a soul, to detach it, and to have it advance more and more, God holds it in this state, it seems to itself that it has fallen into a state of stupidity and folly, since it passes whole days, so it seems to itself, without thinking of anything, no more than a stump or a trunk of a tree would, according to words of those in this state. From this there follows what we call the inability to attend to God or to any good thought.

If the soul wants to reflect, the mind, straying off somewhere, loses sight of itself or remains fully dazed; if the soul wants to pray, all the ordinary acts are lifted from it; if it wants to enter into itself, it doesn't know how to find the way in and discovers itself as if banished, exiled from its own heart, as *The Imitation of Jesus Christ* says.

Finally, if the soul wants to devote itself to pious reading, what St Teresa reports for a similar case takes place: "I was reading," she says, "up to two or three times the same passage in a book, without understanding any more than if it were written in Greek or in Hebrew. What multiplies this inner cross, so mortifying and so annihilating, is to compare this state with the preceding ones. In it we seem to be as if suspended between the heavens and the earth, where we don't receive any consolations either from one or the other, or either from outside or inside."

Is it, perhaps, a savage attack of melancholy or fully natural stupidity?

Not at all, for... in the necessary exchanges with neighbor, the same people during this sorrowful inner condition will, as a rule, not fail to appear to others wholly different from what they feel, in fact, speaking to the point, reasoning, and even writing about divine matters with a facility and a flow at which they themselves are surprised, as thousands of others have experienced....

How do you know that something like this happens?
For this I don't need to consult books, because these people, without wanting to do so, without thinking so, let me know it well enough.

As some people say, it is very distressing, very painful to spend the time of prayer, whole days, being unable either to recollect themselves, pray, read, lift their hearts to God, or even to think of him or settle on anything good. Although they vainly desire it, excite themselves, force themselves, all is useless and lost time; thereupon, they complain like poor people reduced to begging. The sinners, the tepid, and the worldly, don't they have similar difficulty; don't they make the same complaints? But these people simply press on with a most forceful desire to be able to occupy themselves with God during prayer and with the overwhelming difficulty of wanting to do so, and of even vainly trying to do so—and perhaps even too often with efforts that they should never exert. Here, therefore, are hearts completely filled with the best of intentions, filled with holy desires, but that are berated for being unable to engender them in order to have the consolation of having them and perhaps of admiring themselves, which God knows so well how to prevent. Let these people, therefore, humble themselves and remain in peace, happy with their own discontent, since it engenders God's contentment and his good pleasure.

As some others say, in their darkness, their futilities, their stupidity, what distresses them is not this state, so humbling, so crucifying, but the fear of no longer belonging to God, of having lost God, of being rejected, abandoned by God, perhaps even of having given occasion to it by some hidden infidelity; distressing reflections unceasingly occupy them, crucify them. Whence can such feelings come except from an admirable foundation of filial fear or ardent love that devours, that consumes their souls by thousands of impotent yearnings? Nevertheless, just as God "sees fruit in the sprout," ... doesn't he see these yearnings, so hidden and buried that they remain deep in the heart without being able to blossom except in the form of a few sighs that escape?

Let them, therefore, remain in peace, satisfied with conforming to the will of the celestial spouse. Even though they don't see themselves either adorned or embellished as they wish, but rather completely deformed in their own eyes, such a state itself becomes more agreeable to God as they grow in dissatisfaction with themselves, says St Augustine.

Finally, as others say, their condition always gets worse; there is no longer any way of continuing; every means, every support is lacking. Formerly their feelings, even their resignation, served to reassure them, to calm them, but now there is nothing left that is good inside of them. They find themselves unfeeling, hardened like a stone, or discover in themselves a heart that, far from being subjugated, rebels against every act of subjugation that they try to impose.

Such is the summit of their hardness, whence is born a kind of despair that tears at the gut. Here, therefore, they are fully devastated at no longer feeling devastated or fully desperate at no longer achieving any resignation; but it is precisely on account of this that they should remain in peace before God with only this thought: Formerly my feelings, my feeble desires, in accord with my resignation, were rising up from the bottom of my heart towards the throne of God; now there rises despair alone caused by the fear of having lost every remaining good sentiment. Doesn't it speak even more strongly? These are wails more profound, more impenetrable, less comforting for me, but aren't they also more keen, more touching for a God who hears them?

Would you have a major principle to back up your ideas and feelings?
I find it in these very profound words of Jesus Christ: "There where your treasure is, there also will be your heart"; doubtlessly and especially in its feelings and simple movements, which the common people don't consider acts because they aren't counted among reflected, sensible, and tangible ones, and which for this reason they call simple direct acts, as a rule unperceived. The beautiful reflection of St Augustine develops it even better: everything, he says, is moved by its proper weight, the light upward, the heavy downward; my weight, he continues, is my love; by it I am carried everywhere I go. Then he adds that we live less in ourselves than in the object of love, because it is there that generally are found our desires and our affections, which are the life of the heart.

So it follows from this that as soon as a confessor has discovered the dominant tendency of a miser or a rake, he then confusedly catches sight of sin in the heart; I am not speaking of sins which are known and committed by reflected acts, but of another kind, hidden and unknown in an impenetrable abyss of sin, with which an impassioned heart stains itself endlessly by these simple and almost continual movements of the passion of which it has become the slave.

Likewise, once a director has, on the basis of certain traits or words blurted out, recognized the acquired and dominant habitual disposition in one of the people of whom we are speaking, he easily understands that in spite of the faults inextricable from our fragility or human weakness, generally the whole inner life of this soul tends towards God. Why? Because where its treasure is, there also its heart is and will be, by the agency of these simple movements and affections, which are truly acts, although common people don't know this, and more so by all these diverse feelings, whether of love or of hate, of hope or of fear, of joy or of sadness, whether such people perceive them or they don't perceive them. Again why? Because the weight of love often unrecognized, a secret charm that is in the soul, sustains the soul wherever the soul betakes itself—either in mind or heart, with or without reflection, says St Augustine—living in this object more than in itself without knowing it does. Also, as soon as the soul believes that it has found the treasure that it believed lost, inside all is calm and serene; peace and joy gush right up to the surface.

What should we be doing above all else during the time of these trials and similar conditions?
I have already explained this or hinted at the answer: avoid willful troubles and discouragements in order to hold ourselves in peace by means of trust and total abandonment to God; expect solace only from God alone; don't go begging among his creatures, not even among his ministers, except for pressing needs and for necessary instruction.

But what is to be done to arrive at these two levels of detachment?
Once and for all abandon yourself to God without aim, without limit, without any reservations, for it is an established maxim that it is only these reservations which block the flow of grace and the progress of a soul.

Convince yourself once and for all that any great affliction that occurs is wisely arranged by a Providence so loveable, so splendid; and that, if we were to understand the great good which it hopes to draw from these sufferings, we would consider this purgatory as one of the greatest favors of heaven; indeed after we have passed through it and have experienced its precious advantage, we can't give enough thanks.

RECAPITULATION OF ALL THAT HAS BEEN SAID

The paramount aim is to make the direct and intimate acts of the heart well known, and that for five important reasons:

The origin and source of all deliberate and expressed acts, either from the mouth or from purely interior words, lie there in the heart, for everything springs from the free but simple movements of the heart; nothing can come out of it in any way whatsoever unless it is first conceived. Therefore, it is in their earliest stages, if we can speak in this fashion, that we must look on these direct acts, although often we cannot give birth to them, so to speak, in any way at all by reflective acts.

We should all apply ourselves principally to these intimate acts, which ought to animate all our prayers and without which prayer would be no more than a vain sounding of words or a purely mental game.

No one should become discouraged with his prayer even if it is the least of all, which is vocal prayer; no one should believe herself idle as long as her mind or heart abides in her intimate acts.

I have constantly pointed out that with respect to the prayer of simple recollection, a person ceases to fight against it when, from an exact knowledge of direct acts, he or she clearly understood that we are never without acts during this prayer, although they are not at all reflective or expressed in any way.

This same knowledge could serve those who, in order to acquire infused recollection, would have enough courage to subjugate themselves, to constant practice of the four kinds of purity, which are the remote dispositions for this double prayer, and to the exercise of attentive pauses, which are the proximate directions.

What practical conclusion should follow?

It is fully expressed in the following dispositions:

Let all apply themselves with care to their usual prayer, since on the one hand there cannot be attentive pauses without prayer and, on the other hand, none ought to give up their prayer, except insofar as God himself withdraws them little by little when it pleases him, and in the way he wants.

While continuing their prayer in this way, they should let these pauses be more or less frequent and long, depending on how it pleases God to speak, to communicate himself, to make himself felt within the self.

Because God usually only communicates in proportion to the purity of the soul, let them apply themselves therefore to acquire the four kinds of purity.

In proportion to these proximate and remote dispositions, they will enter into and be established in recollection of whatever kind it might be. It is precisely then that those to whom God has given this grace can apply themselves to the three recommendations just given, each according to his or her actual state as either beginner, progressing, or advanced.

In addition I beg certain individuals not to consider fully lost for them the time that I used both to give a rough idea of their prayer and to parry those who attack it only because they lack knowledge of it, since basically all this only tends to anticipate the specious doubts that could come to trouble these people inopportunely.

Moreover, I implore them not to be at all surprised to discover so little instruction for themselves and comfort in this book except towards the end, because I have limited myself to speak only, on the one hand, of the usual simple recollection and, on the other hand, to people at the lowest degree of this prayer. Why? Because I often found that, lacking a firm enough practice of purity of conscience, heart, mind, or action, most of these good souls hardly ever move beyond the lowest degree of simple recollection, the kind we call mixed; that is to say, partly acquired, partly infused, but almost always practiced with a great deal of imperfection and sometimes so feebly that to maintain it they need to return to their first discursive acts, to their old affections formerly expressed and developed interiorly.

In spite of all your warnings, which, so it seems, go very far, can it not truly happen that someone misuses this treatise?

Didn't we say and show in the beginning that there isn't anything that we don't abuse and, furthermore, that if in matters of devotion and piety we must remove all that has so often been misused, there would remain almost nothing; and, moreover, that we would no longer speak about anything, not even preach, except about what is purely necessary? But let what I have written receive the same reception as a sermon: isn't it true that after a solid sermon dealing with non-essential matters but including topics as delicate as they are useful, there can be some minds (and they are found everywhere) who take things somewhat the wrong way? In these circumstances, the usual rejoinder is that the preacher explained himself fairly clearly; too bad for evil minds who will want to make bad use of what was said; good people will profit from the preaching. However, there is a great deal of difference between words that fly by so quickly and a written piece that remains under our eyes. Let us apply the principle that leads people of good sense to speak thus in matters of preaching, by comparing here, as we do in everything, the good of the thing with its shortcomings; that is, the profit for which we can hope—the great number who can profit from it—to the badly founded fears with respect to a very small number....

Principles and means

First of all, to cut out everything that is extraordinary and that could have even the appearance of it, because the Gospel teaches me that all that elevates the spirit of man humbles him before God and that the most humbling prayer of whatever kind it may be is always the best, were it even vocal.

Because self-love and pride are the true sources of every self-delusion and because we observe how they are in everything and everywhere, I did not cease to pursue these two monsters right into their innermost lairs. There's where I tried to cut the roots of every self-delusion, of every disorder, of every imperfection.

Final Prayer

Great God, who for purposes unknown to us have from all eternity orchestrated a collection of small circumstances that all together have contributed to the production of this little book, do not allow the wise or the devout to have any reason to upbraid themselves at death's door for ever having undertaken to block you from the entrance to hearts—how many they are I don't know—because you wanted to enter by a way they didn't like and by a door that was perhaps unknown to them. I am not asking enough. Great God, also make all of us become as small as children, as Jesus Christ commands, and grant that these, once entering by this little door, may soon call thither your good servants, your humble servants, with greater power and effectiveness than I would ever know how to bring about. *Amen,* Jesus.

Ordination of St Ignatius, 1537

PART III

CLAUDE DE LA COLOMBIÈRE

1641-1682

THE SECRET OF PEACE AND HAPPINESS

TRUSTFUL SURRENDER TO DIVINE PROVIDENCE[1]

1. CONSOLING TRUTHS

It is one of the most firmly established and most consoling of the truths that have been revealed to us that (apart from sin) nothing happens to us in life unless God wills it so. Wealth and poverty alike come from Him. If we fall ill, God is the cause of our illness; if we get well, our recovery is due to God. We owe our lives entirely to Him, and when death comes to put an end to life, His will be the hand that deals the blow.

But should we attribute it to God when we are unjustly persecuted? Yes, He is the only person you can charge with the wrong you suffer. He is not the cause of the sin the person commits by ill-treating you, but He is the cause of the suffering that person inflicts on you while sinning.

God did not inspire your enemy with the will to harm you, but He gave him the power to do so. If you receive a wound, do not doubt but that it is God Himself who has wounded you. If all living creatures were to league themselves against you, unless the Creator wished it and joined with them and gave them the strength and means to carry out their purpose, they would never succeed. You would have no power over me if it had not been given you from above, the Savior of the world said to Pilate. We can say the same to demons and men, to the brute beasts and to whatever exists: You would not be able to disturb me or harm me as you do unless God had ordered it so. You are sent by Him, you are given the power by Him to tempt me and to make me suffer. You would have no power over me if it had not been given you from above.

If from time to time we meditated seriously on this truth of our faith it would be enough to stifle all complaint in whatever loss or misfortune we suffer. What I have, the Lord gave me, it has been

[1] Part II, Section IV of *The Secret of Peace and Happiness*, by Fr Jean Baptiste Saint-Juré and Blessed Claude de la Colombière, S.J., translated by Paul Garvin, St Paul Publications, New York, 1961.

taken away by Him. It is not a lawsuit or a thief that has ruined you or a certain person that has slandered you; if your child dies it is not by accident or wrong treatment, but because God, to whom all belongs, has not wished you to keep it longer.

Trust in God's Wisdom

It is then a truth of our faith that God is responsible for all the happenings we complain of in the world and, furthermore, we cannot doubt that all the misfortunes God sends us have a very useful purpose. We cannot doubt it without imputing to God a lack of judgment in deciding what is advantageous for us.

It is usually the case that other people can see better than we can ourselves what is good for us. It would be foolish to think that we can see better than God Himself, who is not subject to any of the passions that blind us, knows the future, and can foresee all events and the consequences of every action. Experience shows that even the gravest misfortunes can have good results and the greatest successes end in disaster. A rule also that God usually follows is to attain His ends by ways that are the opposite to those human prudence would normally choose.

In our ignorance of what the future holds, how can we be so bold as to question what comes about by God's permission? Surely it is reasonable to think that our complaints are groundless and that instead of complaining we ought to be thanking Providence. Joseph was sold into slavery and thrown into prison. If he had felt aggrieved at these apparent misfortunes, he would really have been feeling aggrieved at his happiness for they were the steps to the throne of Egypt. Saul loses his father's asses and has to go on a long vain hunt for them. But if he had felt annoyed at the great waste of time and energy it caused him, his annoyance could not have been more unreasonable as it was all a means of bringing him to the prophet who was to anoint him king of his people.

Let us imagine our confusion when we appear before God and understand the reasons why He sent us the crosses we accept so unwillingly. The death of a child will then be seen as its rescue from some great evil had it lived, separation from the woman you love the means of saving you from an unhappy marriage, a severe illness the reason for many years of life afterwards, loss of money the means of saving your soul from eternal loss. So what are we worried about? God is looking after us and yet we are full of anxiety! We trust ourselves to a doctor because we suppose he knows his business. He orders an operation which involves cutting away part of our body and we accept it. We are grateful to him and pay him a large fee because we judge he would not act as he does unless the remedy were necessary, and we must rely on his skill. Yet we are unwilling to treat God in the same way! It looks as if we do not trust His wisdom and are afraid.

He cannot do His job properly. We allow ourselves to be operated on by a man who may easily make a mistake—a mistake which may cost us our life—and protest when God sets to work on us.

If we could see all He sees we would unhesitatingly wish all He wishes. We would beg Him on bended knees for those afflictions we now ask Him to spare us. To all of us He addresses the words spoken to the sons of Zebedee: You know not what you ask: O blind of heart, your ignorance saddens me. Let me manage your affairs and look after your interests. I know what you need better than you do yourselves. If I paid heed to what you think you need you would have been hopelessly ruined long ago.

When God sends us trials

If you would be convinced that in all He allows and in all that happens to you God has no other end in view but your real advantage and your eternal happiness, reflect a moment on all He has done for you; you are now suffering, but remember that the author of this suffering is He who chose to spend His life suffering to save you from everlasting suffering, whose angel is always at your side guarding your body and soul by His order, who sacrifices Himself daily on the altar to expiate your sins and appease His Father's anger, who comes lovingly to you in the Holy Eucharist and whose greatest pleasure is to be united to you. We must be very ungrateful to mistrust Him after He has shown such proofs of His love and to imagine that He can intend us harm. But, you will say, this blow is a cruel one, He strikes too hard. What have you to fear from a hand that was pierced and nailed to the cross for you? The path I have to tread is full of thorns. If there is no other to reach heaven by, do you prefer to perish forever rather than to suffer for a time? Is it not the same path He trod before you out of love for you? Is there a thorn in it that He has not reddened with His own blood?—The chalice He offers you is a bitter one. But remember that it is your Redeemer who offers it. Loving you as He does, could He bring Himself to treat you so severely if the need were not urgent, the gain not worthwhile? Can we dare to refuse the chalice He has prepared for us Himself?

Reflect well on this. It should be enough to make us accept and love whatever trials He intends we should suffer. Moreover it is the certain means of securing our happiness in this life quite apart from the next.

Loving recourse to God

Let us now suppose that by these reflections and the help of God you have freed yourself from all worldly desires and can now say to yourself: All is vanity and nothing can satisfy my heart. The things that I so earnestly desire may not be at all the things that will bring me happiness. It is difficult for me to distinguish what is good from what is harmful because good and evil are nearly always mixed, and what was good for yesterday may be bad for today. My desires are only a source of worry and my efforts to realize them mostly end in failure. After all, the will of God is bound to prevail in the end. Nothing can be done without His command, and He cannot ordain anything that is not for my good.

After this let us suppose that you turn to God with blind trust and surrender yourself unconditionally and unreservedly to Him, entirely resolved to put aside your own hopes and fears; in short, determined to wish nothing except what He wishes and to wish all that He wishes. From this moment you will acquire perfect liberty and will never again be able to feel troubled or uneasy, and there is no power on earth capable of doing you violence or giving you a moment's unrest.

You may object that a person on whom both good and evil make the same impression is a pure fiction. It is nothing of the kind. I know people who are just as happy if they are sick or if they are well, if they are badly off or they are well off. I know some who even prefer illness and poverty to health and riches.

Moreover it is all the more remarkable that the more we submit to God's will, the more He tries to meet our wishes. It would seem that as soon as we make it our sole aim to obey Him, He on His part does His best to try and please us. Not only does He answer our prayers but He even forestalls them by granting the very desires we have endeavored to stifle in our hearts in order to please Him, and granting them in a measure we had never imagined.

Finally, the happiness of the person whose will is entirely submitted to God's is constant, unchangeable, and endless. No fear comes to disturb it for no accident can destroy it. He is like a man seated on a rock in the middle of the ocean who looks on the fury of the waves without dismay and can amuse himself watching and counting them as they roar and break at his feet. Whether the sea is calm or rough, whichever way the waves are carried by the wind is a matter of indifference to him, for the place where he is, is firm and unshakeable.

That is the reason for the peaceful and untroubled expression we find on the faces of those who have dedicated themselves to God.

Practice of trustful surrender

It remains to be seen how we can attain to this happy state. One sure way to lead us to it is the frequent practice of the virtue of submission. But as the opportunities for practicing it in a big way come rather seldom, we must take advantage of the small ones which occur daily, and which will soon put us in a position to face the greater trials with equanimity when the time comes. There is no one who does not experience a hundred small annoyances every day, caused either by our own carelessness or inattention, or by the inconsideration or spite of other people, or by pure accident. Our whole lives are made up of incidents of this kind, occurring ceaselessly from one minute to another and producing a host of involuntary feelings of dislike and aversion, envy, fear, and impatience to trouble the serenity of our minds. We let an incautious word slip out and wish we had not said it; someone says something we find offensive; we have to wait a long time to be served when we are in a hurry; we are irritated by a child's boisterousness; a boring acquaintance buttonholes us in the street; a car splashes us with mud; the weather spoils our outing; our work is not going as well as we would wish; a tool breaks at a critical moment; we get our clothes torn or stained—these are not occasions for practicing heroic virtue but they can be a means of acquiring it if we wish. If we were careful to offer all these petty annoyances to God and accept them as being ordered by His providence we would soon be in a position to support the greatest misfortunes that can happen to us, besides at the same time insensibly drawing close to intimate union with God.

To this exercise—so easy and yet so useful for us and pleasing to God—another may be added. Every morning as soon as you get up think of all the most disagreeable things that could happen to you during the day. Your house might be burnt down, you might lose your job or all your savings, or be run over, or sudden death might come to you or to a person you love. Accept these misfortunes should it please God to allow them; compel your will to agree to the sacrifice and give yourself no rest until you really feel prepared to wish or not to wish all that God may wish or not wish.

Finally, if some great misfortune should actually happen, instead of wasting time in complaint or self-pity, go throw yourself at once at the feet of your Savior and implore His grace to bear your trial with fortitude and patience. A man who has been badly wounded does not, if he is wise, chase after his assailant, but makes straight for a doctor who may save his life. Even if you wanted to confront the person responsible for your misfortune, it would still be to God you would have to go, for there can be no other cause of it than He.

So go to God, but go at once, go there and then. Let this be your first thought. Go and report to Him what He has done to you. Kiss the hands of God crucified for you, the hands that have struck you and caused you to suffer. Repeat over and over again to Him His own words to His Father while He was suffering: Not my will but thine be done. In all that Thou wishest of me, today and for always, in heaven and on earth, let Thy will be done, but let it be done on earth as it is done in heaven.

2. ADVERSITY IS USEFUL FOR THE JUST AND NECESSARY FOR SINNERS

Imagine the anguish and tears of a mother who is present at a painful operation her child has to undergo. Can anyone doubt on seeing her that she consents to allow the child to suffer only because she expects it to get well and be spared further suffering by means of this violent remedy?

Reason in the same manner when adversity befalls you. You complain that you are ill-treated, insulted, slandered, robbed. Your Redeemer (the name is a tenderer one than that of father or mother), your Redeemer is a witness to all you are suffering. He who loves you and has emphatically declared that whoever touches you touches the apple of His eye, nevertheless allows you to be stricken though He could easily prevent it. Do you hesitate to believe that this passing trial is necessary for the health of your soul?

Even if the Holy Spirit had not called blessed those who suffer, if every page of Scripture did not proclaim aloud the necessity of adversity, if we did not see that suffering is the normal destiny of those who are friends of God, we should still be convinced that it is of untold advantage to us. It is enough to know that the God who chose to suffer all the most horrible tortures the rage of man can invent rather then see us condemned to the slightest pain in the next life is the same God who prepares and offers us the chalice of bitterness we must drink in this world. A God who has so suffered to prevent us from suffering would not make us suffer today to give Himself cruel and pointless pleasure.

We must have trust in Providence
When I see a Christian grief-stricken at the trials God sends him I say to myself: Here is a man who is grieved at his own happiness. He is asking God to be delivered from something he ought to be thanking Him for. I am quite sure that nothing more advantageous could happen to him than what causes him so much grief. I have a hundred unanswerable reasons for saying so. But if I could read into the future and see the happy outcome of his present misfortune, how greatly strengthened I would be in my judgment! If we could discover the designs of Providence it is certain we would ardently long for the evils we are now so unwilling to suffer. We would rush forward to accept them with the utmost gratitude if we had a little faith and realized how much God loves us and has our interests at heart.

What profit can come to me from this illness which ties me down and obliges me to give up all the good I was doing, you may ask. What advantage can I expect from this ruin of my life which leaves me desperate and hopeless? It is true that sudden great misfortune at the moment it comes may appear to overwhelm you and not allow you the opportunity there and then of profiting by it. But wait a while and you will see that by it God is preparing you to receive the greatest marks of His favor. But for this accident you would not have perhaps become less good than you are, but you would not have become holy. Isn't it true that since you have been trying to lead a good Christian life there has been something you have been unwilling to surrender to God? Some worldly ambition, some pride in your attainments, some indulgence of the body, some blameworthy habit, some company that is the occasion of sin for you? It was only this final step that prevented you from attaining the perfect freedom of the love of God. It wasn't really very much, but you could not bring yourself to make this last sacrifice. It wasn't very much, but there is nothing harder for a Christian than to break the last tie that binds him to the world or to his own self. He knows he ought to do it, and until he does it there is something wrong with his life. But the very thought of the remedy terrifies him, for the malady has taken such a hold on him that it cannot be cured without the help of a serious and painful operation. So it was necessary to take you unawares, to cut deep into the flesh with skilful hand when you were least expecting it and remove the ulcer concealed within, or otherwise you would never be well. The misfortune which has befallen you will soon do what all your exercises of piety would never have been able to do.

Unexpected advantages from our trials

If the consequence of your adversity is that which was intended by God, if it turns you aside completely from creatures to give yourself unreservedly to your Creator, I am sure that your thanks to Him for having afflicted you will be greater than your prayers were to remove the affliction. In comparison with this misfortune all the other benefits you have received from Him will appear to have been very slight favors indeed. You have always regarded the temporal blessings He has hitherto showered on you and your family as the effects of His goodness towards you, but now you will see clearly and realize to the depths of your being that He has never loved you so much as when He took away all that He gave you for your prosperity, and that if He was generous in giving you a family, a good position, an income, and good health, He has been over-generous in taking them all away.

I am not referring to the merit we acquire by the virtue of patience. Generally speaking, one day of adversity can be of more profit to us for our eternal salvation than years of untroubled living, whatever good use we make of the time.

It is common knowledge that prosperity has the effect of softening us. When a man is materially well off and content with his state, it is a great deal if he takes the trouble to think of God two or three times a day. His mind is so pleasantly occupied with his worldly affairs that it is easy for him to forget all the rest. Adversity on the other hand leads us as if naturally to raise our eyes to Heaven to seek consolation in our distress. Certainly God can be glorified whatever condition we are in, and the life of a Christian who serves Him when fortune is favorable is most pleasing to Him. But can he please Him as much as the man who blesses Him while he is suffering? It cannot be doubted that a man who enjoys good health, position, wealth, and the world's esteem, if he uses his advantages as he ought, attributing them to God and thanking Him for them, by doing so glorifies his Maker and leads a Christian life. But if Providence takes away what he has and strikes him down, and in the midst of his reverses he continues to express the same sentiments, returning the same thanks and obeying his Lord with the same promptness and submission as he did formerly, it is then that he proclaims the glory of God and the efficacy of His grace in the most convincing and striking manner.

Opportunities for acquiring merit and saving our souls
Judge then what recompense those persons will receive from Christ who have followed Him along the way of His Cross. On the judgment day we shall understand how much God has loved us by giving us the opportunities to merit so rich a reward. Then we shall reproach ourselves for complaining at what was meant to increase our happiness, for grieving when we should have been rejoicing, for doubting God's goodness when He was giving us concrete evidence of it. If such will be our feelings one day, why not anticipate them now? Why not bless God here and now for something we shall be thanking Him for everlastingly in heaven?

It is clear from this that whatever the manner of our life we should always accept adversity joyfully. If we are leading a good life adversity purifies us, makes us better and enables us to acquire greater merit. If our life is sinful it serves to bring us to repentance and obliges us to become good.

3. RECOURSE TO PRAYER

It is a strange fact that though Christ repeatedly and solemnly promised to answer our prayers, most Christians are continually complaining that He does not do so. We cannot account for this by saying that the reason is because of the kind of things we ask for, since He included everything in His promise—all things whatsoever you shall ask. Nor can we attribute it to the unworthiness of those who ask, for His promise extended to everybody without exception—whoever asks shall receive. Why is it then that so many prayers remain unanswered? Can it be that as most people are never satisfied, they make such excessive and impatient demands on God that they tire and annoy Him by their importunity? The case is just the opposite. The only reason why we obtain so little from God is because we ask for so little and we are not insistent enough.

Christ promised on behalf of His Father that He would give us everything, even the very smallest things. But He laid down an order to be observed in all that we ask, and if we do not obey this rule we are unlikely to obtain anything. He tells us in St Matthew: Seek first the kingdom of God and his justice and all these things shall be given to you besides.

To obtain what we want

We are not forbidden to wish for money, material well-being, and whatever is necessary to maintain us in our position in life, but we must wish for these things in their proper order. If we want our desires in this respect to be met without fail we must first of all ask for the larger things, so that while granting them He may also add the smaller ones.

We can take an example from the case of Solomon. God gave him the choice of whatever he desired and he asked for wisdom, which was needful for him to carry out his kingly duties. He did not ask for riches or glory, judging that if God gave him such an opportunity he ought to make use of it to obtain the greatest advantage. His prudence gained for him both what he asked for and what he did not ask for. Because thou hast asked this thing, and hast not asked for thyself long life or riches ... behold I have done for thee according to thy words—I will willingly grant you wisdom because you have asked me for it, but I will give you long life, honor, and riches as well because you did not ask for any of them—Yea, and the things also which thou didst not ask, to wit, riches and glory.

If then this is the order God observes in the distribution of His benefits, we must not be surprised if our prayers have so far been unsuccessful. I confess that I am often moved to pity when I see the eagerness of some people in giving alms, making vows of pilgrimage, and fasting, or having Masses said for the success of their temporal affairs. I am afraid the prayers they say and get said are of little use. They should make their offerings and vow their pilgrimages to obtain from God the amendment of their lives, the gift of Christian patience, contempt for the things of the world, and detachment from creatures. Then afterwards they could pray for return of health or success in business. God would then answer these prayers, or rather He would anticipate them; it would be enough to know their desires for Him to fulfill them.

Until we have obtained these first graces, anything else may be harmful to us and, in fact, usually is so. That is the reason why we are refused. We murmur and accuse God of not keeping His promises. But our God is a Father of kindness who prefers to put up with our complaints and criticisms rather than stop them by gifts which would be fatal to us.

To be delivered from evil

What has been said of benefits can also be said of the ills from which we wish to be delivered. I do not desire wealth, a person will say, but I would be satisfied with not having to suffer hardship. I leave fame and reputation to those who want it, but I would like at least not to be an object of scorn. I can do without pleasures, but I cannot support pain; I have prayed and begged God to lessen it but He will not hear me. It is not surprising. You have secret ills far greater than the ills you complain of, but you do not ask Him to deliver you from them. If for this purpose you had said half the prayers you have said to be healed from your outward ills, God would have delivered you from both a long time since. Poverty serves to keep you humble while your nature is proud, the scorn of the world to free you from your attachment to it, illness to keep you from the pleasure-seeking which would be your ruin. It would be hating you, not loving you, to take away your cross before giving you the virtues you lack. If God found some desire in you for these virtues He would give you them without delay, and it would be unnecessary for you to ask for the other things.

We do not ask enough

It is clear then that we do not receive anything because we do not ask enough. God could not give us little, He could not restrict His liberality to small things without doing us grave harm. Do not misunderstand me. I am not saying that we offend God if we ask for temporal benefits or to be freed from misfortune. Obviously prayers of this kind can rightly be addressed to Him by making the condition that they are not contrary to His glory or our eternal salvation. But as it is hardly likely that it would redound to His glory for Him to answer them, or to our advantage to have them answered if our wishes end there, it must be repeated that as long as we are content with little we run the risk of obtaining nothing.

Let me show you a good way to ask for happiness even in this world. It is a way that will oblige God to listen to you. Say to Him earnestly: Either give me so much money that my heart will be satisfied, or inspire me with such contempt for it that I no longer want it. Either free me from poverty, or make it so pleasant for me that I would not exchange it for all the wealth in the world. Either take away my suffering, or—which would be to your greater glory—change it into delight for me, and instead of causing me affliction, let it become a source of joy. You can take away the burden of my cross, or you can leave it with me without my feeling its weight. You can extinguish the fire that burns me, or you can let it burn in such a way that it refreshes me as it did the three youths in the fiery furnace. I ask you for either one thing or the other. What does it matter in what way I am happy? If I am happy through the possession of worldly goods, it is you I have to thank. If I am happy when deprived of them, it gives you greater glory and my thanks are all the greater.

This is the kind of prayer worthy of being offered to God by a true Christian. When you pray in this way, do you know what the effect of your prayers will be? First, you will be satisfied whatever happens; and what else do those who most desire this world's goods want except to be satisfied? Secondly, you will not only obtain without fail one of the two things you have asked for but, as a rule, you will obtain both of them. God will give you the enjoyment of wealth, and so that you may possess it without the danger of becoming attached to it, He will inspire you at the same time with contempt for it. He will put an end to your sufferings and even more He will leave you with a desire for them which will give you all the merit of patience without having to suffer. In a word, He will make you happy here and now, and lest your happiness should do you harm, He will let you know and feel the emptiness of it. Can one ask for anything better? But if such a great blessing is well worth being asked for, remember that still more is it worth being asked for with insistence. For the reason why we obtain little is not only because we ask for little but still more because, whether we ask a little or we ask a lot, we do not ask often enough.

Perseverance in prayer

If you want all your prayers to be answered without fail and oblige God to meet all your wishes, the first thing is never to stop praying. Those who get tired after praying for a time are lacking in either humility or confidence, and so do not deserve to be heard. You would think that they expected their requests to be obeyed at once as if they were orders. Surely we know that God resists the proud and shows His favors to the humble. Won't our pride allow us to ask more than once for the same thing? It shows very little trust in God's goodness to give up so soon and take a delay for an absolute refusal.

Once we have really understood just how far God's goodness extends we can never believe that we have been refused or that He wishes to deprive us of hope. Rather, the more He makes us keep on asking for something we want, the more confident we should feel that we shall eventually obtain it. We can begin to doubt that our prayer has been heard only when we notice we have stopped praying. If after a year we find that our prayer is as fervent as it was at the beginning, then we need not doubt about the success of our efforts, and instead of losing courage after so long a delay, we should rejoice because we can be certain that our desires will be all the more fully satisfied for the length of time we have prayed. If our first attempts had been quite useless we would not have repeated them so often and we would have lost hope; but as we have kept on in spite of this, there is good reason to believe we shall be liberally rewarded.

In fact it took St Monica sixteen years to obtain the conversion of Augustine, but the conversion was entire and far beyond what she had prayed for. Her desire was that her son's incontinence might be checked by marriage, and instead she had the joy of seeing him embrace a life of holy chastity. She had only wanted him to be baptized and become a Christian, and she saw him a bishop. She asked God to turn him aside from heresy, and God made him a pillar of the Church and its champion against heretics. Think what would have happened had she given up hope after a couple of years, after ten or twelve years, when her prayers appeared to obtain no result and her son grew worse instead of better, adding avarice and ambition to the wildness of his life and sinking further and further into error. She would have wronged her son, thrown away her own happiness, and deprived the world of one of the greatest Christian thinkers.

Obstinate trust

As a final word I address myself to those faithful souls kneeling in prayer before the altar and asking God for the graces He is so pleased to hear us asking for. You who are happy that God has shown you the vanity of the world, you who groan under the yoke of your passions and beg to be delivered from them, you who burn with desire to love God and serve Him as He would be served, you who intercede with God for the sake of one who is dear to you, do not grow weary of asking, be steadfast and tireless in your demands. If you are refused today, tomorrow you will obtain everything; if this year brings nothing, the next will bring you abundance. Never think your efforts are wasted. Your every word is numbered and what you receive will be in the measure of the time you have spent asking. Your treasure is piling up and suddenly one day it will overflow to an extent beyond your dreams.

Consider the workings of Divine Providence and think that the refusal you meet with now is only God's stratagem to increase your fervor. Remember how He acted towards the Canaanite woman, treating her harshly and refusing to see or listen to her. He seemed to be irritated by her importunity, but in reality He admired it and was delighted with her trust and humility, and for that reason He repulsed her. With what tenderness does He repulse those whom He most wishes to be indulgent to, hiding His clemency under the mask of cruelty! Take care not to be deceived by it. The more He seems to be unwilling, the more you must insist.

Do as the woman of Canaan, use against Him the very arguments He may have for refusing you. It is true that to hear me, you should say to Him, would be to give the bread of the children to dogs. I do not deserve the grace I ask, but I do not ask You to give me what I deserve; I ask it through the merits of my Redeemer. You ought to think more of Your promises than of my unworthiness, and You will be unjust to Yourself if You give me only what I deserve. If I were worthier of Your benefits it would be less to Your glory to give me them. It is unjust to grant favors to a sinner, but I do not appeal to Your justice but to Your mercy.

Do not lose courage when you have begun so well to struggle with God. Do not give Him a moment's rest. He loves the violence of your attack and wants to be overcome by you. Make importunity your watchword, let persistence be a miracle in you. Compel God to throw off the mask and say to you with admiration: "Great is thy faith, be it done as thou wishest. I can no longer resist you, you shall have what you desire, in this life and the next."

EXERCISE OF CONFORMITY
TO DIVINE PROVIDENCE[1]

The practice of this exercise is of great importance because of the advantages it always confers on those who undertake it devoutly.

ACT OF FAITH, HOPE, AND CHARITY

First make an act of faith in God's Providence. Meditate well on the truth that God's continual care extends not only to all things in general but to each particular thing, and especially to ourselves, our souls and bodies, and everything that concerns us. Nothing escapes His loving watchfulness—our work, our daily needs, our health as well as our infirmities, our life and our death, even the smallest hair on our head which cannot fall without His permission.

After this act of faith, make an act of hope. Excite in yourself a firm trust that God will provide for all you need, will direct and protect you with more than a father's love and vigilance, and guide you in such a way that, whatever happens, if you submit to Him everything will turn out for your happiness and advantage, even the things that may seem quite the opposite.

To these two an act of charity should be added. Show your deep love and attachment for Divine Providence as a child shows for its mother by taking refuge in her arms. Say how highly you esteem all His intentions, however hidden they may be, in the knowledge that they spring from an infinite wisdom which cannot make a mistake and supreme goodness which can wish only the perfection of His creatures. Determine that this feeling will have a practical result in making you ready to speak out in defense of Providence whenever you hear it denied or criticized.

---

[1] Part II, Section V of *The Secret of Peace and Happiness*, by Fr Jean Baptiste Saint-Juré and Blessed Claude de la Colombière, S.J., translated by Paul Garvin, St Paul Publications, New York, 1961.

ACT OF FILIAL SUBMISSION TO PROVIDENCE

After repeating these acts several times with fervor, commit your soul lovingly to Divine Providence as a child rests and sleeps in its mother's arms. Make your own the words of David: "I will lie down and sleep in peace, for thou alone, O Lord, best established me in hope." Or again in the words of the psalm:

The Lord is my shepherd; I shall not want.
In verdant pastures he gives me repose;
Beside restful waters he leads me; he refreshes my soul.
He guides me in right paths for his name's sake.
Even though I walk in the dark valley I fear no evil; for you
    are at my side
With your rod and your staff that give me courage.
You spread the table before me in the sight of my foes;
You anoint my head with oil; my cup overflows.
Only goodness and kindness follow me all the days of my life;
And I shall dwell in the house of the Lord for years to come.

Filled with the joy these consoling words inspire, the soul can trustfully accept from Divine Providence whatever happens now or in the future with tranquility and peace of mind. Its happiness is that of a child who feels protected and secure. Not that it lives in idle expectation of what it needs or neglects to occupy itself with the affairs of daily life. On the contrary it does all in its power and employs all its faculties in attending to them well. But what it does it does under God's guidance and regards its own judgment as entirely subject to God's. It freely entrusts everything to His governance without expecting any other result from its actions but what is in accordance with His will.

USEFULNESS OF THIS EXERCISE

What honor and glory is given to God by the soul that acts thus? It is a great glory for Him to have a creature so attached to His Providence, so dependent on Him, full of such firm hope and peace of mind in the expectation of what He will send. His concern for such a one is redoubled, He watches over the slightest things that are of interest to him and inspires those who are over him to act prudently; and if for any reason they try to act in a manner harmful to him, He prevents them in the hidden ways of His Providence from carrying out their designs and compels them to do only what is to his advantage.

Thus the Lord keeps those who love Him. If the Scriptures speak of God as having eyes, it is in order to watch over them; as having ears, to hear them; as having hands, to defend them. And those who touch them, touch the apple of His eye. "I shall carry you in my arms," He says by the mouth of the prophet Isaias, "I shall caress you upon my knees. As one whom his mother caresses, so will I comfort you." And in Osee: "I was like a foster father to Ephraim, I carried them in my arms." Long before Moses had said: "In the desert the Lord your God carried you, as a man carries his child, all along your journey until you arrived at this place." Again God says in Isaias: "You shall be nursed with the breasts of kings, and you shall know that I am the Lord your Savior and your Redeemer."

In the person of Noah we can find a figure of the happiness of the man who throws himself entirely upon God. While the floodgates of heaven were opened and the world was laid in ruin Noah was safe and at peace in the ark because God was guiding him. Others remained at the mercy of the waters, losing all they had, their families, their lives. Thus the man who entrusts himself to Providence, lets God be the pilot of his bark, floats tranquilly on the ocean of life in the midst of storm and tempest, while those who try to guide themselves are in continual unrest, and their only pilot being their own blind and inconstant will, they are tossed about by sea and wind until they end in shipwreck.

Let us then trust ourselves entirely to God and His Providence and leave Him complete power to order our lives, turning to Him lovingly in every need and awaiting His help without anxiety. Leave everything to Him and He will provide us with everything, at the time and in the place and in the manner best suited. He will lead us on our way to that happiness and peace of mind for which we are destined in this life as a foretaste of the everlasting happiness we have been promised.

Vigil at Montserrat

THE SPIRITUAL DIRECTION OF SAINT CLAUDE DE LA COLOMBIÈRE[1]

ON PRAYER

As I feel a great attraction toward prayer I asked God, by Our Lady's intercession, to give me the grace to go on increasing in love of this holy exercise until my death. It is the only means of purifying us, of uniting us to God, and of allowing God to unite himself to us and be glorified in us. We must pray to obtain the apostolic virtues; pray that we may use them to help others, and pray also that we may not lose them while serving others. The counsel: pray without ceasing, seems sweet to me and in no way impossible. It includes the practice of the presence of God, and with his help I resolve to follow it. We always have need of God, therefore we must always pray. The more we pray, the more we please him and the more we obtain. I do not ask for consolation in prayer; that God gives where he chooses; I am not worthy of consolation and am too weak to bear it. Extraordinary graces are not good for me; to give them to me would be like building upon sand, or pouring a precious liquid into a broken vase. I ask God to give me a solid, simple gift of prayer which will glorify him and not make me vain. It seems to me that dryness and desolation accompanied by grace are very useful to me, for then I delight in making acts of real virtue: I strive against my bad inclinations and try to be faithful to God.

When we are distracted during prayer and find the time long because of our impatience to pass on to something else, it is good to say to yourself: My soul, art thou tired of thy God? Art thou not satisfied with him? Thou possessest him and dost thou seek for something else? Where canst thou be better than in his company? Where canst thou profit more? I have experienced that this calms the mind and unites it with God.

How can we help our neighbor? By prayer and good works. Preaching is useless without grace, and grace is only obtained by

[1] Selections from *The Spiritual Direction of Saint Claude de la Colombière*, translated and arranged by Mother M. Philip, I.B.V.M., Ignatius Press, San Francisco, 1998.

prayer. If conversions are few, it is because few pray. Prayer for souls is so pleasing to God, it is as though we asked a mother to forgive her son.

In prayer always follow the attraction of your heart, whether God draws you to consider Our Lord's Passion or the joys of heaven; you cannot do wrong in that.

The best book of meditation on the Passion is the Passion itself in the Gospel: read this and meditate upon it, reflecting upon the love and patience of Jesus Christ.

Continue to pray as you feel drawn, but do not worry about it, for worry comes from self-love. You must abandon yourself to the leading of God with no other intention than that of pleasing him, and when you know that you have this intention deep in your heart, you must not waste time in reflecting about yourself and about the degree of virtue you have attained; occupy yourself with him whom you love and bother very little about yourself.

In general, the mere sense of the presence of God is an excellent prayer, and if you can occupy yourself with it without strain, you need think of nothing else: not that you must avoid making acts when drawn to do so, but do not worry about them unless for some reason you feel constrained to make them. Go to God simply, with great confidence that his goodness will guide you; let yourself go confidently as your heart draws you, and fear nothing but pride and self-love....

When you can do nothing at prayer, make acts of humility, comparing your nothingness with God's greatness, your ingratitude with his benefits, your lack of virtue with the purity and perfection of the saints.

It is a great illusion, but a very common one, to imagine that one has little or great virtue according to the many or few distractions one has in prayer! I have known souls raised to a high degree of contemplation who were distracted from the beginning to the end of their prayer. Most of the people who are so much troubled at this wandering of the mind are souls filled with self-love who cannot bear the confusion into which it throws them before God and man and who cannot put up with the weariness and fatigue their prayer causes them. They desire to be rewarded by sensible consolation for the mortification they practice.

Do not be either astonished or discouraged at the difficulties you find in prayer. Only be constant and submissive and God will be pleased with you. Perhaps the lights you have concerning your unworthiness are graces by which God prepares you for the dryness that follows, which is a punishment for past infidelities.

Neither prayer nor recollection call for strain: faults must be avoided, and we must be united to God in heart if we cannot be in mind. Love and do what you will. Nothing is difficult to him who loves, and he only has to make efforts to feel his love. I say feel because it is not even necessary always to express it in prayer. He whom you love sees your heart and that is sufficient. He does not want you to worry about your lack of power to act and to produce affections as easily as you would like. You must submit humbly to his will in this, judging yourself unworthy to raise your thoughts to him. Oh, how happy you would be if you would learn this lesson well and so place your soul in holy liberty and in perfect resignation to God's guidance of you.

The coldness you feel in prayer comes from your too great desire for sensible fervor. You must love God alone with all your heart and be ready to be satisfied with his Cross as the only sign of his love. Take the posture which inconveniences you the least and take care to pray quietly and not to strain yourself.

When you have no consolation in prayer you must endure your impatience to finish it with great humility and stay rather longer than usual so as to mortify yourself.

Despise troublesome thoughts and bear their importunity with resignation. A soul that fears God is not troubled by her fear of committing faults; she goes to her good Master with great liberty of spirit and childlike confidence. When we only desire to please him, we must not fear that he is offended by things that we believe to be well done. Keep yourself as much as possible in the presence of God, humbly tasting the sweetness you will find there: do not fear illusion.

Take great care not to omit your prayer unless you are ill; if you cannot kneel, sit down: it is all the same.

ON RECOLLECTION AND THE PRESENCE OF GOD

You think you would be less distracted if you were away from the circumstances in which God has placed you; I think, on the contrary, that you would have fewer distractions if you accepted things with more conformity to God's will and if, in your work, you thought of yourself as a servant of Jesus Christ whom he employs as it seems best to him and who is equally content in whatever service is exacted from her. Try to live in your present state as though you were never to leave it; think more of making good use of your crosses than of getting rid of them under pretext of having more liberty with which to serve God.

Exterior employment is no obstacle to solitude of heart when the mind is calm and leaves everything in God's hands; when all that one does for others is done with humility and resignation; when we believe that nothing happens without God's permission; when we obey others as God himself; and when we persuade ourselves that their words, actions, temper, conduct, faults, everything in general and in particular, is ordained by the will of God, who knows all that is to happen and who allows and wills it for our good and his glory....

I have promised with God's grace not to begin any action without remembering that he is witness of it—that he performs it together with me and gives me the means to do it; never to conclude any without the same thought, offering it to him as belonging to him, and in the course of the action whenever the same thought shall occur, to stop for a moment and renew the desire of pleasing him.

God is in the midst of us, or rather we are in the midst of him; wherever we are he sees us and touches us: at prayer, at work, at table, at recreation. We do not think of this; if we did, with what fervor and devotion we should live. Let us often make acts of faith, saying to ourselves: God is looking at me, he is here present.

Keep yourself as much as possible in the presence of God, humbly tasting the sweetness you will find there. Do not fear illusion. Despise troublesome thoughts and bear their importunity with resignation. A soul that fears God is not troubled by her fear of committing faults; she goes to her good Master with great liberty of spirit and with childlike confidence. When we only desire to please him, we must not fear that he is offended by things that we believe to be well done....

ON CONFIDENCE IN GOD

In thinking of what could trouble me at death, that is to say past sin and future punishment, this thought came to me and I have made it my own; it is a great consolation to me: at death, when my sins known and unknown trouble me, I will take them all and cast them at Our Lord's feet to be consumed in the fire of his mercy. The greater they are, the worse they seem to me, the more willingly will I give them to him because the offering will be all the more worthy of his mercy. It seems to me that I could do nothing more reasonable nor more glorious to God, and because of the idea I have of his goodness, this will not be difficult. I feel greatly drawn to act in this way. As for purgatory, I do not fear it. I am sorry to have deserved it because it has only been by offending God; but since I do deserve it, I am glad to go there to satisfy his justice as rigorously as possible even to the day of judgment. I know the torments are great, but I know that they honor God and that in purgatory I shall be sure of never opposing God's will and of never complaining of the severity of his justice but of loving it and waiting patiently until it is entirely satisfied.

God sought me out when I fled from him; he will not abandon me now that I seek him, or at least do not flee from him any more.

Cultivate thoughts of confidence as long as it pleases God to give them to you; they honor God far more than contrary thoughts. The more wretched we are, the more is God honored by the confidence we have in him. It seems to me that if your confidence were as great as it ought to be, you would not worry about what may happen to you; you would place it all in God's hands, hoping that when he wants something of you he will let you know what it is.

I do not know what you mean by despair: one would think you had never heard of God or of his infinite mercy. Hold such sentiments in horror, and remember that all you have done is nothing in comparison with your want of confidence. Hope on to the end.

Pray that my faults, however grave and frequent, may never make me despair of his goodness. That, in my opinion, would be the greatest evil that could befall anyone. When we can protect ourselves against that evil, there is no other which may not turn to our good and from which we cannot easily draw great advantage....

My God, I am so intimately convinced that thou dost watch over all those who hope in thee, and that we can want for nothing while we expect all from thee, that I am resolved to live without anxiety in the future, casting all my care on thee. "In peace I will sleep and I will rest for thou hast wonderfully established me in hope" (Ps 4:8).

Men may turn against me; sickness may take away my strength and the means of serving thee; I may even lose thy grace by sin, but I will never lose my hope. I will keep it even to the last moment of my life, and all the demons in hell shall try in vain to tear it from me. In peace I will sleep and I will rest.

Others may look for happiness from their riches or their talents; they may rely upon the innocence of their lives, the rigor of their penance, the number of their good works, or the fervor of their prayers; but for me, O Lord, my confidence shall be my confidence itself. For thou hast wonderfully established me in hope.

This confidence has never deceived anyone. No one hath hoped in the Lord and been put to shame. I am sure that I shall be eternally happy, because I hope firmly to be so, and it is from thee, O Lord, that I hope it. In thee, O Lord, have I hoped; I shall not be confounded for ever.

I know that I am frail and changeable; I know the power of temptation against the most firmly based virtues: I have seen the stars of heaven and the pillars of the firmament fall; but not even this can make me fear. As long as I hope, I am safe from every evil, and I am sure of always hoping because I hope for this unchanging hope. For thou, O Lord, hast wonderfully established me in hope.

ON ABANDONMENT TO GOD'S WILL

I am resigned to sanctify myself in the way and by the means God wants me to sanctify myself: without any sensible sweetness if he so wills; by interior trial and by continual struggle against my passions: all this seems the hardest thing in life for me, yet I submit with all my heart and all the more willingly because I know it is the surest way, the way least subject to illusion and the shortest for acquiring perfect purity of heart, great love of God, and great merit.

Submission to God's will frees us from all other yokes. Because as God wills everything that happens to us, and as we will all that God wills, nothing can happen except what we will. Nobody can oblige me to do what I do not want to do because I desire to do all that God wishes....

ON TEMPTATIONS

Be on your guard against the first movements of passion, especially of the love of pleasure and honor. Love of pleasure includes friendships. Unless I am mistaken, you are very impressionable on this point, and it is hardly in your power to control these passions once you have let them enter your heart. First of all they occupy your attention; then they take up your time and application and make you neglect everything else, so that in the end, when they begin to die down, you feel lost, so to speak, so far away from God. You have strayed off the right path and not knowing how to find your way you are in danger of wandering in any direction to which nature calls you. This is why you must fight against the first movements of passion and prevent them if possible by great recollection.

If you fall under the stress of temptation, rise promptly, ask God's pardon, hope in him in spite of your fall, and with all your heart welcome the humiliation and detest the sin. Your uncertainty as to whether you sin or not is another cross that you must also bear with perfect resignation.

Do not torment yourself about getting rid of thoughts that assail you; all the resistance you should make, you do make in humbling yourself under the mighty hand of God's justice which strikes you and in willingly accepting all that it pleases him to send you. You do not consent to these imaginations, but even if you fell under the strength of the temptation, you must rise courageously and hate the sin with all your heart. I do not advise you to confess these things. If you like you can say in general that you have had all sorts of thoughts, some of them very bad in themselves, but that you do not think they were voluntary. Courage, my child, bear what Our Lord sends you with submission and love. Place yourself on his side and be glad to see him chastising you in proportion to your sins. Try to please him by perfect acceptance of the severest measures of his justice, and this by willingly accepting all that happens, all that is humiliating to body and soul, and especially your confusion and repentance at having used a life so badly that you might have employed so usefully. Let your compunction be mingled with a certain pleasure at the sight of yourself: poor, miserable, humbled, deprived of all merit and virtue.

Despise temptations against faith and remember that you believe what so many saints and doctors of the Church have believed. Be ashamed of your fear of the future. Do you not know that your heavenly Father knows your needs and is all-powerful to provide for them? What do you fear in God's judgments? They are always favorable to souls of good will.

ON PEACE DURING INTERIOR TRIALS

There is no peace except in perfect forgetfulness of self; we must resolve to forget even our spiritual interests, so that we may seek nothing but God's glory.

In meditating on Jesus being taken prisoner in the Garden, two things touched me very much and occupied my thoughts: first the way Christ went forward to meet those who had come to apprehend him: his firmness, courage, and peace just as if his soul had been steeped in calm. His Heart is full of anguish, his human nature is disconcerted, yet amidst it all it turns straight to God the Father; it does not hesitate about taking the way suggested by the highest virtue and self-sacrifice.

One of the greatest gifts the Holy Spirit can bestow on us is to give us peace in time of struggle, calm in the midst of trouble, so that in time of desolation we are armed with so virile a courage that nature, the devil, and even God himself, who seems to be against us, cannot withstand.

The second thing that struck me was Our Lord's dispositions with regard to Judas who betrayed him, to the apostles who abandoned him, and to the priests and others who were the cause of the persecution he suffered. Amidst it all Jesus remained perfectly calm, his love for his disciples and enemies was not altered at all; he grieved over the harm they did themselves, but his own sufferings, far from troubling him, comforted him because he knew they would act as a remedy for the sins of his enemies. His Heart was without bitterness and full of tenderness toward his enemies in spite of their perfidy and of all they made him suffer.

I feel more wretched than I can say: my imagination is foolish and extravagant. All my passions rise in me, hardly a day passes without my being tempted to give way to them. Sometimes real and sometimes imaginary things excite them. By God's grace I suffer all this without consenting to them, yet I am continually troubled by these foolish passions. Self-love hides everywhere; I am very sorry for myself, but I am not vexed or impatient, what would be the good? I pray that I may know what I ought to do to please and serve God and purify myself; but I am resolved to wait peacefully until he works this miracle in me, for I am convinced he alone can do it.

God is touched by our sorrows and does not allow them to last for ever. He takes pleasure in trying our love for a time because he sees that trials purify us and render us worthy to receive his greater graces; but he considers our weakness, and one would even think that he suffered with us, so anxious is he to relieve us. May he be eternally blessed and praised by all his creatures....

No plans we make for God are ever accomplished without trouble. The more the devil tries to upset them, the more glory for God can we hope for.

The time of desolation and dryness is the best for gaining merit. A soul that seeks God easily bears this state and rises above all that passes before the imagination and in the inferior part of the soul where consolation is mostly to be found. It does not cease to love God, to humble itself, and to accept this state even for ever. There is nothing so dangerous and so much to be suspected as sweetness. Sometimes we attach ourselves to it, and when it is passed we find we have less instead of more fervor in doing good. It is a real consolation for me to think that in the midst of aridity and temptation my heart is free and that it is only by my heart (that is, my will) that I can merit or demerit; that I neither please nor displease God by things which are beyond my control, such as sensible sweetness and importunate thoughts which come into my mind in spite of myself.

ON FERVOR

It is strange how many enemies we have to fight as soon as we make the resolution to become a saint. It would seem that everything is let loose against us: the devil with his snares; the world and its attractions; nature with its resistance to all good desires; the praise of the good; the mockery of the wicked; the suggestions of the tepid. If God visits us, vanity is to be feared. If God withdraws himself, we fall into dejection. Despair may succeed the greatest fervor.

Our friends tempt us because we are accustomed to try and please them; the indifferent because we fear to displease them.

Indiscretion is to be feared in fervor, sensuality in moderation, and self-love everywhere. What is to be done? We have no refuge but in thee, O God. "As we know not what to do, we can only turn our eyes to thee" (2 Chron 20:12).

Above all, as sanctity does not consist in being faithful for a day or a year but in persevering until death, we must use God as a shield which covers us completely because we are attacked from all sides.

God must do everything. All the better; there will be no fear of failure. As for ourselves, we have only to acknowledge our powerlessness and to be fervent and constant in asking for help through the intercession of Mary, to whom God refuses nothing; but even this we cannot do without a great grace, or rather without many graces.

The spirit of God inclines us to fervor, but this fervor is calm and causes no trouble either to ourselves or to others; when it meets with obstacles it knows how to stop and submit to God's will. Its only arms are patience and gentleness. You want to be a martyr; you have a daily martyrdom which you endure unwillingly and without resignation! I see nothing reasonable in such a desire and nothing which looks like an inspiration.

ON FAITH

It is an error to think that faith is so entirely a gift of God that it is not in our power to increase and strengthen it. Some admit that they have very little faith and excuse themselves on this account for their bad lives. Therefore when they are reproached for having so little faith, it makes no more impression upon them than if you told them they had not the gift of miracles. They admire faith in the saints as a purely gratuitous grace; they persuade themselves that they can do nothing to increase their own faith and that the only thing to do is to remain passive until God grants them that favor; they will make no effort to grow in faith, saying that to do so is quite useless. "I know my faith is weak," they say, "but it is no good me trying to rekindle it; I cannot do it. I wish I were like those saints who without any trouble were detached from everything but God. What is the good of me wishing for these things if God does not intend to give them to me?"

We must get rid of these ideas, see why it is our faith is so weak, and acknowledge that it is our own fault and that, whatever we may say, the truth is that we do not believe because we do not wish to believe.

Of all states to be in, the most wretched is that of a Christian who has but little faith. It would be better to have none because such a one suffers more even in his pleasures than a man of real faith does in the greatest trials: the little he possesses is enough to damn him but not enough to save him. To him faith is like a light which disturbs the rest one finds in darkness and not like the light which brings the joy of day.

ON SPIRITUAL JOY

By God's infinite mercy I feel a liberty of spirit which fills me with great joy. It seems as though nothing could now make me unhappy. The thought that I am serving God fills me with this joy, and I feel that it is of far greater value than all the favor of kings would be. The occupations of the worldly seem very despicable in comparison with work done for God.

I know no greater joy than to discover some weakness in myself that I did not realize before. I often taste this joy and shall always have it when God gives me his light when I am examining my conscience. I firmly believe, and in this I find joy, that God guides those who give themselves up to his leading and that he takes care of the least things that concern them.

We must serve God with our whole heart and do all in our power to prevent ourselves from sinning, but all this is to be done with joy, liberty of heart, and entire confidence, in spite of all the weakness that we feel and the faults we commit.

ON HUMILITY AND SIMPLICITY

Anyone who thinks of what he is, what he has been, and what he can do of himself will find it difficult to be proud. To shatter pride it is enough to remember that the first sign of real virtue is to consider self as nothing at all. We have only to look at Jesus Christ who emptying himself gave all glory to his Father.

If people praise me, it is a mistake, an injustice done to God. People do not think so highly of us as we imagine: they know our faults, even those we do not see ourselves.

If God uses me for great things, he should be praised and thanked for making use of such a poor instrument, but I myself am not on that account any better; it might even happen that I shall be damned after having helped to save others.

We should imitate Our Lady: she acknowledged that God had done great things for her and that all generations would call her blessed, but instead of attributing anything to herself she says: "*Magnificat anima mea Dominum*" (Lk 1:46)....

We have no reason to despise anyone. A humble man sees only his own faults. It is a sign of little virtue to notice the imperfections of others. A person may be imperfect today who in a little while, recognizing this, may rise to great sanctity.

It is very necessary to walk with great circumspection, humility, and distrust of self in directing others and in one's own spiritual life. We must be detached from our natural desire to make great progress; that leads to illusions and may make us indiscreet. Love of humility and abjection and a hidden and obscure life are the great remedies....

Once God is master of a heart, he does not remain idle. If you saw that you always remained the same, it would not be a good sign even though things seemed to be going on fairly well. When the world is entirely satisfied and even in admiration, a soul that is really enlightened from above finds a hundred things still with which to reproach itself and can only wonder at those who admire its virtue. I do not think there are any souls in the world with whom God is less pleased than with those who imagine they have reason to be pleased with themselves. As soon as we begin to see how lovable Our Lord is, we should have very hard hearts if we did not love him greatly; and when we love greatly, we think we have never done enough for him.

You must overcome everything by humility and simplicity. These virtues are not, as some think, the virtues of stupid people: on the contrary, stupid people are not capable of practicing them. We require a great deal of light to know ourselves and much strength to despise all that is not God so as to abandon ourselves to him and to those who govern us in his name. People who are less docile and who count on themselves because they think they know better are really greatly to be pitied. It would be a strange blindness to think there is any knowledge or prudence above the knowledge and prudence of God, so that we could be dispensed from following the teaching of the Gospel.

ON DETACHMENT

The thought of the greatness of God and of the nothingness of all created things has made me understand the foolishness of those who make themselves dependent upon other people and the happiness of those who depend only upon God.

There is only one way of raising ourselves above our own nothingness, and that is to cling to God: "He who is joined to the Lord is one spirit" (1 Cor 6:17). By doing this we rise above the things of earth and become in some measure like unto God.

There is no peace except in perfect forgetfulness of self. We must make up our mind to forget even our spiritual interests and think only of God's glory.

Thinking of the eternity of God, I imagined it as an immovable rock on the bank of a river past which God sees every creature go by without ever moving himself. Those who are attached to created things appeared to me like people caught in the current, some clinging to a plank, others to the trunk of a tree, others to a mere heap of foam which they mistake for something solid. Everything is washed away by the torrent: friends die, health is shattered, life passes, and we arrive at eternity borne along by these passing props and plunge into it as we do into a sea which we cannot prevent ourselves from entering and where we perish.

Then we see how imprudent we have been not to attach ourselves to the immovable and eternal Rock; we would like to go back, but the waves have carried us on too far; we cannot return but must necessarily perish with all perishable things.

On the other hand, a man who clings to God sees the peril and loss of others without fear for himself; whatever happens he stands upon the rock. God cannot forsake him; he has clung to him alone and feels himself always upheld by the Eternal. Adversity comes and shows him what a good choice he has made. Such a man always possesses God; the death of his relations and friends, separation from all who esteem and favor him, distance, change of employment or of dwelling, age, sickness, or death, none of these things separate him from God. He is always happy and says in peace and joy of heart: "It is good for me to hold fast unto my God: to put my hope in the Lord God" (Ps 73:28).

ON VANITY AND VAINGLORY

I have resolved never to hesitate when an opportunity presents itself of humbling myself and of letting people see me as I am and know me as I have been. This will not be difficult if God gives me the grace to remember that the less we are esteemed by men, the more we are esteemed by God, and it is he alone I desire to please.

I have noticed that when we are very careful to mortify and humble ourselves in everything, we sometimes become depressed and less ready to serve God. This is a temptation which we can conquer by thinking that God only asks these things of us through love. We should aim at humbling ourselves to please God as a good friend tries to please his friend, or a son his father. There must be no constraint but a holy liberty of spirit, for this liberty is one of the best signs of true love. It is easy to do things which we know will please one whom we love.

Do you want to know what you gain from those you try to please? Consider what they gain from you. You are not the only one thirsting for vainglory: nearly everyone runs after the same phantom. Confess that if you had only obtained as much esteem from those around you as you have given them, it would not be worthwhile taking all the trouble you do take. You can be very sure that you certainly do not receive more; it is much if you hold in the esteem of others the same place that they hold in yours.

Beware of vanity. Remembrance of the past is a good antidote. Nothing is more to be feared in the spiritual life than what is extraordinary. Everything that inclines you to humility and hatred of self is good.

ON MORTIFICATION

I can still sin! Wretched condition of this life! Danger which makes life bitter to all those who love God and who know the value of grace! Yet penance and mortification which can prevent this misery make life sweet! Mortification tames the flesh, weakens inclinations to evil, cuts down occasions of sin, removes enticements, and so on: O holy penance!

Try to make yourself worthy of God's favors by always seeking to refuse nature what it demands both interiorly and exteriorly. Do not be self-willed, but try on the contrary always to do what others wish rather than what you yourself wish, even in indifferent things. Thus you will find that Our Lord is close to you and that your hardness of heart will melt away.

Be on your guard against illusions concerning mortification. Be more obedient on this point than on others. Sacrifice to God your desire for austerities, and only do penances which cannot hurt your health: such as interior mortifications.

ON THE DUTIES OF OUR STATE OF LIFE

The good order of things in the world depends upon the fidelity with which each one performs the duties of his state of life. All disorder originates in negligence upon this point. What a grand thing it would be if everyone acquitted himself of his duties! It is, perhaps, the thing that is most neglected even among pious people, indeed probably more often among those than among others. Yet people do not accuse themselves of it. Charles V said to his confessor: "I accuse myself of the sins of Charles, not of those of the Emperor."

More souls are lost for this reason than for any other. Half are damned for not having performed the duties of their state, the other half because others have neglected their duties with regard to them. The duties of one's state take precedence of private duties: for instance, a magistrate must not consider relationship or friendship. Public good must prevail over private good. Jesus Christ, who came into this world to teach us and save us, did not think of his Mother when it was a question of his office as Redeemer: he looked upon others only in so far as they concerned this work of Redemption. Those who cooperated with him are his brothers; those to whom his Precious Blood gives new life are his children; his Mother is she who is perfectly submissive to the will of his Father.

A man who neglects the duties of his state is a discordant voice in the harmony of the world, no matter what else he does. Those who are faithful to all other duties often neglect these; those who do not omit them perform them negligently or through human motives and self-interest. This is not fulfilling their duty.

In choosing a state of life, the human advantages are considered but not the duties. It is impossible to neglect these duties without injuring others, and as God has their interests at heart even more than his own, such neglect is very dangerous.

People would consider it strange for a man to become a religious without knowing to what he was going to bind himself. But what of a secular who has been married for twenty years, or who has held some responsible post in his profession, without knowing the duties these states of life entail.

Sins of omission on this point are easily committed. They are hardly noticed, and consequently reparation is rarely made for them. These are sins that are committed by doing nothing; sins that do not consist in bad actions but which are often the consequence of some good work.

By neglecting your duties, you condemn both yourself and others to punishment: others because you do not teach them their duty and make them fulfill it; and yourself because you do not fulfill your own. The less wicked will be damned for what they have done; the most wicked for what they have omitted to do.

ON THE WORLD

What would you say if I asked you if you can live in the world without offending God? When the dangers are put before you of certain kinds of talk, of certain ways of acting, and of backbiting your neighbor, you answer that you cannot help it, that otherwise you would have to be dumb in society, that people talk of nothing else, that you would have to have a heart of bronze to resist all temptations in the midst of a world which breeds them, and that in fact you would have to live like a hermit if you want to escape them.

All this is frequently said in excuse by those who think it justifies them.

It is impossible to frequent the world without offending God, or at any rate without exposing oneself to the danger of offending him: therefore you must renounce the world.

Every Christian has renounced the world and its pomps at baptism. This vow does not oblige you to live like a hermit, but it certainly obliges you to something. It is not an empty promise.

In the world there is an inner world: a second world which every Christian must avoid, for it knows not God and the devil is its ruler. It was of this world that Jesus Christ said: "I pray not for the world" (Jn 17:9). In this world are found those who live solely for vanity and pleasure; it is where the one aim is to please and flatter, where there is hardly anything that is innocent and good, and where people glory in all that ought to make us ashamed.

How foolish to bother about a world full of such unreasonable people. One is proud of a name which he dishonors by a bad life; another prides herself on a dress which she owes to the skill of a dressmaker and which not merely covers a body made of dust but a corrupt soul; another gives up rest and peace to acquire a fortune he does not know how to use; others get furious over things of no importance or things which do not concern them. There is no charity in this world: men are left to die of hunger, while horses and dogs are fed with food that is refused to those who are created in God's image.

ON PRAYER

What a mistake it is to be tormented and sad because you have no light or consolation in prayer, to strain your head seeking after sensible devotion at Holy Communion, and to neglect little faults, small observances, and occasions for mortifying your own will and desires, for conquering your human respect and for procuring your own humiliation before others! If we were reasonable, we should think only of these last and not make the slightest effort to succeed according to our own ideas; because, as a matter of fact, we never succeed better than when we humbly endure dryness and the privation of this false fervor that nature so loves and that the real love of God despises and even rejects as far as it is able.

If you were ravished in ecstasy twenty-four times a day and I had twenty-four distractions in saying a Hail Mary, but if I were as humble and mortified as you, I would not change my involuntary distractions for all your ecstasies which have no merit. In a word: there is no devotion without mortification. You must always do violence to yourself, especially interiorly. Never allow nature to be mistress, nor your heart to be attached to anything, no matter what it may be; and then I would canonize you and not even ask you how you prayed.

If you only pray when you are obliged or because you are obliged, you will never succeed in prayer, nor will you ever love it, nor ever take pleasure in intimate converse with God.

A soul which exempts herself from prayer when ill or upset through fear of harming herself, does not know how to pray; for, far from harming, it strengthens both mind and heart, it keeps the soul in peace and leaves behind it a consolation which relieves all trouble.

It is neither vows nor promises which should attract you to this holy exercise but the happiness that a faithful soul finds in approaching to her God. I pray that the Holy Spirit may give you the gift of prayer: it is the hidden treasure of the Gospel; but to possess it we must detach ourselves from everything that we may enjoy God and merit his caresses.

ON PEACE OF SOUL

From the moment one has a real desire of giving oneself entirely to God, one enjoys great peace. I am sure that which you have found by Our Lord's mercy is the result of the sincere and fervent will which he has given you to serve him and belong to him without reserve. You would indeed be miserable if there were anything in the world that could trouble you, for there is nothing that can prevent you from becoming a saint, in fact everything may help you to become one. There is nothing, not even our sins, from which we may not gain advantage for our sanctification, through the knowledge they give us of ourselves and by the renewal of fervor with which they inspire us. This being so, I do not see what could happen that could prevent you gaining profit if only you have enough faith to realize that nothing happens to you except by God's permission and enough submission to conform yourself to his will. If ever you have a fit of sadness or trouble, remember that it is because you are still attached to life, or health, or some comfort, or person, or thing that you ought to forget and despise that you may desire Jesus Christ only. Every time your heart feels troubled, be sure that it is caused by some unmortified passion and that it is a fruit of self-love which is not yet dead. Thinking this, throw yourself at the feet of Jesus crucified, and say: My Savior, do I still desire something which is not thee? Art thou not sufficient for me, shall I not love thee alone and be content to be loved only by thee? What have I come to seek, O my God, if not thee? Can I not keep thee? What does it matter what they say of me, or if I am loved or despised, well or ill, occupied with this work or with that, placed with these people or with others? Provided that I am with thee, and thou with me, I am content.

ON GENEROSITY IN GOD'S SERVICE

Many reasons convince me that I must aim at it (generosity) with all my strength. First, God has loved me too well for me to spare myself henceforth in his service: the mere thought of doing so horrifies me. What! not belong to God wholly after his mercy toward me, or reserve something for myself after all that I have received from him? Never will my heart consent to act thus.

Secondly, when I see of how little account I am, and what it is I can do for God's glory by employing myself entirely in his service, I am ashamed at the mere thought of depriving him of anything.

Thirdly, there would be no safety for me in any half-measures: I know myself, and I should soon fall into a bad extreme.

Fourthly, only those who have given themselves to God unreservedly can expect to die calmly.

Fifthly, they alone lead a peaceful and tranquil life.

Sixthly, in order to do much for God, one must be completely his. However little you keep back, you will be unfit to do great things for others.

Seventhly, in this state one maintains a lively faith and a firm hope, one asks God confidently and one obtains infallibly.

ON PUSILLANIMITY

I think you are somewhat slow and pusillanimous. If you are, you will recognize it by these marks: if you are tempted to postpone what you are obliged to do or what you have resolved to do; if you leave off something good that you have begun; if you often change your methods and practices of devotion; if you imagine that things are beyond you and only fit for great saints; if you omit to do something from human respect, through fear of appearing better than you are, fear of importuning superiors, fear lest it should seem you were condemning others, fear of mortifying others; if you are not absolutely sincere with those to whom you ought to disclose your conscience; if you persuade yourself to be content with a mediocre fervor; if you allow yourself to think that anything in obedience is small, that a word does not count, that you can put off obeying instantly ... and so on.

The remedy is not to pardon oneself anything; not to listen to any repugnance; to try always to conquer self and to be quite convinced that one great reason for doing a thing is because you find difficulty in it, and for not doing it because you are inclined to do it, always supposing that you do nothing against obedience.

ON CHRIST OUR FRIEND ABOVE ALL

Jesus, thou art my only true and real friend. Thou dost share all my sorrows and takest them upon thyself, knowing how to turn them to my good. Thou dost listen to me kindly when I tell thee of my difficulties, and thou never failest to lighten them. Wherever I go I always find thee; thou dost never leave me, and if I am obliged to go away, I find thee waiting for me.

Thou art never weary of listening to me, and thou dost never cease to do me good. I am sure of being loved if I love thee. Thou hast no need of me or of my goods, and thou dost not deprive thyself by giving me of thy riches. However wretched I am, no one nobler or more clever or even more holy can rob me of thy friendship; and death which separates us from all other friends will only unite me to thee. All the accidents of age or of fortune will never detach thee from me; on the contrary, I shall never enjoy thee more fully and thou wilt never be so close to me as when everything goes against me. Thou dost bear with my defects with tender patience; even my infidelities and ingratitude do not wound thee in such a way that thou art not always ready to return to me when I call upon thee.

Jesus is in the midst of us in the Blessed Sacrament. What a consolation to live in the same house where he dwells! Yet does it not often seem as though we ignored this happiness? Do we often visit him? Do we go to him in our needs and consult him in our plans? Do we bring him our little sorrows instead of talking about them and complaining and murmuring to others? "There hath stood one in the midst of you whom you know not" (Jn 1:26).

You love the king although you have never seen him and probably never will see him, although he has no affection for you and does not even know you, and if he did know you he would take no notice of you. Yet we find it hard to love God, whom we do not see, it is true, but whom we shall see throughout eternity and who sees us, and loves us, and does us good, and who knows our most secret thoughts! You say you love the king because he is your master. But God is much more than this: he is our Creator, our Father.

I feel myself moved to imitate the simplicity of God in my affections, loving him only, cherishing no other love but this, which is easy since I find in God all that I can love elsewhere.

But my friends: they love me and I love them. Thou seest this and I feel it, O my God, who art alone good, alone lovable. Must I sacrifice these to thee since thou desirest to have me entirely? I will make this sacrifice with my whole heart, since thou dost forbid me to share my friendship with any creature. Accept this painful sacrifice, but in exchange, my divine Savior, be thou their friend. As thou wilt take their place with me, take my place with them. I will remind thee of them daily in my prayers, and of what thou owest them in me in promising to be my substitute. Jesus, be thou their friend, their sole and real friend! Jesus, be my friend, since thou commandest me to be thine.

As Jesus Christ possesses your whole heart, he wishes also to have all your anxieties and all your thoughts. Think of him and trust in his goodness for all the rest. You will see that he will make all things right when you think only of his interests. Reflect very specially on this advice: it contains a great treasure. Experience will show you that I am not deceiving you.

Do not let your peace depend upon what is outside you; you will see that Our Lord will supply for everything when you are satisfied with him alone, and you will find more in him than in all creatures together. Beware of thinking that you have need of anyone whom God withdraws from you. He is too faithful to take away from you any help that he sees necessary for you, so that you may reach the perfection he expects from you.

My Savior, do I still desire something which is not thee? Art thou not sufficient for me, shall I not love thee alone and be content to be loved only by thee! What have I come here to seek, O my God, if it be not thee? What does it matter what they say of me, or if I am loved or despised, well or ill, occupied with this work or with that, placed with these people or with those? Provided that I am with thee, and thou with me, I am content.

ACKNOWLEDGMENTS

Selections from *The Spiritual Teaching of Father Louis Lallemant of the Society of Jesus, Preceded by an Account of His Life by Father Champion, S. J.*, edited by Alan G. McDougall, Benziger Brothers, New York, Cincinatti, Chicago, 1928.

Selections from Jean-Pierre de Caussade, *The Sacrament of the Present Moment*, translated by Kitty Muggeridge, Harper & Row Publishers, San Francisco, 1981. © Harper Collins Publishers. Reprinted with Permission.

Selections from *The Fire of Divine Love: Readings from Jean-Pierre de Caussade*, edited by Robert Llewelyn, Triumph Books, Liguori, Missouri, 1995. © Continuum International Publishing & Liguori Publications. Reprinted with Permission.

Selections from Jean-Pierre Caussade, S.J., *A Treatise on Prayer from the Heart: A Christian Mystical Tradition Recovered for All*, translated, edited, and introduced by Robert M. McKeon, The Institute of Jesuit Sources, St Louis, 1998. Used with permission: © The Institute of Jesuit Sources, St Louis, MO. All rights reserved.

Part II, Section IV and V of *The Secret of Peace and Happiness*, by Fr Jean Baptiste Saint-Juré and Blessed Claude de la Colombière, S.J., translated by Paul Garvin, St Paul Publications, New York, 1961.

Selections from *The Spiritual Direction of Saint Claude de la Colombière*, translated and arranged by Mother M. Philip, I.B.V.M., Ignatius Press, San Francisco, 1998.

BIOGRAPHICAL NOTES

JEAN-PIERRE LAFOUGE is Associate Professor of French at Marquette University. Born in 1944 in Champagne, France, he later studied philosophy at Nancy and taught philosophy in several lycées in France and in Morocco (1962-1976). His academic career took him to the United States where he obtained a Ph.D. in French literature, specializing in nineteenth and seventeen century French and Orientalist Literature. He is the author of several articles dealing with the relationship between art, Orientalism, philosophy, and literature. Jean-Pierre Lafouge is the author *Studies on Eugène Fromentin's Orientalism in his 'Récits Algériens'* (Algerian Travel Memoirs) and is presently assisting in the revision of French to English translations of the writings of Frithjof Schuon.

RAYMOND GAWRONSKI, S.J. is an associate professor at Marquette University who specializes in dogmatic theology with a focus on eschatology and the mystical writings of Hans Urs von Balthasar. He is the author of over thirty articles on various themes, largely touching culture and spirituality, many of which have appeared in publications such as *Communio*, *New Oxford Review*, and *America*. Father Gawronski wrote the chapter "Redemptor Hominis" for *The Thought of John Paul II* and is also the author of *An Ignatian Retreat* (Our Sunday Visitor Press, 2003).

INDEX

Titles in the Treasures of the World's Religions series